EXTRA LEARNING

NEW OPPORTUNITIES FOR
THE OUT OF SCHOOL HOURS

KAY ANDREWS

MT

For Helen Buchanan, Headteacher,
St Clement's Church of England Primary School,
Salford, friend and inspiration.

First published in 2001

Kogan Page Limited
120 Pentonville Road
London N1 9JN
UK

Stylus Publishing Inc.
22883 Quicksilver Drive
Sterling VA 20166-2012
USA

The views expressed in this book are those of the author and are not necessarily the same as those of *The Times Educational Supplement.*

British Library Cataloguing in Publication Data

A CIP record for this book is available from the British Library.

ISBN 0 7494 3343 4

Typeset by JS Typesetting, Wellingborough, Northants
Printed and bound by Biddles Ltd, Guildford and King's Lynn

03|17|04

Contents

Foreword by the Secretary of State for Education and Employment

Study support is an important part of our commitment to ensuring every young person has access to the widest range of learning opportunities to achieve his or her full potential.

This book shows how partnership between schools, parents, voluntary partners, local and central government in a new and shared enterprise has built on one of the best features of this country's education system and has helped to modernise it in the best sense. It also explains, informs and reviews what has already been achieved and what more can be done to reach those young people who are turned off – who have never turned on to the love of learning – and, of course, their families. We know, as all those reading this will know, that the commitment and expectation of the family is crucial, which is why we are now encouraging family learning, family study, and have developed our parenting magazine and parenting pack.

We are proud of what has already been achieved through study support. We also recognise that without the commitment of organisations like Education Extra and schools, pupils, parents and volunteers, none of this provision would be there to be celebrated.

The challenge for the future is to build on the progress made over the past few years to ensure that study support is embedded in the life and ethos of every school and community.

Rt Hon David Blunkett MP

Acknowledgements

Like many books, *Extra Learning* is about a journey that has involved many people, charted many changes in the landscape, and to which there is no end in sight. Without the teachers, the volunteers, pupils and parents who offer, participate in and support out of school learning, there would be nothing to celebrate or to write about. Without the political will and vision that the book documents, there would have been far less to cheer. Without the partners in the voluntary sector who are cited throughout the book, there would be far less good practice and a much-reduced impact. Out of school hours learning and this book itself owe a great debt to all of them.

But there are also a few outstanding characters who have made a critical difference to what has been achieved. The role of Michael Young in the creation of Education Extra is something we take great pride in. The schools and teachers identified in the case studies speak for themselves with typical modesty. Shan Scott, Jenny Evans, Zelda Wilkins and the whole Study Support team at DfEE are exemplary civil servants who have made and continue to make the right things happen and have welcomed all the positive benefits that partnership with the voluntary sector can provide. Shirley Brice Heath encouraged me greatly with her enthusiasm and academic insight.

The trustees of Education Extra, particularly my friend and mentor Ursula Owen, have given us unconditional support at each stage of our growth. Our steadfast funders, who include the Roald Dahl Foundation, the Esmée Fairbairn Charitable Trust, the Paul Hamlyn Foundation and W H Smith, have invested belief as well as money in our work and have brought enjoyment and learning to thousands of schools, families and children along the way. The case studies, unless identified otherwise, are all based on Education Extra project schools, 1999–2000.

My greatest personal debt is to my friends and colleagues at Education Extra who are not named in the text, but whose commitment is evident on every page. In particular, I would like to thank John Crossman, Ian Fordham, Richard Thompson and Pam Boyd, who read and improved specific sections. Saul Hillman researched the case studies with his usual energy and added life and colour to the text. Other colleagues read and commented as the book took shape. All of them put up with an air of distraction and summary demands for detailed information when there were many other things to do. My family simply put up with the distraction, yet again, with their usual forgiveness, and in Jonathan Simpson we could not have had a more sympathetic or meticulous editor.

Although the book represents and celebrates a collective enterprise, any mistakes are all mine. However, the ambitions we hold for the future are shared, not only among ourselves at Education Extra, but also among all those who know what the learning of the future could be, and indeed, should be like.

Introduction

EDUCATION FOR A CHANGE

The ears, the heart and the mind have their own shape for each individual. One of the most important things about an education system is getting people to do what they really want to do. That is where the basis of true excellence lies.[1]

The closing years of the 20th century proved to be a revolutionary period in replacing traditional concepts of where, when, why and how, people learn – a revolution exemplified, externally, by the power of the Internet to overturn notions of information bound by time and place, and, internally, by the moving frontiers of knowledge about how the brain functions and how learning works. Alongside these seismic shifts have come other changes in perception and policy. These include the realisation that lifeskills cannot be entirely delivered by the school curriculum; that families and communities are as important to making successful, lifelong learners as schools themselves; and that influencing what young people do in the time they spend outside school is as important for what they achieve in school as for their success in later life.

Across the UK, the nature, shape, content, scope and boundaries of education itself have provoked over the last two decades an agitated debate about the role of education as economic and social policy, as well as tidal waves of change in the curriculum and government of schools, which are still working through primary and secondary schools. These changes have been matched by growing diversity within the school system (in contrast to an increasingly narrow focus within the curriculum itself), by the increasing autonomy of schools, and by targeted intervention strategies to lift achievement in the most disadvantaged areas of the country. But these

[1] Ben Okri, quoted in *The Times Educational Supplement*, 29 September 2000

initiatives have still not met the demands of those who believe that education in the 21st century needs to be broader and richer, at once more open in terms of learning experience, and more effective in enabling young people to learn and understand for themselves how to manage their learning, their relationships and their world. Above all, it must encourage young people to enjoy and celebrate their own learning.

Those calls for education to be more radical and farsighted are matched by demands that it must also meet immediate needs more effectively. The successful introduction of the literacy hour in primary schools, the National Grid for Learning and the rationale for the new citizenship curriculum are intended to create social as well as economic opportunity. The link between poverty and educational failure is diagnosed beyond dispute, and policies for neighbourhood renewal and New Deal are confronting the root causes of both. But as community life changes and drugs and delinquency and unintended teenage pregnancy mark the rite of passage for many young people to an adult world, so the question becomes: what more can schools do to turn out successful people and good citizens? How will we achieve the changes needed within the context of our traditional school system, given the pace of technological and social change, and the increasing pressures on our great national resource – our teachers?

These are hardly new questions but they are now raised to a new volume. Learning in the future will inevitably have to reflect the increasingly volatile, international and flexible market in skills. Students will have to be able to learn and work more independently; to be as confident with technologies as they are with other languages; to have the generic skills which will open up the new creative and knowledge based industries. More than all this, however, more students must have the opportunity to find out what it feels like to be a successful learner during their years in school and to have that appetite for learning which will sustain them across a lifetime's change.

These imperatives stand in stark contrast with the present reality which includes skill shortages in key areas of the economy, particularly in the knowledge-based industries, including engineering; a stubborn gap in the performance of boys compared with girls; a continuing failure to generate the aspiration and confidence to passport many young people who could perform well into higher education; and a disappointing school experience for many pupils. These challenges are being addressed in many different and urgent ways – and they are hardly unique to Britain. But one of the areas which has distinguished education policy in this country for the past four years has been the attempt to break down some of the barriers to learning and achievement by opening up and organising the time out of school so that young people have more choices, and more chances to enjoy and manage their own learning – and to enrich the whole school experience.

The stark fact is that in the course of the school year, young people spend a third of their waking time inside school and two thirds outside. Given the cultural, personal, family and community contexts in which they develop what they do with the time outside school matters as much as what they do inside school. The search is on, therefore, not only to break down the barriers between in school learning and out of school hours learning (OSHL), but the mental barriers between 'success' and ' failure'. Part of that search is for a new definition of achievement which will be validated by the community at large.

To reach this goal, we must start with the search for ways to motivate young people to learn in the first place. In 1996, Professor Michael Barber pointed out: 'However much schools improve, inspiration and motivation to learn are much more likely to come from children who benefit from involvement in out of school activities as well as formal schooling'.[2] Policy makers, he suggested, would have to think beyond the school, to the elements of learning which had been previously left to chance. One of those areas was learning at home; another was 'organised learning out of school' because:

> The benefits. . . children reap are incalculable. These activities are educationally wonderful. . . They provide a wide range of activities in which young people can discover their talents and find success. They provide opportunities for praise, the key to so much progress. They broaden horizons and excite imaginations. And since they are largely voluntary, they provide regular evidence of the benefits of choosing to learn and to achieve. All this is in addition to whatever discipline or set of skills are being taught. These kinds of opportunities are, therefore, extremely important to young people's all round competence and profile of intelligences and to their self-esteem. Also, because in general they link enthusiastic expert teachers to enthusiastic pupils they can be vital in developing among young people the motivation to learn and to continue learning for its own sake.[3]

The concept of a 'learning day' which extends beyond the boundaries of the school day is the first practical step towards the ambitious plan to make lifelong learners of every individual. Therein lies the concept's great promise. It takes its place among the other initiatives clustered around the concept of lifelong learning, geared to the conviction that learning is an individual choice and an opportunity to be nurtured in the workplace and outside. Initiatives such as the University for Industry, the New Deal, and Pupil Learning Credits, are part of bringing the 'learning society' to life. They take their place alongside changes in further and higher education, and new aims to promote family learning and to link learning and childcare more naturally and closely. The link between school and lifelong learning

---

[2] Barber, M (1997) *The Learning Game: Arguments for an education revolution*, Indigo Press, London, p 257
[3] Ibid p 267

should be self-evident but is not. OSHL and its companion term 'study support', can make that link transparent.[4]

The other link which OSHL can make is between effective learning and effective schooling. The growth of OSHL has been fuelled not only by the search for ways to make learning more enjoyable and more effective, it has also been driven by the desire to obtain better value from schools as community institutions. At a fundamental level, OSHL is a way of opening up libraries, computer suites, and swimming pools outside school hours. But OSHL can also enable the school to play a role in community regeneration by bringing families into schools, providing opportunities for adults to build up confidence and key skills, and to support their children effectively. Alongside this has come the recognition that informal learning outside the school day or the school year is a welcome opportunity for opening up new ways of teaching as well as learning.

MODEST PROPOSALS, MAJOR REVOLUTIONS

Education offers visionary ideals which may not survive the realities of the classroom. This book describes how OSHL offers a radical vision of how and where learning can happen outside the traditional boundaries of time, space and the school curriculum; but it also shows how in practice schools and partners are making that a reality, assisted by new and practical resources for doing so. Like many British revolutions, the radical nature of this development is disguised by the fact that it builds on habit, goodwill and good practice – in this case a distinguished feature of liberal education, the voluntary commitment of time by teachers to extra-curricular activities. The concept of OSHL or study support is a development of those principles to meet the challenges of a modern education system.

Where OSHL/study support differs from traditional extra-curricular activities is that, building on the voluntary commitment of time of students and staff involved, it aims for a greater awareness and is more deliberately linked to learning benefits; it aims to be inclusive of all pupils but with a particular care for those who can benefit most; it aims to be built in rather than bolted on to the school experience and objectives; and it brings with it a set of principles for organisation, effectiveness and partnerships which very few traditional programmes encompassed. Where OSHL differs from the in-school curriculum is primarily that it finds time and space for a learning rather than a teaching environment, and for extending, enriching the curriculum as well as enabling students to enjoy learning and access the curriculum in different ways.

---

[4] Throughout this book, the term out of school hours learning (OSHL) is the preferred term to indicate the breadth and scope of all the programmes and partnerships which are on offer or in development. Study support, the term which preceded it (see Chapter 2) is used as appropriate, depending on the context

The emphasis on learning links, on organising both a balanced and an effective programme, on finding new resources and partners, and on involving different pupils, takes many different forms in different schools. But the crucial difference is that 10, even 5 years ago, OSHL activities would have been seen by most schools as peripheral to the 'real' business of schools. While extra-curricular activities flourished in many schools the shadow of the relatively new National Curriculum, together with new systems of testing and target setting, had cast a long shadow over the virtues and benefits of learning outside the 'classroom'. A great many schools were deterred from setting up or supporting new programmes or from maintaining what had become traditional because, increasingly, time was fully occupied with planning, reviewing and reorganising.

This was the background to the invention of Education Extra in 1992 – on the initiative of Michael Young (Lord Young of Dartington). The picture has changed radically. A new vocabulary and new scope, new enabling frameworks, new proof of benefit, new sources of funding, and new models of provision and practice which aim to offer something for all pupils irrespective of age and ability, are now in place. This sits alongside the regeneration of ideas of community education for the 21st century which gives schools a key role in community regeneration. The history of these changes is charted in Chapter 1.

What has not changed is that the majority of activities still rest on the voluntary commitment of teachers and students. Like every other aspect of school life, successful OSHL programmes rest on leadership and on generating extra enthusiasm and capacity for learning. The leadership which inspires the teacher, the classroom assistant or the caretaker to take part in the extra-curriculum programme, as well as enthusing the reluctant, almost invisible student to get involved, may well prove to be the fulcrum of far greater changes inside the school. Professor Tim Brighouse once described the positive changes wrought in one school thus: 'One staffroom traced it all back to an 'activity week' when the timetable had been suspended, and suddenly, everybody's real interests had been revealed and celebrated'.[5]

The 'added value' which OSHL brings (see Chapters 2 and 3) is not simply measured in the accumulative findings of raised self-esteem, enthusiasm, and achievements, it is reflected in the range of strategies which are now in place to find new ways of engaging young people with learning. Learning at different times – particularly in the summer – takes its place alongside learning at different places (most notably, in Premier Division football clubs through the Playing for Success Initiative), and in the new schemes for accelerated and intensive learning pioneered by the University of the First Age in Birmingham. These new ways of learning and teaching

[5] Brighouse, T and Woods, D (2000) *How to Improve your School*, p 52, Routledge, London

are being put in place across national and local initiatives ranging from the Education Action Zones to Excellence in Cities, and policies for promoting healthy living to reducing juvenile crime.

Many schools are putting into practice Ben Okri's wise words and finding out and following the enthusiasms of their pupils – whether that is for robotics or rap, line dancing or lace making, maths clubs or music mixing. Some schools may open up a traditional drama, music and sport programme in different ways to different pupils; some have thrown open libraries, music and computer suites, swimming pools and playing fields, across the year; others have restructured the school day so that extra time is built in for an extensive and timetabled range of extra activities, shading from homework provision to family learning, with mentoring programmes involving local business, outreach provision in local libraries and a range of experts on regular attendance. Curriculum links are everywhere, and, as Chapter 4 notes, so is the potential for making the extra that is offered a clear part of the whole school development plan, so that parents, governors, staff and students alike can see the value derived from it. That is also seen as the way to bring in the extra commitment, resources and ultimately, quality which will sustain and enhance the programme.

This commitment to adding value through OSHL is illustrated throughout the rest of the book with case studies of good practice which cover school-based settings (see Chapters 5 and 6) as well as links with social inclusion and new partnerships (see Chapters 7 and 8). Throughout these chapters and the case studies, which have been drawn from the work of Education Extra and its partners (primarily the National Development Programme for Study Support), the fundamental point emerges that self-esteem is the root of successful learning. As the Fryer Report on lifelong learning puts it, along with the physical barriers to learning (time, costs and accessibility), a lack of interest and motivation are 'a major set of obstacles to establishing a learning culture for all'.[6]

Replacing a negative experience of schooling with a positive and enjoyable experience which leads every student to leave school wanting to go on learning is the great challenge. The alternatives are stark – and are hardly unique to the UK. Within a wide framework, the Carnegie Council on Adolescent Development reflected on the fate of the country's 20 million adolescents in 1994:

> The passage through early adolescence (10–15) should result in positive outcomes. For increasing numbers of young adolescents, that is not their experience. Instead of economic security, they face uncertainty; instead of

---

[6] Department for Education and Employment (2001) *Learning for the Twenty-First Century*, DfEE, The Stationery Office. See also Fryer, R H (2001) *The Second Report on the National Advisory Group for Continuing Education and Lifelong Learning*, p 20

intellectual stimulation, they face boredom and stagnation; in place of respect, they are neglected; lacking clear and consistent adult expectations for them, many youth feel deeply alienated from mainstream society.

The damage to individual young lives is staggering. In the United States, society pays heavily for such outcomes. We pay in the diminished economic productivity of future generations. We pay the increasing bills for crime, welfare and health care. We pay the immense social cost of living with millions of alienated people. And we pay the moral cost that we are producing millions of young adolescents who face predictably bleak and unfulfilling lives.

In particular, the report went on to emphasise, graphically, the different life chances implied by the different choices young people made for the time they spent outside school. 'For many, these hours harbour both risk and opportunity. . .' On the one hand well-supported young people could look to time 'with friends, to play sports, pursue interests and engage in challenging activities'. But there were also the others, for whom the 'out of school hours presents serious risks for substance abuse, crime, violence and sexually transmitted diseases, including AIDS'.[7]

In Britain the children who are sometimes seen as overloaded with opportunity and activities, rushed from ballet lessons to maths tutoring on a daily basis, provide stark contrast with those who may lose out for a lifetime because leisure centres, sports clubs, music lessons, museums, theatres, films, and outdoor activities are a remote and expensive choice. OSHL aims to do more than fill the gap between these children's opportunities. In its most recent manifestation its potential for promoting social inclusion and citizenship matches its potential for promoting creativity and achievement across a spectrum. The recent Green Paper on Education (*Building on Success*, February 2001) makes it clear that OSHL will grow and expand; that children have the right to a rich school experience, and OSHL is a part of that; and for some children there will be extra support, through Pupil Learning Credits, to access experiences which others can take for granted.

None of this would – or will – happen without the commitment of teachers. It is to their enormous credit that, despite the pressures they face on a daily basis, which are now widely recognised as changing the nature and expectations of teaching, teachers across the UK have not only welcomed this opportunity, they have seized it as a way of overcoming some of the most stubborn problems they face. As one teacher succinctly put it: 'On balance, I think the extra enrichment, participation and variety has outweighed the extra stress and the lack of a lunchbreak to call your

---

[7] Carnegie Council on Adolescent Development (1994) *A Matter of Time: Risk and opportunity in the out of school hours*

own. I've decided that school life is definitely more interesting when you add the "extra" factor' (Gemma Warren, Latymer School, LB Enfield). Such teachers deserve every thanks, and every support. In the case studies throughout this book, they speak for themselves about the pleasure and the effort it takes to make the 'extra' happen for young people.

Also, throughout the book, the young people involved speak for themselves – and it is in their words which reflect their hard work, their excitement, and the pride they take in themselves and their achievements, that the real benefits of OSHL become irresistible. And, as one very gifted headteacher has expressed it: 'Through the after-school activities, our children know that we value every moment of their time in this school'. (Helen Buchanan, headteacher, St Clements (Egerton) CE School, Salford).

There can be no better start to life-wide as well as lifelong learning.

1

OSHL: framing and funding policy

This chapter briefly examines:

- The changing social and economic context of OSHL and its place in educational culture as a whole.
- The challenge of raising achievement and what is meant by that in the context of wide gaps in opportunity and performance of pupils; the links between educational failure and social exclusion; and the place of OSHL in those policies.
- The role of voluntary and statutory partnership in the framing of study support OSHL policies after 1997.
- The key steps involved in creating a framework, linking Extending Opportunity to social inclusion policies (Schools Plus).
- The introduction of funding for OSHL through the New Opportunities Fund (NOF).

The whole area – crucial to a young person's education – is notable for the absence of policy surrounding it. Occasionally, it has been cut across by government writing unworkable guidelines on charging for school activities or by concerns about the safety of adventure centres but these isolated debates have not resulted in policy makers thinking coherently and system-atically about learning out of school as a policy issue.[1]

OSHL: FACTS AND FICTION

Extra-curricular activity is hardly a new idea. It is an old idea with a history of voluntary commitment and excellent practice. The developing concept and practice of OSHL/study support invests both concept and practice

[1] Barber, M (1997) *The Learning Game*, p 257, Indigo Press, London

with new significance, reinforced by new knowledge and applied to new imperatives. While schools do make a difference, there is a mounting conviction, informed by academics, teachers, pupils and parents, that they do not make *all* the difference; and that what happens outside school matters just as much as what happens in school, since it reflects the complex set of relationships and influences that impact upon the school-age child. The key change over the past five years is the recognition of how much learning does take place out of school hours, how this can be most effectively organised and evaluated, and how valuable this is in terms of short- and long-term educational objectives.

OSHL has, however, a long tradition, not least in the history of the community school which, by definition, sees its role as a learning centre for the community, open all hours and for all ages and abilities. Historically, the idea of the community school is perhaps the most perfect expression of the links between schools, families and communities and the concept of social inclusion.[2] Most recently, this fusion has been made clear in the blueprint for greater mutual involvement of schools and communities in the Policy Action Team report *Schools Plus: Building learning communities* which made a series of recommendations for the promotion of community education and lifelong learning as levers 'with which to promote schools as a resource for the whole community'.[3]

Another early and innovative strand of provision in OSHL was the growth of supplementary schools, run by minority ethnic groups in the UK.[4] There are over 1,000 supplementary schools in London, reflecting the fact in part that over 250 minority ethnic languages are spoken in London schools. They operate as supplementary schools, Saturday schools, ethnic minority language classes, or community classes: 'Whatever the name, they are independent educational providers that operate outside state-maintained education. . .' Some of these supplementary classes focus on the National Curriculum subjects, particularly maths, English and science, and sometimes Black history and culture; others on mother-tongue classes and culture. The provision, the organisers stress, is 'entirely supplementary and. . . a positive response to the minority ethnic child's socio-educational needs. . . Its mission is to contribute to the holistic development of the child

[2] See, for example, Ball, M (1998) *School Inclusion: The school, the family and the community*, Joseph Rowntree Foundation, for a typology of the range of links and developments on the ground. For a review of evaluative and research literature in this field in the UK since 1988, see Dyson, A and Robson, E (1999) *School, Family, Community: Mapping school inclusion in the UK*, Joseph Rowntree Foundation
[3] Schools Plus Policy Action Team 11 (2000) *Schools Plus: Building learning communities: improving the educational chances of children and young people from disadvantaged areas*, p 39 (Hereafter, *Schools Plus*)
[4] For further details, see the guidelines published by the DfEE and the Support Unit for Supplementary and Mother Tongue Schools, *Towards More Effective and Supplementary and Mother-Tongue Schools* (1999)

without being a substitute for formal schooling.' All of them aim, through the strong cultural input, to 'give children a real sense of their position in society'.[5]

Alongside this modification of an older ideal, however, extra-curricular provision for school pupils threads its way through the history of schools themselves.

FORTY YEARS ON: THE EXTRA-CURRICULAR HABIT

The modern phenomenon of extra-curricular activities *per se* provides a transparent link to the defining characteristics of Victorian liberal education. This tradition, in itself, took many years to develop. For the early part of the 19th century, at schools such as Harrow, Marlborough, Uppingham, Lancing and Loretto, 'masters atoned' for their obsessive concerns with the classical curriculum ' by an almost total indifference to the way in which a boy employed his leisure'. The boys' free time was their own, and games were hardly part of an extra-curriculum which consisted largely of roaming the 'glorious, unspoilt countryside'. At Marlborough, for example:

A large part of the boys' free time was spent in exploring the countryside, fishing, hunting small animals, poaching and nesting. . . duck hunting and beagling. . . they were [also] given to frog-hunting and killing. The diary of one schoolboy in 1851 recorded playing 'chess, music practice, egg blowing, watching bathing, lying around in fields, high jumping, and general packing.[6]

Gradually, the freedom to ramble over the countryside, go fossil hunting or killing birds gave way to long afternoons given over to team sports, the competitive institutions of houses, mission badges and shields, and the notion of service to the school and the community.

For the majority of people, the image of the public school, outside personal experience, is principally informed by the school story – or by its cartoon companion. Specialists in children's literature have observed that this canon is primarily a narrative of exploits, activities, relationships, developing outside the classroom. Indeed, without any reference to what went on outside the classroom, most school stories would be very thin gruel. While sports offered the opportunity to develop leadership, discipline, and team work, the natural history societies, so popular among adults as well as pupils across the 19th century, enabled the public schoolboy and the city grammar school pupil to connect with a rural memory.

---

[5] Ibid pp 5–6; p 13

[6] I am grateful to Professor Sally Tomlinson, Department of Education, University of Oxford, for directing me towards this source: Mangan, J A (1981) *Athleticism in the Victorian and Edwardian Public School: The emergence and consolidation of an educational ideology*, Falmer Press, London, pp 18–19

The grammar and secondary modern school traditions, faithfully modelled on the public school, reproduced the positive practice of voluntary activities after school, reflected in the traditions of school sports, debating, natural history, music and drama clubs, offered and accepted on a voluntary and school-spirited basis. The major difference, however, was that unlike the public school with its long, free afternoons, these activities in the maintained sector of education were on offer after the school day had ended.

In many instances fictional grammar school pupils seem to have had a richer and more successful life outside the classroom. The activities of the Colham Grammar School Natural History and Field Botanical Club (CGSNHAFBC) – or 'Cigars and Nuts' as it was known to Willie Maddison and Jack Templeton – proved a welcome outlet and also reflect some contemporary concerns:

> On Saturday and Wednesday afternoons, membership of. . . Cigars and Nuts provided an alternative to the playing of games and the rambles of the Club were conducted by Mr Worth. In giving his consent to the formation of the club Mr Rore had insisted that its members should remain together and take notes of their observations. For this reason chiefly membership of Cigars or Nuts was considered a poor escape from more strenuous forms of exercise and too much like work. The club suffered from a paucity of members that was more or less permanent except for a transitory swelling at the commencement of term, when new boys were wont to join with the spontaneity of newly-hatched flies blundering into the most hoary spider's web in the corner of a potting shed.[7]

In the post-war world, the personal histories of Jennings and Darbishire are almost entirely a record of their out of school hours exploits, leaving Mr Carter to observe in Jennings' first end of term report at Linbury Court, after a story-length saga of selection for the First Eleven, that Jennings 'enters very fully into all out of school activities and takes a lively interest in the corporate life of the school'. They both exemplify the 'inventive, industrious and high-spirited' activities in their after-school hobbies which contrasted formidably with their lack of serious purpose in lessons:

> In the common room, the noise made by a group of twenty boys suggested that to be active indoors meant creating enough sound to raise the roof and shake the foundations of the building. Odd pieces of wood were being hammered and chiselled into model yachts; biscuit tins were being beaten into gleaming aeroplane wings; the stage manager of the puppet theatre. . . was imitating rolls of thunder with a tea tray and a gong stick. . . Near the rattling windows members of the wireless club with home-made sets tuned

[7] Williamson, H (1983) *Dandelion Days*, Zenith, Feltham p 55

to rival stations, relayed grand opera, military bands, and talks in Norwegian all at the same time.[8]

Parallel with the supply of after-school activities in public and maintained schools has also come a concern with the need to divert and control young people's behaviour outside school. Organised activities, scouts, guides, temperance movements, or youth clubs are part of the dense weave of voluntary provision reflecting public concern with morality, public health and social order which have emerged over the past century. These organised community-based activities, traditionally separate from schools, have been served by different social and voluntary agencies, and been independent of educational policy.

The need to organise the idle hands of children and young people seems to have accelerated, as with so many other aspects of provision for children and families, during wartime. The First World War posed, at national level, the problem of juvenile delinquency. 'A central juvenile organisation committee (JOC) was set up with local JOCs to organise diversions, like games leagues, and were the first recipients of the first grants to voluntary organisations.'[9] The Second World War provoked further action on juvenile delinquency, in this instance inspired by the rise in juvenile crime evident by 1941. Intriguingly, in a memorandum issued in June that year, the Home Office and the Board of Education pointed to the fact that the number of children under 14 found guilty of offences in the first year of the war had risen by 41 per cent and by 21 per cent for those between 14 and 17. 'It was felt that a major cause of these increases, besides lack of discipline, was the closure of leisure facilities due to the war.' In response, in London, 'play centres were opened in all areas and staff were sent to the reception areas to organise out of school activities. For older children mixed youth recreation centres were opened, for young people to 'meet in social inter-course and recreation'.[10]

And, of course, to bring the story up to date, Harry Potter himself presents a heroic figure in the Quidditch tournament as surely as he does in facing his adult enemies.

[8] Tucker, N (1986) Anthony Buckeridge: the last of the line?, in National Centre for Research in Children's Literature, Digby Stuart College, Roehampton Institute, (NCRL Paper 4) *School Stories from Bunter to Buckeridge*, ed N Tucker, p 86. Most recently, Anthony Buckeridge, in the *Observer*, 27 August 2000, crafted an entire story around Jennings and Darbishire's out of school creativity involving a school play, a moustache and a revolver

[9] Armytage, W H G (1964) *Four Hundred Years of English Education*, p 211, CUP. See the following pages for an account of the growth of the National Association of Boys Clubs and the eventual formation of the Youth Service

[10] Brown, M (2000) *A Child's War: Growing up on the home front*, p 100, Sutton Publishing, Stroud

THE 1990s: CHANGING LIVES AND CHANGING PRIORITIES

Over 40 years, therefore, the pattern of provision of OSHL changed very little. The extra-curricular tradition, although recognised as fundamentally important to the ethos and practice of the good school, still tended to be seen as extra to the school (and to the community). Moreover, it was characterised as:

- closely linked to the curriculum itself;
- offered on a personal basis by committed teachers;
- unsupported by the school in terms of funding and organisation;
- largely disassociated from the school's learning objectives;
- unpaid and unprovided for;
- accidental in its benefits;
- undertaken by the already motivated and confident.

By the 1990s, however, the widely held perception, after a decade of difficulties in schools around issues of pay and conditions, was that after-school activities had perceptibly declined.[11] This, accompanied by the loss of playing fields and playgrounds, and the increasing proportion of mothers returning to work, saw increased concern about what school-age children were doing outside school hours. At the same time, social and economic changes began to intensify the conflict between the needs of parents and children at the end of the school day. The 'long hours culture', which means that parents may be financially rich but time poor, is now mocked by a school-day timetable still fixed by the role of children in gathering in the harvest. At the same time, while very few women worked at the beginning of the last century most mothers of school-age children are now in paid employment. The result is that schools and timetables have simply not kept up with the realities of family and working lives – a perception reinforced by the sight of playing fields, swimming pools, tennis courts, not to say libraries, music and art rooms and gymnasiums, standing idle when they might be available to bored children and frantic parents at the end of the day, on weekends and during the holidays.

These changes and perceptions do not, in themselves, simply make a case for a changed or extended teaching day or teaching year. That argument also reflects a range of other concerns.[12] Indeed, the majority of schools do not – and have never – closed down at 3.30 pm. Rather, they illustrate the greater difficulties that now face working families (many of which include teachers themselves) and employers alike. Britain, in

[11] For evidence of the decline in after-school activities in London, for example, see Education Extra, *Capital Gains* (1996)

[12] See, for example, the recent report by the Association of Local Government on the School Year (2000)

particular, has had a poor record compared with the rest of Europe of making childcare for working families accessible and affordable – and, until very recently, has neglected the positive investment that comes from pre-school provision for the youngest.[13] Given the fact that most women return to work after children have reached school age,[14] providing for after-school care for school-age children has been a matter of informal private arrangements, with much parental juggling of time and resources, until very recently. For many families finding care for the very many 'latchkey' children, and keeping them safe and off the streets, has been a huge stimulus to the expansion of the idea of OSHL as regular, reliable provision alongside the protection of children and childcare after school.

Finding safe and stimulating childcare for primary-age children in particular is even more urgent when families contemplate other changes in the lives of their children compared to their own childhood. With no safe place to play or no chance to walk to school, opportunities to meet and make friends even at a young age outside the school are more limited than they were. Concerns about the right of children to play informally, to organise their own time, to become independent and to learn to negotiate with each other sit alongside the other practical needs of children and parents for care and activities during holidays and after school.

One response to mounting pressures to meet the needs of parents and children outside school hours came in the form of the Out of School Childcare Initiative introduced in 1993 to give grant support to help towards new after-school childcare for school-age children. By mid-1996, 71,500 childcare places had been created and 40 per cent of parents had seen some improvement in their labour market position.[15] To support this, the first childcare benefits were made available in 1994, to help with the costs of childcare. The incoming Labour Government in 1997 had pledged to make a national childcare strategy a definitive policy and one of the priorities for the New Opportunities Fund was for after-school childcare. By November 2000 a further 119,000 places had been created.[16]

The key purpose of out of school childcare for younger children has been to provide high-quality, safe, and guaranteed childcare – and enjoyable stimulating play. Play and learning are interdependent but for older school-age children, in recent years, a key issue has been the opportunity to provide some help with homework alongside playcare where children make and play with friends and develop their social skills.

[13] See, for example, Daycare Trust/Childcare Vouchers (1999) *Childcare changes lives: The benefits of investing in childcare*

[14] *Parents' Demand for Childcare*, National Centre for Social Research, DfEE research report RR 176 (March 2000) (National Centre for Social research)

[15] From DfEE Consultation Document (1996) *Work and Family: Ideas and options for childcare*, Oct 1996, p12

[16] NOF, Monitoring Information Bulletin, November 2000, p 5

However, not only social skills suffer due to lack of opportunities for active play. A recent research study into sport and family life in Britain found compelling evidence of sedentary lifestyles and of the fears which stop parents from allowing their children out alone, to play informally or organise their own activity. The report also found that four fifths of children watched over six hours' TV a week, and one fifth of children more than 21 hours a week. A fifth of parents surveyed said their children played with computer games for over seven hours a week; a third, however, said that their children did not play computer games at all. The same report also exposed the paradox that whereas adults believed that children were less active than they themselves as children, there was an equal perception that opportunities for children to engage in sport had increased.[17] The report concluded that there was clearly a role for after-school clubs to 'satisfy the public's desire to see more children, regardless of their ability, gain the benefits of active participation in sport, without increasing the burden on family budgets'.

Another major concern, however, is with the school itself. The school curriculum has never, in its long history, satisfied the demands of employers[18] but today's complaints are not about the lack of specific vocational or technical skills, but the lack of generic, or key skills, which are not learnt on the job but laid down throughout the years in school. A recent report showed, for example, that in London in July 2000, the majority of employers surveyed were looking not for specific subject related skills, but for generic skills which could be translated into management and problem solving skills in a complex environment.[19] These generic skills, such as communication, ICT, problem solving and leadership, once effectively learnt, can be taken into every new situation no matter what the challenge or, indeed, into any country in which someone makes his or her future. Such skills are critical to any national ambition to raise achievement.

THE CHALLENGE OF RAISING ACHIEVEMENT

There is now clear evidence of a chain linking childhood poverty to teenage parenthood, reduced rates of staying on at school at 16, increased chances of contact with the police and higher risks of low wages and unemployment.[20]

More than anything we need to make our schools as good as yours.[21]

[17] Nestlé Family Monitor, no 59, Introduction, Professor David Kirk
[18] See, for example, the continual complaints about the inferior nature of English technical education compared to that of Germany and France throughout the late 19th century and early 20th century – exemplified in the Royal Commission on Technical Instruction, 1882–84
[19] Report on skill shortages in *Focus,* London, 2000
[20] *Schools Plus,* Annex I: The scale and costs of underachievement, p 55
[21] Parent quoted in *Bringing Britain Together: A national strategy for neighbourhood renewal,* Social Exclusion Unit, 1998, p 33

Raising achievement means several things – and in each case inspires a role for OSHL/study support. It means:

- Raising overall standards of all pupils to stand in good comparison with those in the highest achieving countries across the world.
- Raising the levels of achievement of *specific groups of pupils* – those who are underachieving for different reasons. This may include pupils living in areas of social or economic disadvantage or from minority groups. It may mean boys, or it may mean gifted and talented pupils who are failing to reach potential. Or it may mean the student who is likely to get a D grade at GCSE although he or she could get a C or even higher.
- Raising the standard of achievement in *different areas of the curriculum* – particularly in relation to literacy and numeracy or in terms of key skills such as communication.
- Raising the *standard of motivation for all pupils* – particularly the disaffected, and engaging them more enjoyably with the business of learning – and keeping that spark alive.

In each case it means learning to think more confidently and successfully as well as having the skills to study successfully and to prove to yourself, your peers and teachers that you can do it!

The debate over school improvement, and the anxiety to close the gap between pupils and schools who were doing well (or 'improving') and those who were failing to do so, and the blaze of initiatives that has marked the Labour Government since 1997 has been conducted in the knowledge that in 1999:

- 24 per cent of pupils in disadvantaged areas gained 5+ GCSEs grades A–C compared with 46 per cent nationally.
- 6.1 per cent (35,000) pupils left school without GCSEs and 7.9 per cent failed to get GCSE in English or maths.
- 27.5 per cent of 11-year-olds failed to reach level 4 English and 28.9 per cent failed to reach level 4 maths.
- There is a persistent gap between boys and girls in terms of achievement, reflected in comparative achievement up to and including A levels.
- A third of all children live in households below half-average income.[22]

Raising achievement also means reducing the barriers to learning for those young people and adults. Those barriers, cultural (eg class, ethnicity, gender and age), structural and personal, explored by the Campaign for Learning, are much higher for some children than others. Alec Clegg has drawn up a

---

[22] See *Schools Plus*, Annex 1: The Scale and Costs of Underachievement, pp 54–58

list of 33 'differences and difficulties' that disadvantaged children face.[23] This list includes the following facts, which set disadvantaged children apart from other children:

- more disadvantaged children die young;
- more have parents who left school as soon as they were able;
- more come from homes where books are few;
- more are taught by teachers who do not live in the area;
- fewer hear school English spoken in their homes;
- fewer talk often with adults;
- fewer read to their parents;
- fewer have parents who read to them.

For our purposes there are four items of particular significance that suggest the gap in opportunities for enjoyment, enrichment and taking responsibility:

- fewer disadvantaged children than other children receive extra-curricular help;
- fewer are taken to galleries and concerts by their parents;
- fewer become prefects;
- fewer are members of school teams.

The structural barriers, which can include money, time, childcare and lack of provision can be at least alleviated by education and school policies. The personal barriers identified are more systemic. They include:

- lack of motivation;
- lack of confidence;
- lack of family culture;
- low self-esteem;
- peer pressure;
- lack of support.

For children growing up in the 'worst estates' and neighbourhoods these barriers are highest of all. In 1997 the Social Exclusion Unit was given the task of putting forward coherent policies which would dismantle those barriers of poverty, inadequacy, unemployment, poor housing, community breakdown and 'bad schools'.[24]

---

[23] Clegg, A (1997) Teaching and learning in secondary schools, in Maxted, P (1999) *Understanding Barriers to Learning: A guide to research and current thinking* pp 58; 74, Campaign for Learning

[24] See *Bringing Britain Together: A national strategy for neighbourhood renewal* (1998), Social Exclusion Unit

The Unit's report identified 44 districts of England where social indicators showed complex disadvantage: where, for example:

- two thirds or more adults were unemployed;
- there were higher mortality rates than in other districts;
- there was worse housing than in other districts;
- there was four times the proportion of ethnic minority residents than in other districts.

In terms of educational failure, in these districts:

- there were five times as many schools on special measures than in other districts;
- one child in four had no GCSEs (this is five times the national average);
- truancy levels were at four times the national average;
- adults were more likely than average to have no qualifications and lower skills.

Throughout the blueprint and the policy which has unfolded in the past two years lies the assumption that educational improvement and individual success in school has a fundamental role to play in lifting these communities out of poverty and distress. The report cited examples and evidence of how a broader role for the school in the community could make a major difference.

EXTRA

Moss Side Youth College

A partnership between schools, colleges and youth, community and business agencies, 'offers targeted provision to address the educational and training needs of disaffected and underachieving young people and pays special attention to the needs of African-Caribbean pupils'. Among its strategies in 1997 were:

- A coordinated package of education outside school for excluded and self-excluded pupils between 13 and 16 – offering an alternative curriculum and work experience.
- Strategies to tackle disaffection in local high schools – using initiatives such as IT literacy schemes and 8 'til late homework clubs.

Some 1,800 students were helped throughout the overall programme, including 78 excluded or self-excluded students.[25]

---

[25] Ibid, pp 49–50

Alongside new policies for young children (Sure Start), and employment (New Deal for Communities), a new development of community schooling (Schools Plus) was also flagged by the decision to set up Action Teams devoted to Schools Plus which presented its final report in February 2000. This took shape within policies already in place to support a national concept and framework for OSHL.

PARTNERSHIPS, PRESSURES AND POLITICS

The process whereby OSHL moved from the margins to the centre of educational policy between 1996 and 2000 was encouraged, not only by the search for new ways to close the achievement gap, but also, during the early 1990s, by the growth of voluntary sector advocates and partners, and by changes in government attitudes towards partnership with the voluntary sector. Four complementary voluntary agencies proved to be particularly important.

Education Extra was set up in October 1992 to bring after-school activities within the reach of every child. In order to recognise the work of teachers and others outside school hours and to help schools do far more, it created a National Award for After-School Activities which enabled small grants to be made to schools ready to develop their activities and clubs, and to take the next step. This first public act of recognition proved extremely popular, with hundreds of schools entering for the award, articulating the value and benefits of after-school activities and joining the new national network set up to define and spread good ideas and good practice.

By 1994, with about 700 schools in its national network, Education Extra was engaged in a range of research and development initiatives in both out of school learning and childcare for older pupils, and had set up a series of demonstration projects across the UK to show what could be done outside school. It had begun the work of creating professional development materials and pathways for teachers and adults, and by providing a portfolio of specialist advice and good practice. In 1996 it was given the task of managing the first publicly funded 'homework' schemes set up under the Conservative Government; in 1997 it was responsible for setting up the first National Summer Literacy Schemes under the Labour Government. Over the years it has become the leading voluntary sector organisation, enabling thousands of schools to start or develop new activity programmes, managing exemplary national projects, and spreading good practice with the aid of a UK-wide network of over 5,000 schools. Its work has been supported by a proactive research and development capacity, and close partnership with all statutory and voluntary agencies across the UK.

The Community Education Development Centre (CEDC) is the national centre for community-based learning, working in the fields of education, health improvement and economic and community development. The charity is dedicated to addressing disadvantage and to enabling community development and regeneration through education. Its education work includes supporting parents, carers and children learning together. It has been heavily involved in formulating the concept and practice of the Schools Plus initiative.

The Prince's Trust began its work in study support in 1992. It played a key role in promoting study support across the four countries of the UK, working with key local authorities, TECs and schools to develop effective study support centres focused in particular on academic revision, homework and curriculum extension work and personal development activities. In 1997 it hosted a national evaluation programme designed to track students over a period of three years, identifying what study support contributes to achievement and how it does so. Eleven partner authorities took part in the project and 50 schools. That work is now continued by the National Evaluation and Development Programme.[26] The Prince's Trust also produced the first Code of Practice for Study Support, a self-evaluation tool to support secondary schools wanting to develop more robust and effective programmes of learning support after school. The Code was revised and reissued in partnership with other voluntary partners in 1999, and other codes, for primary schools and libraries, have been developed alongside the original.

The Kids Clubs Network (KCN) began its work in the mid-1980s when concern about the lack of childcare for working parents was first articulated. In the past 15 years, as the leading charity in the development of after-school childcare, it has established quality frameworks, training programmes, and delivery mechanisms in most areas of the country. Most recently, along with the umbrella organisation, the DayCare Trust, it has played a major role in the implementation of the National Childcare Strategy.

Three partners – CEDC, Education Extra and KCN – came together in 1997 to present a joint manifesto which called for a national development strategy for OSHL. Ahead of this manifesto, advocacy, diagnosis and prescription and proof of benefit, as well as a growing body of innovative practice, had already begun to make an impact on the three major political parties. The Liberal Party, supporting the joint manifesto from the three voluntary sector bodies, made its commitment clear. Paddy Ashdown went on record saying:

> The under-use of Britain's schools is a national scandal. Schools are still seen by too many as 8.30 am to 3.30 pm. . . In the education revolution this country needs our schools must become, instead, a resource for the whole

---

[26] This work is led by Professor John Macbeath, Professor Kate Myers, and Tony Kirwan of the Quality in Study Support initiative

community – 'centres of community learning' which, in partnership with others, offer a whole range of educational opportunities for all ages, throughout the day, all through the year.

The Labour Party went into even greater detail:

After-school activities have been shown to have a crucial bearing not only on individual pupil attainment but on the overall ethos and success of a school. . . We will. . . recommend that after-school activities be included in every school's development plan so that their contribution is clearly linked into the school's core objectives. . . Rather than being seen as a peripheral add-on, such activities should be seen as core to a school's whole ethos and attainment. . . I invite you all to join with us, to work towards making this vision of after-school activities in every school, and an after-school club in every community, a reality. (David Blunkett, speech to KCN Annual Conference).

HOMEWORK AND HIGH HOPES

The immediate context for the development of study support was a growing concern to improve the consistency and standard of homework set and marked as a way of raising achievement overall. The process had begun with the Conservative Government (1992–1997) which had set in motion exemplary schemes for homework after school.[27] There had been wide-spread anxiety about the quality and consistency of homework for some years – and an increasing concern for the many children (primary and secondary) known to have no place to study, no family support to do so, and no resources. An Ofsted report published in 1995 updated earlier findings and noted that only a quarter of primary schools had a written policy on homework, many of the policies were very recent and the average amount of homework set varied widely. Ofsted recommended that schools should have 'an agreed, written homework policy' in order to be fully effective, and that senior management should ensure it was properly planned, clear and closely monitored.[28]

The clinching argument emerged in 1997, with the publication of a DfEE funded study which provided evidence of the clear link between successful

---

[27] Education Extra (1997) *Succeeding at Study Support: An evaluation of 12 model projects in primary and secondary schools*

[28] See Ofsted (1995) *Homework in Primary and Secondary Schools*. Homework policies were formalised in homework guidelines published in 1998 which were intended to help schools to draw up and implement consistent policies for homework. The guidelines suggested, *inter alia*, a minimum commitment of time for pupils of different age groups, related to the curriculum and Key Stages

schools and the amount of homework and extra-curricular provision. The report covered curriculum enrichment ('by which we mean traditional extra-curricular activities such as sport, drama, chess, photography and other clubs and societies'), curriculum extension ('by which we mean study support opportunities provided before or after school or during the breaks in the school day, such as homework clubs, extra revision classes and extra after-school tuition, whether undertaken voluntarily or as a result of teacher direction') , and 'homework'. This was the first systematic attempt to map the place of extra-curricular activities as a whole against an Ofsted cited (ie 'successful' school) and the report concluded: 'Our results indicate that academic performance and high levels of participation in extra-curricular provision go together'. The research evidence revealed:

- an enormous range and depth of extra-curricular provision;
- a very high value placed on extra curricular provision by headteachers and schools;
- a high value placed on extra curricular activities by pupils – with two-thirds of all pupils believing that curriculum extension and enrichment were important;
- a positive correlation between the quality of a school as reflected in Ofsted inspection and the provision of curriculum enrichment;
- elements of good practice, eg a committed leadership, whole school policy, pupil involvement, and opportunities for self-study;
- a clear link between the amount of homework done and the overall performance of the school.[29]

However, researchers also commented that, despite the very wide range of benefits identified by the schools, it was 'perhaps surprising to find that only three of the fourteen heads have a formal policy for extra-curricular provision, while two others say that there is reference to it in their school development plan'.

These findings provided the incentive and guidance for the government to set up the first publicly funded homework projects to define and disseminate good practice in OSHL. The 12 projects showed how, in 12 different primary and secondary schools, many different ways could be found of providing learning support through activities out of school – from primary school library and ICT clubs, to secondary school 'homework hotlines' and structured subject clubs for revision. The one special school included (Chesnut Lodge) developed an outstanding new technologies club whereby pupils undertook CREST projects as part of the school's commitment to environmental studies.[30] Each of the different model projects

[29] Barber, M *et al* (1997) *School Performance and Extra-curricular Provision*, DfEE, January
[30] See Education Extra (1997) *Succeeding at Study Support*

recorded significant gains in terms of student participation, learning gains and positive attitudes towards school, recording academic improvements in relation to KS levels, informal tests and predicted GCSE grades.

EXCELLENCE, OSHL AND THE LABOUR GOVERNMENT

There are many opportunities outside the classroom to bolster pupil confidence and motivation and boost achievement at school – from homework to learning about the world of work. Such out of school activity can reinforce the ability and willingness to learn. It is especially valuable in helping disadvantaged individuals and groups.

Out of school learning and play are. . . crucial for many children and their working parents. We want to see a national network that builds on the work of organisations such as Education Extra and Kids Clubs Network in developing these plans. Research shows that in both primary school and secondary school these activities raise pupils motivation, improve school skills and encourage participation in other activities.[31]

With the mantra 'education, education, education' resounding through Whitehall, one of the first White Papers off the stocks after the election of the Labour Government was on Excellence in Schools which contained the first promise of OSHL as a prime agent for change – and as another way of addressing both disadvantage and underachievement. The White Paper signalled the intention of making provision for homework through homework clubs, and made it clear that out of school hours activity was to have a key role in the national achievement strategy: 'We want all young people to have access to a range of activity in addition to normal classroom teaching and learning designed to improve their achievement.'

The challenge facing the incoming government was to give OSHL a status, visibility and clear educational purpose; to create a framework which would nourish the voluntary character while linking it explicitly to higher standards and formal education; to provide some key funding and foundation stones for sustainability and above all, to enthuse staff, parents and children.

Most importantly, the White Paper anticipated the idea of a National Framework for Pupil Motivation – from which was to emerge the National Framework for Study Support and new funding through the People's Lottery to expand and improve national provision and open up new opportunities. The resulting document, *Extending Opportunity – A national framework for study support*, was the first national attempt to create an enabling framework for study support which would raise awareness of

---

[31] DfEE *Excellence in Schools*, July 1997, pp 58, 60

study support, define its language, purpose and scope, extend its boundaries, set out agreed principles of good practice and emphasise the partnership prospects for OSHL as a whole. Apart from providing the key definitions, it also set a blueprint for good practice. Its publication marked the defining moment in establishing the difference between traditional extra-curricular activities and what was officially labelled 'study support'. This official definition, set out in some detail in *Extending Opportunity*, established the generic term as: 'learning activity outside normal lessons which young people take part in voluntarily. Study support is, accordingly, an inclusive term, embracing many activities –with many names and many guises. Its purpose is to improve young people's motivation, build their self-esteem and help them to become more effective learners. Above all, it aims to raise achievement.'

The report also placed a very high value on learning partnerships in study support: 'The National Framework is intended to help all those who play a part in study support – whether as local or national policy makers or as providers working with young people in schools, community centres, libraries or other settings. It aims to offer guidance and support, and to raise awareness of what study support can achieve. . .'[32]

It also emphasised the need to link new programmes with the school's overall learning objectives: 'Ad hoc activities can help to meet needs – this is often how study support activities begin. Ideally, however, study support should be planned as a coherent programme to address all pupils' needs and to complement and support what goes on in the classroom. Such a programme should encourage a broad range of learning activities which fall within a common set of purposes and values.'[33] *Extending Opportunity* invited schools and other partners to look at ways of taking learning outside the traditional boundaries of time and place, and to look for new ways of creating an effective learning environment. Among the many examples cited was that of the Highway Youth Club:

EXTRA

The Highway Youth Club

Established in 1995, the Highway Youth Club was established in Broadwater Farm, Tottenham, London, and aimed to help young people reach their full potential. The club primarily provides supplementary help in maths, English and science and is guided by the National Curriculum. The club is open every Saturday from 10 am to 1 pm. It also organises a four-week summer school for about 50 pupils. In 1995, 40 children, mainly from West African countries, were taught by eight volunteer teachers. 90 per cent of pupils attended the Broadwater Farm Primary School. The club's organiser, Reverend Alex Gyasi,

---

[32] DfEE (1998) *Extending Opportunity: A national framework for study support*, para 1.2
[33] Ibid para 1.5

emphasised that the club had made a very positive contribution to the community: 'The children have learnt to respect themselves and other people irrespective of their racial backgrounds. Parents are happy with the improvements they observe in the standards of their children.'[34]

As well as publishing *Extending Opportunity*, the DfEE put in place a raft of research and development into the extent of study support in schools and LEAs, patterns of participation, research reviews, and a project development programme which generated a bank of innovative and replicable provision.

A year later, the equivalent framework document for Wales, *Unlocking Potential* – a framework for extending out of school hours learning opportunities in Wales – was published, reflecting the different partnerships and emphases of Welsh education and community. The document emphasised the strong base on which lottery funding and the new provision would build and the potential to make 'a real difference for young people in Wales'.

PATTERNS OF PARTICIPATION AND PARTICULAR CHALLENGES

Finding out what schools were already doing, what students were attending and why and what new provision would be most effective was clearly an essential first step. The first attempt to survey what schools were doing, why and with what effect outside school hours was the indirect result of the Education Extra National Award for After-School Activities. Given that an award of only £7,000 was being offered, by an unknown and untested voluntary body, it proved that schools wanted recognition for their extra efforts in after-school activities as much as extra help with funding them. Over 300 schools entered for the first award, bringing with them stories of extraordinary efforts and activities, hopes and fears for their pupils, and a sense of urgency that more could be done. The information provided formed the first national database on extra-curricular activities.

While the sample might not have been representative, the positive enthusiasm which the teachers demonstrated have consistently proved to be. Each year, the Award has given Education Extra the opportunity to rediscover how after-school activities inspires and enthuses schools, and is an outstanding expression of the best of the school in action. That information has now been extended and supported more systematically by national surveys commissioned by the Scottish Office and the DfEE.

In Scotland, drawing on a narrower definition of study support as supported homework, revision and study, researchers found that whereas

[34] Ibid p 24

78 per cent of secondary schools said that they had study support in one or more forms, only 22 per cent of primary schools did. Even so, 'very large differences in the profile of provision from school to school emerged' and in participating numbers as well as differences between the primary and secondary curriculum.[35]

In England, in the first survey undertaken by the NFER, in 1998, 1,000 headteachers and 9,000 pupils provided significant clues for future policy and planning.[36] It found, first, that virtually all mainstream schools (98 per cent of primary and 99 per cent of secondary) and 72 per cent of special schools took part in some form of 'out of school lesson time' for their pupils. And, while 90 per cent of secondary schools said they were providing out of school lesson time activities in the broad area of study skills (and a third planned to introduce more), only 10 per cent of all secondary pupils said that they had attended such activities during the survey week.

At some stages, schools were also found to be performing better. No significant differences were found between schools with different levels of provision at the end of KS2 or KS3 English exams. However, at GCSE level, schools with lower GCSE grades (ie with 25 per cent or fewer pupils achieving five or more GCSE grades at A*–C) 'were found to provide fewer types of out of lesson time activities (ie a narrower range of specific activities)'. Likewise, schools with more than 31.5 per cent of pupils eligible for free school meals were also found to provide fewer out of school lesson time activities. [37]

The survey showed, moreover, uneven patterns of participation with declining numbers as pupils progressed through secondary school (40 per cent of KS4 pupils, 48 per cent of KS3 pupils and 56 per cent of KS2) in the single survey week. The same pattern of lower participation was seen in the participation rates for the whole year: 74 per cent of KS4; 83 per cent of KS3 and 84 per cent of KS2. There were also wide differences in levels of participation, with 20 per cent of all the pupils attending three or more activities during the survey week. At all three key stages, more girls than boys attended an activity, and were more likely than boys to have attended a creative and performing arts activity; whereas boys were more likely to have attended a sports activity.

Activities were most likely to take place either at lunchtime or after school. 'Relatively few activities took place at other times.'[38] The OSHL curriculum of primary and secondary schools also differed. The majority of primary schools provided activities clustered around sport, leisure and

---

[35] See Macbeath, J (1999) *Study Support in Scottish Schools*, p 3, Quality in Education, University of Strathclyde, and The Scottish Office

[36] DfEE/NFER, *Out-of-lesson-time Learning Activities: Surveys of headteachers and pupils*, RR 127 (July 1999)

[37] Ibid p 18

[38] Ibid

board games, or the creative and performing arts. The secondary schools provided activities in those categories, as well as in:

- mathematics, science and information technology;
- study skills;
- English language, reading and writing;
- humanities, foreign languages and community studies.

Within these categories, the most popular activities among all pupils were team sports and computer/IT clubs. Other popular activities included:

- library/book clubs;
- singing/choir;
- drama;
- arts/crafts/design technology.

The importance of finding something individual pupils enjoyed was borne out in the main reasons pupils gave for taking part. In order of frequency, pupils made these comments about OSHL or clubs:

- 'I like the things we do there.'
- 'It is one of my hobbies.'
- 'My friends go there.'
- 'It is interesting.'
- 'I like learning new things.'

However, most significant, there was evidence that 'perceived achievement levels, educational aspirations and home background factors were positively associated with attendance at out of school lesson time learning'.[39] For example, pupils who were *more* likely to attend more frequently were those who:

- perceived themselves as among the best in their class at school work;
- intended to continue in full- time education after 16;
- came from homes with more books.

In short: 'those who take part in a range of activities outside school are better motivated and achieve better results in school'.

The report concluded that 'pupils from less favoured home backgrounds' were less likely to take art in out of school lesson time activities than those from more favoured backgrounds, and that there was a need to 'target activities that appeal to:

[39] Ibid p iv

- pupils who perceive themselves to be poor at school work;
- those with low academic aspirations;
- those from less favoured home backgrounds'.[40]

These highly significant findings were consistent with others which show that children from poorer families are *less* likely to know about and to have access to opportunities out of school overall. A recent research study found, for example, that while 28 per cent of children aged 3–14 were involved in 1–3 hours of out of school activities during the week, 'Only 12 per cent of children participated in more than 6 hours of activities. . . In line with the previous findings on childcare use and key socio-economic factors, a link was also found between use of out of school activities and household structure, employment and social class. . . Families from lower social levels [were] less likely to say their children used out of school activities. The level of use ranged from 27 per cent among social classes IV and V to 47 per cent in I and II.' Moreover, there were regional differences too. Only 30 per cent of children in London and 32 per cent of children in Wales were likely to do after-school activities compared with 44 per cent in East Anglia.[41]

Evidence therefore shows differences between levels of provision in schools, the links between disadvantage and lack of opportunities out of school, and lack of achievement in school matched by lack of participation out of school. These facts provided clear guidance to policy makers concerned as much with how out of school provision could help lift achievement and promote social inclusion. They were to prompt and reinforce the way in which OSHL was presented, framed in national and local strategies, and delivered at the level of the school itself.

SCHOOLS PLUS

With a national framework in place, and a national map outlining the contours of unequal opportunities, OSHL was already flagged up as a new way of promoting raising achievement in areas of high disadvantage and, therefore, as an agent of social inclusion. Growing out of the Neighbourhood Renewal report of 1997, therefore, the Social Inclusion Unit set up two action teams which had a particular interest in what OHSL could do: Policy Action Team (PAT) 10 on the role of arts and sports in social renewal and PAT 11, Schools Plus.

PAT 10, led by the DCMS, looked at the way that participation in sports and arts could help young people and adults to become confident, creative and successful and emphasised that: 'Participation, and the provision of

---

[40] Ibid p 45
[41] Ibid pp 34–35

services to support participation, in arts and sport, can help address neighbourhood renewal by improving communities' "performance" on the four key indicators of more jobs, less crime, better health and improved educational attainment.' The report concluded that schools should be encouraged 'in the use of creative and sporting activity to support the drive to raise standards of literacy and numeracy and through the use of these activities as part of PSHE to build students' confidence and self-esteem'.

The report cited many different examples of good practice in sports and the arts. The role of the arts is discussed in more detail in Chapters 3 and 8, but the most far-reaching of the reports was that of PAT 11, *Schools Plus: Improving the educational chances of children and young people from disadvantaged areas*, which set out the most radical of all policy options in terms of the role that OSHL could play.

The aim of the Schools Plus policy was 'to develop a coherent and comprehensive approach to supporting the learning of every child in deprived communities'. Alongside the requirement that teaching should be 'focused, stimulating and productive', the twin theme was that schools should be 'fully utilised as agents for broader change in communities'. Among the changes needed was to break the established link between failure at school and delinquency out of school.[42]

The Report marshalled an impressive set of statistics about the 'enormous' costs of educational failure and the links between underachievement and criminal behaviour. Looking at the way schools had transformed themselves through partnership with communities and external agencies, the report concluded that a more coordinated approach would bring greater rewards for schools and communities. The Report contained examples of schools which had turned themselves around from 'failing' to 'improving' schools. One school cited at length was Westgate Community College, Newcastle upon Tyne .

EXTRA

Westgate Community College

In the mid-1990s, Westgate Community College had been placed under special measures to combat very high levels of truancy, vandalism and very low achievement rates. The school was in the bottom 5 per cent of all schools nationally. Alongside robust new management strategies and teaching strategies, with zero tolerance of poor behaviour, and targeted policies for attendance, the school also embarked, with the help of Education Extra and the local TEC, on a systematic programme of OSHL, with breakfast clubs, lunchtime clubs and a summer literacy school.

The school was chosen by Education Extra as one of the first 12 model schools to pioneer out of school homework support in 1997 and was able to

---

[42] *Schools Plus*, p 4

provide enhanced and extended study facilities and ICT provision during lunchtimes and after school hours for years 7 and 8 with the aim of raising standards of literacy and promoting independent learning. The result of the confidence shown in the school and the pupils led to an increase in 'passes' for the learning centre from 30 to 90 students, with 25–30 attending on a daily basis. Measurable (although variable) gains were recorded with a maximum gain of 19 months over a year by a pupil for whom English was a second language. The headteacher reported: 'We found significant evidence of low-attaining children focusing on their own standard of learning and getting all too rare satisfaction from a sense of their own success. Visitors to the project have commented that the room is alive with confidence and motivation. The Chair of Governors, seeing the queue, found the sight unbelievable.'

Among the priorities *Schools Plus* identified was the need to 'provide motivational and confidence-building activities *around the school day for all pupils*'. The title of *Schools Plus* signalled ways of adding value to schools in two specific ways: by extending the services offered by schools to their pupils, and by greater involvement of the community in the school and the school in the community.

The conclusion of the report was clear: 'The PAT recognises the important part that study support can play in helping to raise attainment. It wants those at most disadvantage to have the opportunity to benefit from a targeted expansion of funding for study support.'

The report recommended the following targets:

- The opportunity for pupils in every school where there is 35 per cent or more entitlement to free school meals to have at least three hours' study support each week, including various activities over the weekend.
- The development of a 'Tap-in' programme for both primary and secondary schools offering individual programmes of study and support to pupils at the risk of leaving or students rejoining mainstream education, whether because of absence through truancy, exclusion or long-term absence. The programme would concentrate on addressing language and other core skills and make extensive use of ICT, and would be linked to SEN funding streams.
- Extended opening hours at some schools allowing pupils extensive access to study support-type activities, including enrichment activities. Individual programmes of study to be developed which would also take into account the disrupted life of some pupils.

These far-sighted policies give OSHL a role of immense significance within the national educational and social strategy for improvement. They also take OSHL beyond education and into other policy areas such as the arts, environment and employment. Moreover, they sit within other policy recommendations for closer links with business to develop mentoring schemes and improve work experience opportunities; and alongside initiatives developing the community role of schools, including Community Learning Champions, a National Community College Network, supported by a Community Education Fund and Schools Plus Teams. Parents and young people themselves were recognised as having a key role in making a success of the whole initiative.

CREATING NEW OPPORTUNITIES

Inspired by the central place afforded to it in the White Paper *Excellence in Schools*, OSHL has grown in capacity, significance and quality in the past three years because policy and funding opportunities have developed hand in hand. The White Paper was closely followed in 1997 by the Lottery White Paper, *The People's Lottery* , which identified out of school hours activities as one of the first three priorities for new funding. (The first two initiatives were Healthy Living Centres and ICT.) The paper stated: 'The New Opportunities Initiative will help establish out of school hours activities which help to raise pupils' achievements. By 2001 we want high quality programmes of regular learning activities established in at least half of all secondary and a quarter of all primary schools.'

The New Opportunities Fund (NOF) was set up in 1997–1998. Its remit, unlike other National Lottery Boards, was circumscribed by policy directions which govern content and overall direction. NOF began distributing funds in April 1999 with final bids timed for March 2001 and with funds of:

- £180 million for OSHL to be distributed across the UK by the NOF (April 1999–2003).
- £25 million for summer schools.
- £20 million from the funding for childcare, for schemes which integrate childcare and learning (apart from the £220 million made available for out of school hours childcare *per se*).

These OSHL funds have been dedicated to 'help children and young people to enjoy active learning, improve their academic performance, learn new skills and increase their self-confidence'. The funds enable new schemes to be started and those already in place to build on and improve existing good-quality provision. The definition of activities to be funded through NOF is effectively the same as that in *Extending Opportunity*. NOF also stressed the importance which partnership can play in study support and lists as potential partners: community and voluntary organisations, other educational institutions and services, the Youth Service, childcare organisations, libraries, museums, galleries, businesses, arts and sports organisations. More traditional partnerships are also important: 'One of the most important partnerships can be the informal partnership developed with parents and carers, and with local residents.'

NOF funds have been intended, in large part, to benefit children and young people 'of all backgrounds and abilities' but 'particularly those who suffer disadvantage and who would benefit most from help to raise achievement'. Consequently, 50 per cent of primary school funding was reserved for the 'most disadvantaged' 15 per cent of primary schools, and 50 per cent of the secondary school funding for the most disadvantaged 25 per cent of secondary school with 'some priority' going to Education Action Zones and its equivalent in other countries of the UK. Each bid has to identify at least one named school to ensure that the funding was linked, directly, to school policies.

NOF funding, in effect and scope, created an immediate need for local authorities to develop a strategy for out of school learning. Two bidding routes had been set up; the first, by which schools themselves could bid for funds, or, a second and, in practice, preferred route, which was seen as providing a guarantee that schools in disadvantaged areas would receive their allocated share of funding, LEAs could put in a coherent bid (or bids) for schools which fell within the targeted scope of the funding, and thus carried an implicit guarantee of success.

At the same time, it was announced that the government was also ready to fund study support through the Standards Fund. In April 2000, the first £20 million for study support was made available to local authorities; to be followed by a further £60 million in April 2001. At the same time, £10 million was made available from the Excellence Fund for Scotland.

CONCLUSION

From small beginnings, study support has grown into a national movement of immense significance.[43]

In four years, therefore, a new approach has been laid down for the provision of OSHL. Building on historical practice of voluntarism and goodwill, evident in the vast majority of schools, despite some loss in the 1980s, OSHL has been reframed nationally without losing its voluntary quality and potential. While building on the best of extra-curricular provision, it is now seen that:

- it is highly and publicly valued as part of policies to raise achievement and promote social inclusion in its widest sense;

[43] Macbeath, J (1999) *Study Support in Scottish Schools*, p 3, Quality in Education, University of Strathclyde, and The Scottish Office

- it exemplifies wider definition of achievement in which enrichment as well as extension activities play a critical role;
- it brings together in a coherent focus a wide variety of different learning opportunities, styles and partnerships inside and outside schools;
- it emphasises the need for organisation as a way of making it both more inclusive and effective;
- it emphasises its links with whole school policies and school development policies;
- it is seen to have a particular role to play in lifting motivation and aspiration as well as achievement within disadvantaged communities;
- it is articulated within a transparent, dynamic and flexible national framework;
- it is funded from public sources.

Most significant of all, however, have been the clear statement that the benefits of OSHL must not be a chance option but an entitlement for all children, and in particular, for those who are disadvantaged. In a speech to the Social Market Foundation on 15 March 2000, David Blunkett made this commitment clear:

> We intend to establish an out of school hours entitlement for older primary and secondary pupils. . . We want to develop the concept of a learning day in which activities in school – both during and outside the formal school day – at other locations such as football clubs and youth centres, and work done at home are seamlessly linked. Beyond the school day and the school gates there are wonderful opportunities for experts from across society to support schools and to offer young people a wide range of role models and a rich diet of opportunities. Only when first-rate schooling is combined with these wider opportunities can we be sure that each young person will make a successful transition from school student to lifelong learner.

The following chapters examine the implications of those changes for effective learning, effective schooling and effective community learning partnerships.

2

Informing policy: proving the benefits

This chapter looks at:

- the development of the language and concepts of study support;
- current understanding and new ways of learning and thinking;
- the research and development which suggests that out of school hours learning offers a highly dynamic and effective learning environment;
- patterns of pupil participation and particular challenges with regard to pupils who could benefit most.

The worst news since double Latin, chizz. Molesworth would grone as any fule no. It turns out that all those Fotherington-Thomas extra-curricular activities to which middle-class children are bribed, cajoled and bullied by their high-achieving parents really do help you to get a better job in later life. . . True, the research was done in America but we gloomily predict that the results would be replicated here.[1]

USING OUR BRAINS DIFFERENTLY

Increasing demands on the curriculum to accommodate the knowledge explosion translate into increasing pressures on teachers. . . It is less and less possible for pupils to pass examinations and go on to further study simply on the basis of what they do in the classroom. The capacity for homework, study and independent learning in your own time is the single most powerful determinant of ultimate success and failure.[2]

[1] *The Independent* leading article, 25 September 2000
[2] MacBeath, J (1999) *Study Support in Scottish Schools*, p 3, Quality in Education, University of Strathclyde, and The Scottish Office

Because study support can create a differently shaped learning environment – whether that is outside school hours or outside school itself, the opportunity exists for young people, their tutors and teachers, to explore different ways of learning and different, personal styles of learning. The previous chapter looked at the way in which policy and practice took shape over the last decade. This chapter looks at some critical research into the way children learn and perform from a young age – and at findings which have thrown a particular and new light on the value of learning out of school. It also looks at how policy has been informed by many different changes and perceptions in terms of language, concepts and knowledge.

In recent years, there has been an explosion of knowledge about the nature of intelligence and learning. As John Macbeath has observed, 'Learning is a subject about which we have probably learned more in the past decade and a half than in the previous 200 – and what we have learned. . . has helped to overturn the historical idea of intelligence, formed around the beginning of the century, which has dominated educational thinking and practice for many decades.'[3] Some students who do not learn well in classrooms, where motivation and ability can be depressed, 'can learn more effectively in a more responsive environment such as a study centre'.[4] The 'decade of the brain' brought forward in education the theory of multiple intelligences as well as emotional intelligence.[5]

The theory of multiple intelligence, ie that each person possesses eight kinds of intelligences – albeit differently balanced and blended – each of which should be nurtured through different entry points in the learning system, plays to the great strengths of OSHL.[6] In brief, these entry points offer a toolkit for ensuring that each individual exploits his or her broadest personal capacities for learning. Individuals may learn best using a linguistic approach, or by using quantitative analysis; but they may also learn by using a logical, analytical approach, or through kinaesthetic experience – where learners learn by performing learning-related activities. The in-school curriculum has focused on the linguistic and logical intelligences; the out of school hours opportunities offers the chance to use all the entry points – not least those which emphasise inter- and intra-personal understanding.

As with multiple intelligences, developing emotional intelligence is about finding new ways to become not merely a successful learner, but a more successful and balanced adult. Emotional intelligence, it is argued, shows the clear interdependence between reason and emotion, and the role of

[3] Quoted in Tom Bentley (1998) *Learning Beyond the Classroom: Education for a changing world*, Routledge, London, p 21
[4] Quoted in the Princes Trust-Action (1997) *Learning to Achieve*, p 5
[5] Goleman, D (1996) *Emotional Intelligence: Why it can matter more than IQ*, Bloomsbury, London. See also Gardner, H (1983) *Frames of Mind*, NY Basic Books, New York
[6] See, for example, Brice Heath, S (2000) Seeing our way into learning, *Cambridge Journal of Education*, **30** (1)

emotion in determining life chances, success in work and in life. The role of the school – although not dominant – offers many opportunities for young people to develop their emotional intelligence in terms of understanding and managing their own emotions, motivating themselves, recognising and respecting emotions in each other, and handling their relationships. Again, organised OSHL offers unique opportunities for young people to work together, voluntarily, in their own time, negotiating their own learning and activities, and drawing on their own emotions and experience. More importantly, developing emotional intelligence enables learners more effectively to learn in other ways.

In Britain one of the most successful experiments in using OSHL as an environment for pioneering new ways of learning – particularly accelerated learning – has been carried at the University of the First Age (UFA) in Birmingham. Theirs is the forerunner of what is now becoming a national programme.[7] As one enthusiastic participant put it: 'Here we are shown how to learn better – we are shown how our brain works – I like that.'

The UFA began with a summer school in 1996 for around 600 pupils from six secondary schools. Established by Professor Tim Brighouse, Director of Education in Birmingham, the programme has expanded since then and now provides OSHL activities throughout the year and reaches around 2,500 pupils at some 40 schools. The aim is to provide exciting opportunities for children and their families which encourage teaching and learning in different ways.

The UFA is training a wide range of people to deliver its programmes – from teachers to library staff and parents. It is also involved in developing study support programmes for use by teachers in schools.

The UFA's core principles are to transform learning through:

- introducing new approaches to teaching and learning;
- creating unique and positive learning environments;
- developing learning communities;
- valuing individuality and difference;
- ensuring quality, support and accountability.

The core activities are:

- involving students in consultation and democratic participation through the Young People's Parliament;
- providing training for secondary school leavers;
- providing Vacation Enrichment Schools for over 1000 young people;

[7] For information about the UFA peer tutoring project in relation to the concepts and practice of successful learning as developed in the UFA, see, for example, http://www.qiss.org.uk/sgp/ufapeertutor.htm

- operating extended learning centres out of school hours in all partner schools and community organisations;
- presenting Super Learning Days;
- offering an Accelerated Literacy Programme for over 900 students;
- running a parent/community/peer tutor training programme;
- recruitment and training of learning teams;
- running Summer schools for gifted and talented pupils.

So successful has this project been that the government awarded the scheme £400,000 to replicate the model elsewhere, forming a National Project working, for example, in Middlesbrough, Blackburn, Kirklees in Yorkshire and Enfield in north London. Individual local authorities are also using intensive periods to enable more effective learning.

In summer 2000 the London borough of Newham organised Project SuperCamp at its outdoor education centre near Maldon, for 50 Year 9 students to learn 'more about how to learn more quickly while staying in the centre's beautiful rural setting – very different from the inner city where the students live.' Project SuperCamp 'aimed to build confidence and improve academic performance with 'accelerated learning methods' using the latest research findings in psychology and brain function to coach and support students in the rediscovery of how learning can be fun 'and what remarkable learning abilities we all have'.

Most recently research has been published on the relationship between high self-esteem and success in school and in life. The London School of Economics Centre for Educational Performance, using the British Cohort Study, has followed the fortunes of all babies born in Britain in a certain month. Their research has shown 'clear evidence' that low self-esteem, even when combined with high academic achievement, can lead to 'significant under-performance in the jobs market' – and boys, in particular, who were antisocial and had low self-esteem at 10 were 'at greater risk of unemployment in early adulthood'. The researchers also made a link between high self-esteem and parenting skills which instilled a sense of worth, confidence and ambition, and concluded that 'Schools are geared to helping pupils achieve good exam scores, not to help individual children achieve their psychological growth.'[8] The *Observer* concluded on the basis of this research, for example, that:

Parents' interest in the education of their child and whether they exhibit hostility to the child are also 'hugely important'. . . The LSE author, Leon

[8] See, for example, reports of the research by Leon Feinstein and colleagues, quoted in the *Daily Mail* (25 September 2000); *Observer* (24 September 2000); *Guardian* (27 September 2000). See the author's summary of research findings in *CentrePiece*, LSE, Autumn 2000, p 17. On the value of self-esteem, see Lawrence, D (1996) *Enhancing Self-esteem in the Classroom*, 2nd edn, Paul Chapman, London

Feinstein, has also argued that 'There may now be grounds for arguing that school performance should be assessed not only in terms of maths, reading or science scores but also in terms of the success or failure of helping children to develop in other ways'.

NEW LANGUAGE AND CONCEPTS: MAKING SENSE OF STUDY SUPPORT

Against this background of experiment in teaching and learning styles one of the most significant and sometimes confusing changes in recent years has been the shift in language, from extra-curricular or even after-school activities to the terms OSHL and study support. The term study support was first used, narrowly, to describe the range of support being developed to support academic work in schools – and championed by the Prince's Trust from 1992 onwards. Now, although the definition has broadened far beyond that, to embrace all aspects of extra-curricular activity , the term study support is rather a pallid reflection of the richness of what is possible and is being done in its name after school.

As John Macbeath, the leading academic in this field for many years, has observed: 'The term "study support" is acknowledged as an inadequate one to cover the range and variety of activity which falls within that compass. . . If there is confusion over what study support is and where its boundaries begin and end it is in part because provision has grown over a decade from different roots and in different directions.'

As this book explains, the term study support has given way in many areas to the more inclusive and dynamic term OSHL. The different directions have also prompted a range of strategies which promote social benefits, school improvement and individual learning, as well as the overall goal of raising achievement by widening the learning experience.

The earliest forms of provision, again to quote MacBeath, were 'nothing more elaborate or pretentious than a warm welcoming place to go after school' for homework; or a residential weekend, for year groups to revise for exams or catch up. However, 'As study support has matured there has been a growing emphasis on study support or learning skills. That is going deeper than homework to examine the underlying competencies which young people need in order to be able to succeed in academic work, in examinations and in life beyond school' – ie the 'real understanding' through which information becomes knowledge and knowledge wisdom: moving through the 'strategic learning' whereby learning is specifically applied to the challenges of tests to the 'metacognition' – 'learning below the water line of the iceberg' and which involves students thinking about thinking.[9]

[9] See Macbeath, J (1999) *Study Support in Scottish Schools,* p 3, Quality in Education, University of Strathclyde, and The Scottish Office

The practitioners in the field are approaching the linguistic dilemma more pragmatically. One OSHL officer put it thus:

> I have entered a world where the environment is 'live' and the parameters are changing almost daily. So OSHL, 'Study Support', 'supplementary education', 'enrichment', the words vary depending on the funding agency or the audience. However the strategy is clear: to secure the Government's vision of an inclusive, continually learning society, which challenges the causes and consequences of deprivation, and provides children and indeed whole communities, with access points to continual enrichment.[10]

THE CURRICULUM OF OSHL

If the school curriculum is acknowledged as a structured series of experiences to achieve certain learning outcomes, OSHL is part of the whole school curriculum – built in rather than bolted on as a series of activities focused on different content and skills. Within this assumption, however, two other issues can be explored further: How does OSHL differ from in-school learning in terms of activities and learning styles? And how, precisely, does it differ from the traditional practice of 'extra-curricular activities'? *Extending Opportunity* set out a very broad definition of study support as:

- homework clubs (facilities and support to do homework);
- help with key skills, including literacy, numeracy and ICT;
- study clubs (linked to or extending curriculum subjects);
- sports, games and adventurous outdoor activities;
- creative ventures (music, drama, dance, film and the full range of arts);
- residential events – study weeks or weekends;
- space and support for coursework and exam revision;
- opportunities for volunteering activities in the school or community;
- opportunities to pursue particular interests (science, ICT, law, archaeology, languages);
- mentoring by adults or other pupils;
- learning about learning (thinking skills, accelerated learning);
- community service (crime prevention initiatives, environment clubs).

The differences between classroom and study support learning can be defined, for example as follows.

OSHL is 'unashamedly pupil centred'. In OSHL:

- Pupils (and staff) are there by their own choice. The activity is driven by personal interest and commitment.

[10] Andrew Goodman, the newly appointed Out of Schools Learning Officer for Tower Hamlets, quoted in *Extra Strategy* (Summer Term, 2000) Education Extra

- The learning groups are smaller than in school.
- The emphasis is on learning through activity and enjoyment.
- Individual students can decide what they need, what they want to do and how.
- The emphasis is upon learning rather than teaching, Learning is, however, rarely an individual or self-sufficient activity. It is usually social, shared and supported by other people.
- OSHL is more likely to involve different people. They may be teachers, but they can be other school staff, outside 'experts' and volunteers, older students.
- The curriculum is different. The school curriculum has structured and sequenced content. It is directed by teachers and timetabled in discrete segments. Study support on the other hand is driven by what students bring to it and is tailored to their learning needs. Its 'programme; is whatever students need at a given time to help them retrieve ground, taste success, to build confidence or increase their chances of success. . .'.
- The school curriculum is determined by teachers for students; study support provides an opportunity for tutors to learn alongside students.
- The opportunities for partnership with other organisations is greater.
- The management of study support does not necessarily require the same processes or structures as management of a school but the principles and skills of management are likely to be similar. OSHL enables a lighter touch and more open and collaborative management than is possible in the classroom.[11] The critical differences are, essentially, the creation of a flexible, active, and voluntary learning environment with the emphasis on students learning for themselves, independently, and supporting each other's learning.

In materials created specifically for teachers involved in study support, and drawing upon existing materials already in use, educationalists such as Maggie Farrer, first Director of the UFA, have described how study support can create the optimum conditions for effective learning.[12] These can be identified as:

- high challenge but low anxiety;
- the opportunity for pupils to control their own learning;
- support for pupils to develop and use their different intelligences;
- flexibility to accommodate different learning styles;
- accelerated learning techniques and thinking skills work;
- support for pupils learning from outside the school.

[11] Many of these differences are noted, for example, in the Study Support Secondary Code of Practice (1999)
[12] See DfEE and Partners, TESS 1 Materials, Module 1

When looking at the differences between OSHL and traditional extra-curricular activities, we find that OSHL is also different because:

- it expresses the clear link with educational outcomes and benefits;
- it makes purposeful and organised what has been traditionally accidental;
- it aims to make universal provision for what might previously have been available only to the few.

In practice, successful OSHL schemes aim for:

- An awareness that all enjoyable activities offered outside the school day (whether that is homework clubs or hockey) can have a learning outcome – especially when they are seen to be a fundamental part of the school's commitment to motivating pupils and helping them to become successful students and citizens.
- A commitment to planning and the pursuit of quality and sustainability which, to be really successful, reflects the involvement of the young people themselves in the choice of activities and they way that they are delivered. It invites schools and local authorities to plan and coordinate what can be offered to pupils alongside other strategies to raise achievement. This implies building in evaluation as a natural part of the process of improvement.
- A role for partners outside the school to become involved in what, traditionally, has been seen as something only schools do. OSHL can be provided by many different people and it need not be on school premises – it may take place in libraries (for example with homework clubs) or in sports clubs. This creates a link between OSHL and other forms of informal, lifelong learning which take place in the community and are available for adults and young people.
- New ways of learning and sharing knowledge – whether this is in new places, with new people, or involving new types of activities.

Moreover, OSHL is what it says: it covers *all* the out of school hours. Activities can be offered before and after school hours, during lunchtimes, at weekends and during holidays. OSHL can be led by, or linked to schools and although the activities usually take place within school premises, the involvement of other partners can mean that they are based in libraries, museums, galleries, youth clubs, sports clubs, community centres or even local businesses.

EXTENDING, ENRICHING, ENABLING, ENJOYING

The three elements of OSHL, defined and refined by Education Extra over a number of years, are extending, enriching and enabling and these show the interlocking elements and strengths of what can be offered. Above all, it is not just about homework and revision. Overlapping with each area is the Big E – enjoyment. To work for young people, OSHL simply must be enjoyable. Within this framework, the taxonomy includes both 'curriculum extension' activities and 'curriculum enrichment' activities. Each of these implies a different sort of link with the curriculum, but equally implicit and explicit curriculum links overlap in many areas and may be explicit or implicit (see Chapter 4). Within these definitions there is a great deal of scope for developing the basic, key and creative skills that tomorrow's learners will need.

Curriculum extension activities

Building on the original Barber definition (1997) these are the activities which, by definition, extend what is possible during the school day in the delivery of the curriculum itself. They may include, for example:

- homework activities;
- study clubs;
- revision opportunities.

Curriculum enrichment activities

These are activities that would never form part of a formal curriculum but that are easily attached to it. They may include clubs which encourage pupils own special interests, for example:

- rocket clubs and radio clubs;
- art activities – such as film making or ceramics – which the curriculum cannot provide for;
- individual or 'street' sports.

Enabling activities

These activities enable students to access the curriculum or develop life skills. They can include:

- reading clubs;
- maths clubs;
- volunteering or community activities.

The diagram Figure 2.1 demonstrates how these three areas overlap with multiplying effect.

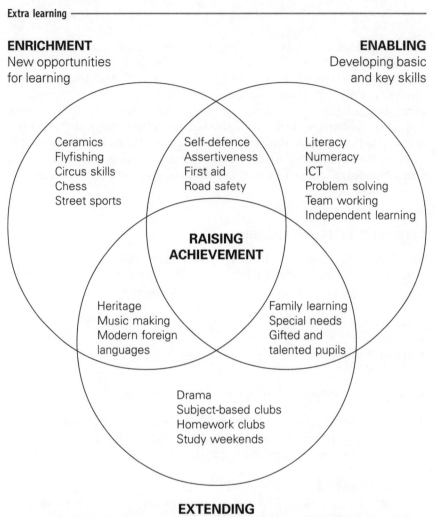

ENRICHMENT
New opportunities
for learning

ENABLING
Developing basic
and key skills

Ceramics
Flyfishing
Circus skills
Chess
Street sports

Self-defence
Assertiveness
First aid
Road safety

Literacy
Numeracy
ICT
Problem solving
Team working
Independent learning

**RAISING
ACHIEVEMENT**

Heritage
Music making
Modern foreign
languages

Family learning
Special needs
Gifted and
talented pupils

Drama
Subject-based clubs
Homework clubs
Study weekends

EXTENDING
Building on existing class-based activities

This version from Study Support: A Code of Practice for the Primary Sector, DfEE 2000,
adapted from the original framework produced by Education Extra

Figure 2.1 *Out of school hours framework*

BASIC SKILLS AND KEY SKILLS

The boundaries of this three-way definition are hardly watertight; nor do
the activities categorised promote only one set of skills. Another taxonomy
shows how different types of activities will promote particular types of
skills. In relation to the basic skills of literacy, numeracy and ICT, the
opportunities are self-evident and can be built into most OHSL programmes. For example:

- A reading club where pupils bring and read books for pleasure, visit the local bookshop, or take on a 'Readathon' for charity will primarily promote reading skills; but will also support the key skills of communication, cooperation and organisation.
- A circus club, where children might learn juggling or balancing will promote specific spatial and sports-based skills, but will also promote literacy as pupils prepare posters, write letters and programmes to advertise and promote performances and shows.
- An 'Impact Maths' club after school where maths games and board games which promote numeracy are available, can challenge pupils at different ability levels – and can involve family members too.

All activities can be audited and enhanced in relation to the benefits which can be identified as part of building high-quality and inclusive opportunities for students.

However, another strength of study support is the specific opportunity it offers for promoting the six key skills among pupils of different ages and abilities. These key skills are:

- communication;
- application of number;
- IT;
- working with others;
- improving own learning and performance;
- problem solving.

Each of these skills can be evaluated in different ways in terms of OSHL:

- **Communication skills** are fundamental to all performance art; to every mentoring situation; to debating societies, schools councils, and volunteer work in the community.
- **Application of number skills** can be brought into sports activities (time-keeping, scoring; probability, etc) as easily as into technology clubs where the task is to build a radio or a rocket.
- **Information technology** is often the key to attracting the most reluctant of students – but there are many choices as to how this can be done. A technology club in a special school will bring pupils together socially, may involve local visits to see alternative energy in action, and will promote lifeskills in many different ways.
- **Working with others** is a transparent requirement of any form of teamwork from sports clubs to designing and planting arrangements for the school gardening club. Leadership skills are often a key feature of programmes planned around mentoring and teamwork activities.
- **Improving own learning and performance**. Homework and revision clubs, study clubs and curriculum clinics are not only the places where

students can improve their performance and practice their skills. They are also the places where they can experiment with their own learning and find their own learning styles, at their own pace – whatever that might involve.

- **Problem solving** is inherent in any club or activity which involves bringing a shared concept to life – a performance, a display, a fashion show, a concert, or building a school windmill.

In addition, there are other sets of skills some of which overlap with key skills, such as the 14 Enterprise Skills, developed by the charity Changemakers, which has pioneered new ways of involving young people in creating, setting up and maintaining their own activity based in and outside school hours. These are the skills which 'are essential to the development of skills relating to employability, citizenship and lifelong learning'. They include, for example, the ability to:

- assess personal strengths and weaknesses;
- make decisions;
- plan time and energy;
- carry through responsibilities;
- develop negotiating skills;
- deal with people in power and authority;
- resolve conflict;
- cope with stress and tension;
- evaluate self-performance;
- develop presentational skills.

EXTRA

The Deanes School

The Deanes School joined the Changemakers network in 1995. Teacher-directed projects were already firmly established but student-led action was less prolific. Projects emerging from Year Council or individual initiatives began to bloom throughout the school, particularly projects linked to fundraising for charities. They included:

- A garden at a local junior school created by Year 11 boys.
- The restoration of a local 23-mile footpath in association with Essex County Council.

Help also came from the Trident Trust and Barclays New Futures Award in each case. In 1998 Changemakers reported that 'The student led councils are portraying a positive image and encouraging pupils to involve themselves with projects. The proactive message of their actions is: "We can do it for ourselves. . ."'[13]

---

[13] Changemakers (1998) *Young People Shaping Their Future*, pp 45–46

CHOOSING TO LEARN

It's fun – not like doing homework at all. I couldn't stop finding things and making things. (Pupil at Peters Hill Primary School, West Midlands, about an Internet story-telling project)

Teachers spend time running clubs for us when they could have been at home. It's great. . . It's like the school is part of your family. (Pupils at Torridon Primary School, LB Lewisham)

It can well be argued that promoting all the skills identified through OSHL is redundant because it represents the express task of the in-school curriculum. What, therefore, can OSHL bring that is extra? Where is the added value? The consensus among teachers, tutors, mentors and students in recent years has been that OSHL works to make learning enjoyable and effective essentially because:

- It is a voluntary commitment – example: the child who is easily distracted in class but who takes an active role in choosing and sharing books in the Bookworm club.
- It enables students to follow individual interests and enthusiasms – example: the 15-year-old with predicted grades below C who turns up to the video club and discovers a flair for 'directing'.
- It puts a high premium on enjoyment and activity – example: the academic child who enjoys aerobics.
- It enables students to work and learn together – example: the children who live in high-rise flats and who can never play outside have the opportunity to create and enjoy the school allotment.
- It enables students to work out what learning style suits them – example: the children who attend the Student Care club and find out that they can learn by teaching others what they know.
- It enables students to develop positive relationships across age ranges and with other adults – example: the child who fails to make any contribution in class but who helps the librarian catalogue and display books.
- It is a safe environment in which risks can be taken – example: the children who think they are no good at art but who find out, by working with 'experts', that their ideas, and their art, is praised and valued.
- It more closely connects with real-life situations–– and a real life environment.
- It is fun.

The unique 'microclimate' of OSHL is an amalgam of purpose, curriculum, the situation, and the duration of the project as well as the commitment of pupils and staff – each in a new learning situation. While organisational principles for good practice can be laid down and reproduced, the learning dynamic, although more difficult to dissect, is explicit in the way in which students and staff report and reflect on the experience. Some of the organisational features which can be 'designed in' to the rich learning environment outside school, for example, are opportunities:

- for students to have ownership of the curriculum, timetable and evaluation;
- for greater interaction between learners and 'teachers' who may be mentors, older students and adults other than teachers;
- for ensuring a learning and teaching environment which is very interactive, intense, and constantly monitored;
- for setting individual learning targets which can be negotiated on a daily basis and mediated by parents or mentors;
- for introducing incentives, rewards and new experiences as part of the learning programme.

Since 1998 a series of development projects, funded through central and local government and charities, have created these conditions and catalogued the common experiences and successes which have emerged consistently. The unique response of staff and students is reflected, for example, in the words of those who have participated in different summer projects.

The reactions of students were generally overwhelmingly positive. Perhaps this was partly because they had expected to be doing conventional school work and had been pleasantly surprised to find they were having so much fun. The scheme organisers had received so much positive feedback that the overwhelming impression was on enthusiastic enjoyment. As one participant put it: 'Even if you're ill you'll want to come. You've got to pretend you're not ill – well , I did when I had a headache.'[14]

Teachers' observations were almost consistently positive:

> There have been no behaviour issues. I know some of these children and I was aware that we could have had some problems. . . I'm very pleased. . . In fact, I'm a little surprised at some of the enthusiasm that they've shown. We have a punctuality problem in school but these kids are at the summer school early! During activities, they're saying, 'Can I do this?' 'Can I do that?' when I would not have imagined it during regular school.

> . . .Our success rate is high because we use lots of games stimulus. It means that students end up doing maths without realising it's maths. When they do realise, it's too late, they've already enjoyed it! [15]

[14] DfEE/NFER (1999) *Study Support in Summer School Pilots*, p 56
[15] Ibid pp 57–58

The things I do in the name of literacy! I didn't bank on this much enthusiasm and involvement – I've got 70 children arriving in my classroom after school next Wednesday. Any suggestions?' (Gemma Warren, teacher at Latymer School, LB Enfield)

And – from a very wide selection of pupil experiences, the pupils' words reveal the excitement, enthusiasm and pride in showing what they can do:

You can learn good stuff here. I like the stories and all the work. It's better than playing out. I'm not very good at reading but I can see I'm getting better. (Swansea pupil, Summer Literacy Scheme in Wales, 1997)

It gives you opportunities that you wouldn't have in school time. (Hartcliffe school pupil, Year 10)

It's brilliant. It's class. Look at him, he's enthralled by it all. (Older brother of a pupil on the Boots Family Learning Project)

I never knew I was so arty. (Pupil, ArtOut project)

You get to do performances and get trophies and certificates and things. My mum is right proud of me just now. (Pupil, Torridon Primary School, LB Lewisham)

These observations are borne out by a growing body of evidence which, as evaluation techniques develop, has begun to probe beyond the immediate impact on attitudes to learning, confidence and self-esteem towards the analysis of more subtle and potential links with grades and attainment – and beyond students themselves to the staff involved, and the families and the communities who have also participated. Much of this evidence is scattered throughout this book in the text of the case studies themselves. Despite differences in scope, methodology and in the design of the projects themselves, the findings reveal a remarkable consistency both in terms of the experience of the students and schools involved (reflected in self-evaluation and observation) and in terms of the external evaluations conducted. The growing body of evidence supports a view that participation in study support activities brings specific outcomes and new opportunities in terms of individual learning benefits, resources and relationships. Table 2.1 shows the most commonly reported benefits identified by students and teachers across the Education Extra projects.

THE RESEARCH EVIDENCE

In recent years there has been growing academic interest in the value and effect of out of school and informal learning upon personal achievement

Table 2.1 Commonly reported benefits

Benefits for pupils	Benefits for teachers and the school	Benefits for parents and the community
Learning/teaching – opportunity to: • Access targeted support in areas of weakness • Work with teachers in a different environment • Have somewhere to complete homework and receive help • Catch up on work not understood in class • Find new ways to learn • Learn at their own speed • Enjoy learning (including active learning) and learn in depth • Achieve more at school • Provide specific learning gains in mainstream areas • Improve attitudes to school: 'It's cool to learn' • Develop interpersonal, communicative, social and leisure skills • Provide opportunities for integration between pupils with special educational needs and mainstream pupils/adults • Offer choices to those with often restricted and highly structured lives (particularly for special schools) • Discover new talents, interests and skills in areas such as the arts, sports or foreign languages	**Learning/teaching – opportunity to:** • Improve school ethos, status and performance • Raise standards of achievement • Develop a deeper understanding of how pupils learn • Enhance relationships and motivation • Develop interests and experiences beyond the National Curriculum • Enrich and extend pupil's learning experiences • Improve teacher/pupil relationships, in particular the ability to take on new roles • Individually support pupils • Work with pupils in different contexts • Involve parents in their children's education • Widen range of community partnerships • Enhance the status and reputation of the school • Improve pupil attendance • Work with pupils in mixed age groups • Explore a wider concept of learning • Contribute to (whole) school improvement • Learn and teach without an emphasis on formal assessment • Help children from disadvantaged backgrounds	**Learning/teaching – opportunity to:** – Share a skill or interest or to help out – Develop better working relationships with teachers – Get more involved with the school – Break down barriers between school and community – Develop community spirit around the school – Register improvements in young people's behaviour within the community – Support social and economic regeneration – Promote inclusion through integration with mainstream/other schools

Benefits for pupils	Benefits for teachers and the school	Benefits for parents and the community
	• Help those in need of support with their learning, particularly literacy or numeracy skills • Improve school homework policies	
Personal benefits – opportunity to: • Be recognised for success in many different fields • Improve fitness and health. Work in groups and with new friends • Have fun in a safe environment • Raise/consolidate self-esteem • Enjoy a range of extra sports/arts activities • Increase skills, in particular lifeskills, leadership, independence, emotional stability and assertiveness • Broaden horizons and increased access to/equalising opportunities • Increase motivation/demonstrable success • Have better relationships with teachers • Increase sense of purpose and direction • Meet new role models	**Personal benefits – opportunity to:** • Enhance the esteem of teachers and tutors • Increase job satisfaction • Acquire more or different skills • Get to know pupils/parents in a different context	**Personal benefits – opportunity to:** – Acquire new skills and qualifications – Make new friends – Know their children are happy at school – Become a learner as well as a parent – Support their children in making improved progress in learning
Resources – opportunity to: • Have access to a wider range of facilities and resources	**Resources – opportunity to:** • Try out materials and ideas • Have better use of existing resources and generation of more resources for the school • Reduce vandalism • Increase enrolment	**Resources – opportunity to:** – Reduce vandalism and graffiti/develop a more secure community – Have care activity in a secure known environment – Access school facilities

and, more recently, school performance.[16] The positive impact on those that participate in OSHL has been confirmed in recent years by a growing body of academic research and evaluation. Like other aspects of educational research, however, there are acknowledged limitations to the methodology and the hazards of attempting to link cause and effect. But, as researchers would argue, this means taking greater care over the use of evidence and explanations of ambiguities. In the UK, looking at the impact of OSHL on school effectives is obviously subject to the same limitations and hazards, but in this very recent area of research, accumulated evidence and evaluation is pointing to consistent and positive findings.

The longitudinal study of the impact of study support on school effectiveness, undertaken by the Study Support National Evaluation and Development programme which had begun under the Prince's Trust in 1995, had not made its final report when this book was written. However, early evidence confirmed a strong link between participation in curriculum-linked study support and GCSE achievement as well as more positive attitudes to school. A review of methodology suggested, however, that the data were 'likely to reveal an overall significant study support effect but. . . sharp differences in added-value from school to school, centre to centre, and activity type to activity type'.[17] That study, based on 54 schools in disadvantaged major conurbations, was significant also for the partnership expressed between the local authorities involved.

Large-scale studies in the United States have shown a consistent link between participation in out of school activities (both attached to and detached from school), adolescent development and individual success in later life.[18] Recent studies have argued that 'positive youth development is facilitated by involvement in constructive leisure activities. . .' either a link between involvement in activities and later educational attainment, occupational status and income, or reduced chances of school drop-out and criminal offending. Leading US academics in this field, Bonnie Barber and Jacquelynne Eccles (1997), showed that 'the total number of activities and diversity of involvement predicted better grades, attachment to school and later college attendance', and linked activities to both positive and risky mid- to late adolescent outcomes and to formation of social identities.

Most recently, Barber and Eccles have extended their work into young adulthood. Looking at 2,200 students aged 11–27 in Arizona, over a period of 17 years, their research has found that participating in after-school activities has had a profound effect on students' success in later life. Barber

[16] See, for example, MacBeath, J and Turner, J (1991) on *Learning out of School*, SED
[17] Unpublished paper, Studying the Development of Study Support: What's the evidence of increased student achievement?' John MacBeath, Kate Myers, and Tony Kirwan, International Congress for School Effectiveness, Toronto (January 2001)
[18] See, for example, the bibliography in the DfEE/NFER report (RR 110 July 1999) *The Benefits of Study Support: A review of opinion and research*

observed that: 'The long term accrued benefits of activity participation . . . extend well beyond adolescence. The extracurricular activities are not just a way of passing time. These extracurricular activities extend a richness of possibilities a teenager wouldn't get by just attending school and doing homework with no outside interests.' One particular benefit was the power of developing a shared value system with a peer group through activities 'that kept them out of trouble and focused them more on academics'. But other benefits over the 17 years were manifest in the ways in which they contributed to the community, belonged to a valued group, established supportive networks of adults and peers and worked in a challenging setting.[19]

The researchers determined five categories of activities: pro-social (eg going to church or doing voluntary or community service); performance (eg taking part in a school band or drama); school involvement (eg being a prefect); team sports; and clubs (eg participating in debating, language or chess clubs).

They found that children who did one of these activities:

> generally did better academically than more 'bookish students'; if the children
> played sport they were more likely to go to college than any other group
> (but also more likely to drink excessively); if they did theatre, drama or music,
> they were less likely to truant or use drugs or drink; if they attended church
> or did extra curricular activities they had a higher academic performance. . .

In the UK, the first body of academic work was that pioneered in Scottish schools and undertaken by Professor John MacBeath of the University of Strathclyde, who provided the academic foundation for the Prince's Trust Study Support Programme. In 1993, his research into curriculum-linked study support provided by 12 schools in Strathclyde[20] found that among the benefits identified by students were greater confidence in class and in relation to exams; improved homework grades; better understanding of the tasks; better relationships with teachers; and help with homework. The report demonstrated the need for schools to construct a homework policy; as well as the need to convince parents of value of study support.

A number of individual reports based on initiatives across the UK have looked specifically at the links with attainment. MacBeath's earlier findings were confirmed in 1999 in a survey of Scottish schools which found that the overwhelming reason why primary schools offered study support was as a way of 'enhancing self-esteem', followed by 'teaching learning skills' and 'extra subject support'. Special schools followed a similar pattern but there were conspicuous differences in secondary schools, which identified

[19] For a summary, see www.newswise.com/articles/2000/9/ACTIVE.UAZ.html
[20] MacBeath, J (1993) *Learning for Yourself: Supported study in Strathclyde schools*

'extra subject support' as the main priority, followed by 'developing study habits' and 'a place to do homework'.[21]

Tower Hamlets probably has the widest and most developed provision for study support in any local authority (including after-school and breakfast clubs, Saturday schools, revision schemes, and a summer university for over 2.000 young people each year). In 1997 the borough undertook its own assessment of the impact of study support on pupils' achievement at GCSE. The study analysed the effect of Easter revision programmes in 14 schools in the borough. The study found an overall increase of 30 per cent in the average proportion of students gaining five or more A*–C grades at GCSE between 1994–96 in the eight schools which offered study support. The average increase in the six schools in the borough without provision for study support was 3 per cent.[22] Although the results varied in direction and magnitude there was a positive correlation between the length of time schools had offered study support and the increase in the proportion of students gaining good scores. Also, a higher proportion of revision attendees achieved better grades than predicted (although no tests of statistical significance are reported).

There is also some evidence drawn from initiatives intended to help ethnic minority students to raise their standards of performance too, which, for African-Caribbean, Bangladeshi and Pakistani pupils, 'have been consistently below average'. A recent DfEE report highlighted the factors which make the difference to underperforming groups:

a strong emphasis on raising expectations; inclusive curriculum; support for bilingual pupils; ethnic monitoring; mentoring and study support. . .[23]

In some schools teachers run homework and revision sessions at lunchtime, after school and even in the Easter holidays. Pupils are targeted as individuals, particularly those beginning to fall behind with homework or those who already feel marginalised. Good schools recognised that some young people and groups face many external pressures that work against good school performance. . .

In one area:

A Homework Club has been established as an after school activity providing an opportunity for pupils to revise and get advice on their work. It is invaluable for students with little support at home. Efforts are made to target those

---

[21] MacBeath, J (1999) op cit p 8
[22] See Tower Hamlets Study Support Project (1997) *Closing the Gap*, reviewed in the DfEE/NFER report (RR 110 July 1999) *The Benefits of Study Support: A review of opinion and research*
[23] DfEE (February 2000) *Removing the Barriers: Raising achievement levels for minority ethnic pupils (guidance for governors, heads and teachers)*, p 12

least likely to attend from choice. Good science results from black students in 1997 were directly attributed to these after school classes. Homework clubs are timed to fit with Muslin students'evening classes at the Mosque.

EVALUATING THE EVIDENCE

Some of the most conclusive evidence in recent years has come from the National Foundation for Educational Research, charged first with reviewing research and development in this field, and second with evaluating the government's own funded programme of research and development.

In 1999 the NFER published a review of research into study support based on 62 projects and research studies dating from 1989–99.[24] The review looked at evidence not only on study support in schools but also at the impact of general participation of young people in activities outside school hours on their range of achievements. The literature review included large-scale studies conducted in the United States which had examined the relationship between students' extra-curricular participation (in sports and arts clubs, student government, church and community service) and their progress in school and 'extra curricular involvement was found to be significantly related to a range of positive outcomes, such as academic self-concept, time spent on homework, good attendance and academic achievement'.[25] Significantly, other researchers had found a negative link between time spent in 'unnamed activities' and academic performance, whereas time spent in organised activities was beneficial to disadvantaged children and 'prevented them from becoming involved in anti-social behaviour with deviant peers'.[26]

Several other studies were discussed in detail as bringing positive benefits to mathematics and reading. A study in 1989[27] found that secondary pupils' participation in a number of specific extra-curricular activities was 'positively related to their attainment and progress in maths and reading' irrespective of background factors, such as gender, social class and ethnicity. Brooks *et al* (1997) found a statistically significant relationship between the reading performance of eight-year-olds and their involvement in a range of activities outside school (eg playing with friends, involvement in sports) and that those who were involved in several activities did even better.[28]

The NFER concluded that: 'The review has found a consistently positive picture of study support. Study support is considered to offer a range of benefits to young people in relation to social, personal and academic development. There would appear to be a particular need for access to

[24] DfEE/NFER, RR 110 (July 1999) op cit
[25] Camp, Marsh (1988, 1992); Bradford Brown and Steinberg, (1991) quoted, ibid p 5
[26] Posner and Vandell (1994), ibid p 6
[27] Smith *et al* (1989) *The School Effect: A study of multiracial comprehensives*, PSI, London
[28] Brooks *et al*, NFER p 6

study support for children from disadvantaged backgrounds'.[29] The researchers concluded that, while making it clear that a positive association between participation in study support and achievement was 'suggestive rather than conclusive' it was clear, for example, that study support was: 'almost universally considered to be a good thing. It aims to help young people to develop their personal and interpersonal skills, self-esteem and motivation to learn. It provides opportunities for young people to develop particular interests. . .' it also offers benefits to teachers, parents, schools and the local community.'

But, in addition, it was: 'possible to state that the research evidence has established a link between young people's participation in a range of activities outside school hours and a number of desirable outcomes, including improved attitudes to school, attendance and academic achievement. . .' Significantly, the report went on: 'But, as many commentators have argued, access to organised activities is often dependent on the social and financial resources of a child's family. This suggestion is confirmed by research evidence that children from poorer families are less likely to take part in organised activities outside school.'[30]

The evidence reviewed by NFER confirmed the findings of Barber *et al* in 1997: that benefits could come from both curriculum extension and curriculum enrichment. It was, however, suggested that the academic benefits from curriculum extension were more direct and transparent while those from curriculum enrichment were likely to be less easy to detect but also more socially beneficial: 'Research into curriculum extension has shown positive relationships with a range of outcomes, such as self esteem, confidence, motivation and academic performance. . . Curriculum enrichment is associated with positive personal and social outcomes and there is some evidence of a positive association with academic achievement.'[31]

These findings also confirmed those of the NFER's own survey of extra-curricular provision (quoted in Chapter 1) that disadvantaged and hard-pressed schools were less likely to be provided for or to be providing the extra that was needed. The findings have also been extended by the NFER's own evaluations into a range of government funded initiatives over the past two years, namely:

- Playing for Success (September 1999).
- Out of School Hours Learning Activities: An evaluation of 50 pilot schemes (December 1999).
- Study Support Summer School Pilots: An evaluation of 25 schemes (May 2000).

---

[29] DfEE/NFER (July 1999) RR 110 op cit p vi
[30] Ibid p 15
[31] NFER, RR 110 (July 1999) Summary of Evidence

The Playing for Success initiative, which has placed underachieving pupils in inner city areas into OSHL clubs based in First Division football clubs, has also noted significant improvement in basic skills. 'Playing for success has contributed to improved attitudes, motivation and self-esteem', particularly in regard to reading and mathematics, and 'Pupils made significant progress in both mental arithmetic and reading. On average primary pupils improved their reading scores by the equivalent of six months and secondary pupils improved their reading scores by about eight months. Teachers noticed particular improvements in pupils' ICT and study skills. Parents felt that the Centres had helped with many aspects of their child's learning, including ICT, mathematics, reading, writing and homework'.[32]

The evaluation of the 50 pilot schemes concluded that, across a very wide range of different models, with different content, curricular, catchment areas and structures: 'Many project providers were pleased with the outcomes that had emerged during the period of the research. Providers and pupils regarded easing children's transfer from primary to secondary school as particularly successful. Other successes centred on the personal development of pupil mentors, the increased motivation shown by participants and improvements in their personal/social skills and standards of work.'[33]

The evaluation of the 25 summer school pilot schemes, which covered the whole curriculum, rather than simply literacy and numeracy, noted that they had generated 'significant changes in participants' overall. . . reading enjoyment. There was also a significant impact on participants' attitudes to maths, with participants overall finding maths less difficult, more enjoyable and more useful at the end of the summer school compared to the start. Also children/young people's attitudes to school work had significantly changed with regard to appreciating the usefulness of school work.'[34]

Evidence-based links with school performance overall are, relatively, in their infancy. Chapter 4 explores some of the potential links in relation to school objectives and this will clearly be a fertile field for future research. In the NFER survey of OSHL activities, however, the survey of 465 secondary schools which participated in the survey relating to achievements at GCSE, researchers found that schools with 25 per cent or fewer pupils achieving five or more GCSE grades at A*– C were found to provide fewer types of out of lesson time activities than other schools (ie a narrower range of specific activities). However, a smaller sample of secondary schools also

---

[32] DfEE/NFER, RR 167, *Playing for Success: An evaluation of the first year*, pp i–ii

[33] DfEE/NFER, RR 178, (December 1999) *Out of School Hours Learning Activities: An evaluation of 50 pilot schemes*, p iii

[34] DfEE/NFER, RR 200 (May 2000) *Study Support of Summer School Pilots: An evaluation of 25 schemes*, p vi

revealed that there were no significant differences between schools with different levels of performance at KS3 English examinations.[35] While researchers point to the conflicting evidence contained in these two findings, the potential link between a narrower range of activities and GCSE results overall seems well worth exploring.

Indeed, most recently the link between extension activities and academic success has been endorsed by Ofsted which, in the report, *Improving City Schools* (2000), identified study support as a key factor in improvement of city schools in severely disadvantaged areas. 'What marks these schools out is an upward trend in standards. They are improving against the odds, often at a greater rate than schools overall.' One of the main findings was that 'Many of the schools put strong emphasis on the arts and sometimes on physical education. Homework has an important place and is supported in secondary clubs by supervised sessions and revision clubs.' And, in more detail:

> Students value the opportunity to work with teachers and others outside normal lessons: examination results testify to the success of study support, with rises in the number of higher GCSE grades associated with the best programmes.
>
> Aside from study support, many schools provide other out of school opportunities for pupils to extend their experience. Often, with the support of charities and other donors, some schools invest very heavily in these opportunities, which include field trips, visits and residential courses as well as arts and sports activities. The best of them enable pupils to develop interests and skills which they otherwise might never have had.[36]

RAISING ACHIEVEMENT BY RAISING CONFIDENCE AND SELF-ESTEEM

Of all the evidence accumulating for the positive impact of study support, the most consistent finding across many different types of projects and evaluations seems to be that study support gives children and young people greater ownership of their own learning, and of the school itself – and for many, a taste of success which has hitherto eluded them in the classroom. It helps to raise confidence and self-esteem which, in turn, helps to raise aspirations and achievement.

Studies by Education Extra are rich in examples of children showing improved levels of self-worth; a sense of achievement and success, a sense of independence and the willingness to take on more responsibility.

[35] DfEE/ NFER, RR 127 (July 1999) *Out-of-lesson-time Learning Activities: Surveys of headteachers and pupils*, p v
[36] Ofsted (2000) *Improving City Schools*, pp 7, 33

It's a good feeling when you've done something, like when you've done courses like computing. (Year 11 boy participating in the Hartcliffe project)

It makes you feel happy with oneself. (Participant in the Boots Family Learning Project)

You feel good about yourself. (Report on study support in special schools)

You get certificates and medals – it is important. (Sedgehill School report)

One of the first and most powerful demonstrations of this effect was the 1997 summer schools literacy programme which set up 50 summer literacy projects during the summer holidays to provide enjoyable, focused learning for Year 6 pupils with low-reading skills. The 50 schemes without exception showed that intensive practice in reading and writing could be fun; that children would work hard and enthusiastically over a holiday period, given the right encouragement, support, and incentives; and that intensive focus on individual learning could help to raise self-esteem, self-confidence, and bring specific learning benefits. They showed, too, that teachers and other staff could enjoy the opportunity as much as the pupils themselves, and that the whole community, once informed about what was planned, could help in different ways to make the children's commitment a success.[37]

EXTRA

Patcham High School

While Patcham High School in Brighton did not run internal tests, among the measures of success set was that every one of the 30 children reached an individual target of reading. Some children reached and even exceeded the top target of 12 books. The school took particular pride in the girl 'who [had] read very little and who read 14 books in a fortnight; and the child who said: 'I didn't like reading before summer school and I do now'. The school offered a two-week scheme at the end of August. Each day started with an intense two-hour teaching session with much emphasis on National Literacy Project word and sentence development. Afternoon complementary activity workshops reinforced and extended the structured teaching of the morning. Cooking, poetry and song workshops and sports were all included. The scheme was led by the head teacher and SENCO and the literacy adviser praised the organisation and the quality of teaching as well as the involvement of children in the second session when they created menus, made books and played games with a literacy focus.

---

[37] See *Education Extra: An Evaluation of Summer Literacy Schemes* (1997)

In 1999, other summer schools were set up for 800 gifted and talented students. Again, the NFER research found that the summer schools had a positive effect on student self-confidence and academic self-image. As a result of the summer school, more students had confidence in their ability to do well.

The result of improved self-concept and better relationships in the school context clearly has an impact in terms of motivation, attitudes to school and learning, and overall behaviour. Looking at a sample of evaluations from projects in recent years managed by Education Extra we can hear the authentic voice of delighted teachers and parents. . .

> By nature, some are scallywags, but motivation and interest in school itself has increased; they are less destructive, more caring of the facility. The school 'belongs' to them. They have more ownership.[38]

> She loves it. She wasn't very well one day but because she didn't want to miss this she made herself come to school.[39]

Children were more willing to have a go whereas initially they had hung back from explaining or taking part in a challenge.

> He has not been this enthusiastic ever in school before. Now he wants to come home and tell me about a book or continue with a piece of writing.

> When the library was closed due to a flood there was a great disappointment that there would be no 'Book-it' until we dried out.[40]

Pupils voices are, perhaps, even more authentic:

> It keeps ma Ma off ma back and I can ask the stupid questions that I couldnae ask in school. (East Lothian pupil)

CONCLUSION

This chapter has reviewed the cumulative evidence that OSHL can create time, opportunities and environment for learning to flourish. Many evidently successful ways of teaching and learning are offered within the classroom by many successful teachers. But the weight of experience and evidence suggests that it can be very successful to use the novel conditions of time, space, and voluntary commitment outside the school day, when

[38] Childer (1996) Thornton Primary School, *Education Extra: Succeeding out of school*
[39] Brittain, M, Morgan, A and Webster, P (September 1999) *The Boots Company Family Learning Project: An end of Year 1 report*
[40] *Education Extra: Evaluation of Book-it Clubs* (2001, unpublished)

students can afford to take risks with their learning, working together in a safe and non-competitive environment where 'failure' is not an issue.

The emphasis on using the activities on offer to promote learning does not compromise or diminish the enjoyment which pupils and teachers express. Indeed, the evidence suggests that students respond to the challenge. Longitudinal evidence conducted by the Study Support National Evaluative Development Programme is only now within reach in the UK, confirming the specific academic benefits of study support. This research, which also shows higher attendance among students participating, as well as improved GCSE grades, will open up the way for further examination of how effective different areas of activity, different situations, and different schools, can work in different and better ways. This will remain a fertile field for research for many years to come.

One of the most significant findings, however, has been to show that those students who are least likely to take up the extra-curricular offer are those who could make best use of it in terms of their family circumstances and overall performance in school. This poses a major challenge for schools and policy makers. The following chapter looks at some of the ways in which national and local initiatives have responded to this, and to the challenge of spreading best practice as a whole.

3

Delivering OSHL: policy and practice

This chapter looks in more detail at the implementation of policies for OSHL and specifically examines:

- how out of school learning is being put in place to raise standards through innovative schemes for learning at different times and ways;
- the relationship between arts and sports and OSHL in terms of motivating and innovating experiences;
- key initiatives for tackling disadvantage;
- local strategies for implementation.

> I am really in favour of out of school learning. I think if a lot more of this was done, if this type of provision could be available to all children – that is all types of children – then it helps to create a better, more responsible child, and then in turn a better, more responsible adult.[1]

INTRODUCTION

The challenges and opportunities facing study support as part of the national achievement strategy are complex. However, it offers new opportunities to:

- motivate and maintain the habit of learning as pupils grow older;
- improve the performance of boys and certain groups which may also have additional needs (eg Asian girls);

[1] DfEE/NFER (December 1999) *Out of School Hours Learning Activities: An evaluation of 50 pilot schemes*, RR 178, p 130 (parent of child at Medway Summer University quoted)

- increase the participation of less successful and disadvantaged pupils in school life;
- raise self-esteem and the chances of success among low-achieving pupils;
- help schools in acutely disadvantaged areas to improve.

Two major challenges for this emerging area of public policy are the dissemination of good practice, and the direction of resources to where they can be most effective. The first section of this chapter looks at some of the swiftly increasing innovative and successful models, and how schools can learn from them. The second section of this chapter looks at the broad range of policies which impact upon and which can be enhanced by OSHL and at the challenge that poses for local authorities. The final section of this chapter looks at the development of local policies and their implementation.

LEARNING: DIFFERENT TIMES, PLACES AND WAYS

Summer school was the best idea in the world. (Pupil from Beeches Primary School in Peterborough, 1999)

Whereas summer camps have been an almost mythical feature of growing up in the United States, there has been nothing to compare with them in the UK apart from private initiatives and occasional initiatives by individual schools. However, a different model – summer learning – has emerged over the past few years. Since 50 pilot schemes were set up in 1997, summer learning schemes have developed in many guises. The first concept of 'summer literacy' expanded to become 'summer learning', with schemes which extend beyond the single secondary school and its feeder schools, to multiple partnerships which cover all curriculum subjects. These schemes may cater for gifted and talented pupils as well as for promoting the transition from primary to secondary school and accelerating literacy and numeracy. Fully funded by Standards Funding 2000 such summer schemes ran for LEAs across England in summer 2000, focusing on activities for the age range between Years 6 and 9, including the important progression groups.

The summer learning schemes established early on that one of the most effective outcomes was to steer primary children into secondary school, giving them a taste of the secondary curriculum, and access to their new teachers and schools before they actually started work. The positive impact has been noted, consistently, as one of the most outstanding benefits of the schemes as a whole.

EXTRA

The Woodlands Summer School

This school, in Basildon, Essex, was funded in 1999 to run a two-week summer school, targeting Years 7–11 and Year 6 children from its local feeder primary school. Building on the highly successful experience of two previous summer schools, there was a high emphasis on literacy and numeracy and student numbers had increased from 180 to 300. The summer school was aimed at raising self-esteem and achievement for all participants, but for Year 6 children it specifically aimed to:

- support the transition phase;
- create a sense of inclusion.

Year 6 children included a 'target' literacy and numeracy group and a general mixed-ability group. Each student had a five-hour learning day – with hours for literacy, numeracy, cross-curricular topics, creative arts and PE. Progress in reading took the form of a reading passport. The curricular work, conducted in a relaxed yet intensive atmosphere, was complemented by trips for students and individual groups. The impact on transition was summed up by the summer school coordinator: 'The general teasing problems that are apparent in September will be less. There will be fewer children saying that they have no friends, far fewer saying they can't find particular rooms. They will have met teachers and friends. They've gone from a school where they had one teacher all day to a school which is a lot bigger. This now will not faze them.'[2]

EXTRA

Welsh Literacy Summer School

Summer literacy schemes in Wales have often been focused on the Welsh language.

In August 1998 the first Welsh Literacy Summer School was opened at Ysgol Gymraeg Cwmbran, organised by Torfaen LEA. Pupils from Years 4 and 5 were invited to attend a school day programme of fun activities to improve their literacy and oral skills. Volunteers from the sixth form at Ysgol Gyfun Gwynllyw played a critical role in the success of the scheme, acting as mentors and role models for the pupils. Torfaen's Welsh Advisory Service gave full support to the scheme, which culminated in the production of a children's magazine and a musical show. The magazine *Tafod Torfaen* provided an opportunity for the pupils to write on a variety of subjects, producing content including comic strips, interviews, news, poetry, puzzles, jokes, recipes, letters and sport. The musical show was directed by the sixth-form pupils and was an outstanding success. The summer school finished with a fun day out at Techniquest, the science discovery centre in Cardiff.

---

[2] NFER (May 2000) *Study Support Summer School Pilots*, RR 200, p 80

As Chapter 2 outlined, the cumulative evidence over three years suggests strongly that the schemes have fostered in pupils a more positive attitude towards learning and a sense of their own creativity, and had a positive effect on self-confidence – with a particular benefit in terms of smoothing the transition from primary to secondary school.

One of the most significant parallel developments has been the growth of summer universities – short, intensive periods of active learning across a very wide range of subjects and teaching and learning styles. In July 1998, Tower Hamlets Summer University conducted a survey of 14 local summer colleges or summer universities involving a wide range of students, and different curriculum and organisational forms. They were all student-centred programmes that attracted young people to learning at a range of venues, which may have included school sites, but not necessarily those attended by the student during term time. Most of the projects were local authority managed, or managed through Education Business Partnerships or local universities. Many of them have been strongly influenced and supported by the teaching and learning style of the UFA.

Significantly, all the schemes focused on transitional phases in the lives of young people: from primary to secondary; GCSE to A level; school to higher and further education; and beyond study to the world of work. Most schemes focused on 14- to 16-year-olds, facing the challenges of further education or work. A particular emphasis was put on the skills for employ-ability through the volunteer schemes, work projects and vocational courses and also in the teaching styles and course content.

Nor is summer learning limited to school-age pupils: Tower Hamlets Summer University has been running summer courses for 14- to 25-year-olds since 1995. The programmes combine academic and vocational study, arts, sports, electronic media, and personal development. In summer 2000, 150 courses were run for 1,793 students. This summer university has gained considerable popularity and success due to the way in which it involves young people in the organisation and delivery of the courses. Students are encouraged to become involved in the organisation, contributing ideas and acting as peer mentors.

However, in recent years the idea has taken on even greater significance. In the context of the controversial debate over the selection of university students for Oxbridge, universities and schools alike are beginning to look for new ways of introducing and enthusing students to higher education, in much the same way as the first summer schools gave primary pupils the chance to get to know their new secondary schools and teachers as well as the challenge of the secondary curriculum. In 2000, another generation of summer schools were run in over 50 universities for young people aged 16–17, to raise their sights and ambitions in terms of higher education.

These strategies are now extended down the age range into KS2 and more broadly across other parts of the country. Master classes and special weekend or residential schemes bring together pupils from different schools, and links are made with external partners who can offer enriching experiences, using a variety of funding sources. Tower Hamlets, for example, has put in place weekend workshops for study skills for pupils approaching GCSEs. These take place at an outdoor activity centre on the Norfolk coast and the workshops are designed not only to boost examination skills but to raise self-awareness and self-esteem. But activity sessions are also built in to ensure that the fast pace and concentration is maintained. These are run by the Tower Hamlets EBP and supported by the Skillswork Single Regeneration Budget.[3]

Learning in different places: Playing for Success

Another innovation has been the decision to create new learning environments outside school, in places where young people feel particularly comfortable. In 1997 the government established the Playing for Success initiative, in partnership with the Football League and its clubs.

> The chance to meet Alan Shearer and other players – or at least to work in the players' lounge, to see their changing room and to walk through the players' tunnel and on to the pitch – is a powerful incentive for pupils. And for the club, the centre is an educational resource, used by the under-17 side to study for BTEC sports studies, and by the coach, former Scotland International, Tommy Craig, who is learning ICT skills for the first time.[4]

The broad aim of the Playing for Success initiative was to contribute to raising educational standards, especially in urban areas, through the establishment of Study Support Centres in football clubs. Using the medium and environment of football, the target was to raise motivation by engaging pupils underachieving at KS2 and 3 in activities focused around literacy and numeracy, ITC and study skills. All activities were to take place after school, at weekends and during the holidays. The initiative targeted underachieving pupils in inner city areas. Underachievement and low self-esteem were the main criteria used by participating schools to select the pupils to take part.

The Leeds United Study Support Centre opened in October 1998, taking groups of pupils every weekday evening and on Saturday morning for two-hour sessions. Courses for individual students are run for 10 weeks. The first session was attended by children from four primary schools and the second session for students from four high schools. On Saturdays the centre was open for two morning sessions of one and a half hours. The centre

---

[3] See *Insight* (Summer 1999) pp 16–17, DfEE
[4] *Insight* (Summer 1999) Newcastle Football Club: Playing for success, p 13

established a close relationship with the 27 schools involved. Schools nominated a link teacher, and there was close communication on participation and progress.

Operating the centre was an extension of existing commitments set up by Leeds United FC to the local community and the initiative was supported by IKEA, Packard Bell, Planet and Macdonald's, which donated furniture, computers, food and drinks and certificates for the students. The centre was established at Elland Road itself under the South Stand and NFER evaluators observed that 'visitors cannot help but be impressed by the standard of accommodation and furniture' – and the cybercafé.

The target group of pupils, chosen by the schools, were those who were felt to 'deserve a chance' and a Study Support Centre manager was appointed, supported by additional staff, including an ICT technician and students from local universities and colleges. Curriculum materials and projects related to many aspects of the Leeds football ground – and were subsequently developed by the centre manager to make use of 'all the possibilities, the communication systems, the safety systems, the personnel, the local history. . . If you only relate the activities to the game of football then you miss 90 per cent of what is going on.' The scheme is primarily focused on ICT and basic skills, but a high priority is also given to practical and creative work. Freedom for pupils to work in their own way at their own pace is matched by the range of interesting and exciting learning activities. 'The rooms are seeded with ideas for them to take up rather than pushing out ideas onto them.' Significantly, some young people had some difficulty with the concept of freedom of choice.

The centre has proved extremely popular with students and schools and feedback had been very positive. 'Schools have commented on the fact that children's confidence, enthusiasm and skills have been sustained back in school long after their course has finished. . .' and as one pupil said: 'It's a great place to be'.[5]

As Chapter 2 outlined, the NFER evaluation of the scheme confirmed that the centres were very popular with students, parents and schools, that they had reached the target group intended and that they had contributed to improved attitudes, self-esteem. . . academic skills and achievement'.[6] Of the 49 eligible clubs, 40 are committed to opening centres. By Spring 2000, 29 centres were open, with others in development.

While the project initiatives described so far helped to establish and inspire good practice, evidenced by high levels of pupil and school enthusiasm and defined learning outcomes, they were specifically designed to demonstrate what could be done. Since 1998 has come a whole raft of new policy initiatives to improve schools, and challenge underachievement.

[5] DfEE/NFER (1999) *Playing for Success: an evaluation of the first year*, RR 167, pp 15–27
[6] Ibid pp i–ii

These new policies take their place, significantly, alongside others which have articulated, on the one hand, the impact that school failure has on individual and community failure and stress within highly disadvantaged neighbourhoods, and on the other, the need for an educational system driven by excellence and serving diversity. As these policies have emerged, and as education and social policy have converged, study support is taking its place as a unique and effective agent across both areas.

INNOVATION AND DEMONSTRATION

In 1997, an England-wide programme was set up, funded through the DfEE, which was designed to explore and demonstrate good practice in study support in a wide range of situations. Fifty national projects were identified, ranging from the single small primary school-based projects to more elaborate partnerships between schools and other learning partners.

These projects were targeted at pupils with identified learning needs, from disadvantaged communities, liable to be disaffected, and who had little access to support and facilities to learn. One school involved explained its reason for opting in: 'Low aspirations and poor exam results, lack of facilities and opportunities for young people locally, racial tension, drugs, unemployment and widespread poverty, make this initiative a priority.'

Typically, as the organiser of one rural project explained, the aim was 'to address and reverse the poor achievement of young people'. . . In this project the intention was 'to take study support out into villages of a remote, rural and scattered population area. . . a priority because there is little to do in the evenings, public transport is virtually non-existent; young people become bored and disaffected.'[7]

Projects set up ranged from the relatively traditional, such as homework or computer clubs, to enrichment activities, involving interactive music, gardening, recreational activities, personal health and safety. Transition projects involving primary and secondary schools were very popular.

EXTRA

The Medway Children's University

I want to encourage my daughter to learn outside school as well as within it. To come to a university campus as part of the Children's University is so appropriate. It makes the whole thing so important – so adult like, to that child's eyes. I think they respond to that and my daughter has most definitely responded. (Parent of a child who attended the Children's University in 1998)

The Children's University scheme, which has recently spread to a number of locations throughout the country, offers short, intensive courses in a variety of subjects to children in Years 5 and 6. In 1998, the Medway Children's

---

[7] DfEE/NFER (December 1999) *Out of School Hours Learning Activities*, RR 178

University involved 19 primary schools and covered a wide range of curriculum areas presented in attractive and innovative ways. The venues included secondary schools and the University of Greenwich. Each term 250 children were involved on four Saturday mornings. Teachers, sixth-form pupils and Year 11 students working as course assistants and other adults (eg school governors) were involved.

Against a background of low achievement the Children's University worked to:

- offer children the opportunity to explore new subjects and learn new skills;
- make learning exciting and fun;
- build children's self-confidence.

In short, as one pupil put it: 'to do lots of things you don't usually do in class'. These involved, for example, cookery, sports and the arts; palae-ontology ('everything you wanted to know about fossils'); computer movie magic; history detectives (using historic sites in Canterbury); aspects of flight (model-aircraft building and other flying objects). All the courses incorporated practical activities involving skills such as constructing, experimenting, exploring, creating and practising. The most obviously practical subjects were very popular and over-subscribed.

Teachers and parents were as enthusiastic as the parents. As one teacher said: 'It was something I had never done before. It sounded a fun thing to do. I'm a better educator at the Children's University than a teacher in school.' The difference in the pupils' response to the challenge was also marked. As one parent commented: 'My daughter has started using the Internet at home because palaeontology has whetted her appetite'.[8]

Overall, the 50 innovative projects were highly successful, with schools and local authorities using the experience as the opportunity to develop a longer-term programme, in many cases funded through the New Opportunities Fund, to build on what had been achieved within the year. The achievements were:

- high levels of enthusiasm and motivation;
- more confidence and willingness to organise their own learning;
- improved personal and social skills;
- improved key skills, particularly ICT.

The Billy Elliot syndrome: arts policies and schemes

It is clear to anybody that the arts – with their clear links to media, design and fashion – play a vital part in young peoples' lives. But apart from their value in themselves they contribute to education as a learning activity by helping young people to acquire those skills most needed in tomorrow's society: communication skills, team skills, questioning skills, problem solving, lateral thinking, flexibility and adaptability.'[9]

---

[8] Ibid p 125
[9] Gerry Robinson (Chairman of the Arts Council) speech at the *New Statesman* Art Lecture in June 2000

The arts are flourishing out of school – and the way in which participation can enhance achievement across the curriculum as well as giving children a sense of belonging to school and to the community is very powerful.

EXTRA

Llanbister Primary School

Llanbister Primary School's drama club began three years ago in response to what many perceived as poor speaking in the school. Children come from a large and remote rural area, with very little exposure to the arts other than what they may see on cable or satellite TV.

The club runs for two hours once a week after school. From the very beginning, the level of interest was great with most children wanting to attend. The drama club's productions have ranged from *Charlie and the Chocolate Factory* to *The Tempest*, a notable success in which a boy with specific learning disability took the lead of Prospero and managed to learn all the major speeches. 'His confidence zoomed – he has since gone on to high school where his results continue to surprise everyone.' (Teacher).

All productions have been improvised rather than directed, with children generating their own ideas from the stories.

The school's film project, part-funded by Education Extra, is in its infancy. The project had arisen when the school took part in the filming of a Channel 4 series called *Achieving Schools* which focused on the development of the history Web site. This interest in film-making was fuelled further when a local cameraman helped and advised with what was needed to make short films for S4C and Channel 4. To date, the school has bought a new and extremely powerful computer, professional editing software and a Canon digital camera. Currently, they are producing two sets of films with two teams working separately, the first on a series of documentaries of the lives of local 'celebrities', the second being a series of fictionalisations of stories that celebrities have told the school. Both projects involve extensive inter-viewing, discussion and planning, and the pupils are expected to develop an understanding of lighting, costumes, sets, scripting, storyboarding and many other skills. It is hoped in time to involve the wider community more.

As well as improving their knowledge and skills as outlined above, the children in the drama club are preparing for a successful future. The creative industries are a source of new careers and wealth. It has been estimated recently that these industries are worth a staggering £57 billion a year to the UK.[10]

---

[10] DCMS, 1998, quoted in DfEE/DCMS (1999) Robinson report, *All Our Futures: Creativity, culture and education*, p 19

Arts performances or exhibitions can help a school community to express and celebrate its identity and achievements internally, and to the local community. Educational research also confirms that arts activities encourage and help develop independent thinkers. Teachers know that participation in the performing arts in particular helps to develop students' confidence, social skills and awareness of other cultures. They help to open up other areas of the curriculum, enable pupils to work together, to solve problems, to develop their critical and reasoning skills, and their aesthetic understanding. The arts are as critical to the development of emotional intelligence as to aesthetic sensibility. Best of all, most children find the arts fun, creative, and absorbing.

The arts have now taken on a wider significance in terms of learning in the context of new awareness of the power of all forms of creativity. The Robinson report, *All Our Futures: Creativity, culture and education* (1999), argued for a national strategy for creative and cultural education and emphasised that creativity was not only the source of culture, linking arts and science, but that together, creativity and cultural education would help to raise overall standards of achievement, emphasising that: 'The greatest disincentives to achievement are low self-esteem and lack of motivation. Creative and cultural programmes are powerful ways of revitalising the sense of community in a school and engaging the whole school with the wider community.'

Recently, the role that the arts play in statutory education has changed significantly. Schools are no longer required to teach the full programme of the arts curriculum at levels 1 and 2. Many arts-trained teachers have frustratingly few opportunities to use or develop their art forms and skills – which bring so much pleasure to teachers as well as students. As one gifted teacher put it: 'The single experience I most enjoyed as a schoolboy was acting the part of Sir Andrew Aguecheek in *Twelfth Night*. . . The achievements of which I am most proud in my career as a teacher. . . are some of the plays I directed. . .'[11] However, pupils are expected to achieve basic skills and competence in the areas of visual arts, music and dance. These include:

- in art: developing skills for working in two or three dimensions, observational drawing and painting;
- in music: learning how to make, shape and control sound to create music;
- in dance: displaying the ability to compose and combine basic actions and to be able to express feelings, moods and ideas through movement.

Providing pupils are able to achieve certain basic skills in these priority areas, teachers are, to all intents and purposes, free to dip into the

[11] Jonathan Smith (2000) *The Learning Game*, p 145, Little Brown, London

curriculum as and how they like. As a counter-balance to this relaxation of arts teaching in school time, the government has put in place a number of new initiatives to give the arts out of school hours a definite boost. The New Opportunities Fund itself emphasised the importance of partnerships and has led to funding bids across the UK involving arts partners and organisations. These initiatives include the restructuring of the Arts Council and the devolution of policy and funding for the arts to Regional Boards in order to boost local access to the arts. Other initiatives include:

- A new National Advisory Committee for Culture and Arts in Education made up of leading figures from education, arts and entertainment. Its role is to make recommendations to the government on the creative and cultural development of young people through formal and informal education.
- £10 million for a new Youth Music Trust to breathe new life into school music provision across the country and £40 million additional funding for school music.
- £40 million for new Creative Partnerships in highly disadvantaged areas to stimulate young people's access to and participation in the arts. See in particular DCMS (2001) *Culture and Creativity: The next ten years* for a view of how out of school learning opportunities in the arts might be extended.

As a result of all these changes (see also Chapter 8) many arts organisations across the country have now become very proactive partners in the design and delivery of study support activities. The following case study shows how one school in a particularly disadvantaged area has responded to the challenge of a changing culture.

EXTRA

Minsthorpe Community College

This community college is located in South Elmsall in Wakefield, in an area where social and cultural identity has been dramatically eroded by the loss of the mining industries over the last 10 years. The school has responded to the changing climate by developing a crucial role for itself as a focus for arts, culture, training and employment. The school has become a lifeline for many people within the local community, redirecting and refocusing interest and energy. The school has recently employed a writer to work with pupils at KS3 to help them develop a social history project into an exciting piece of theatre which will tour through the three local mining villages of Upton, South Elmsall and South Kirkby. The Head of Expressive Arts at the school emphasises that the school has:

a very strong tradition of going out from the school into the community. We have regularly run programmes of exhibitions of work by professional artists and local people which have proved extraordinarily successful in terms of bringing the community into the school.

I strongly believe that the great respect and sense of care that our students have developed in relation to visual arts, exhibitions and performances is born out of their continual exposure to an exciting and stimulating aesthetic environment.

OUT OF SCHOOL LEARNING AND SPORTS

I've seen lots of children who are not really into sport – some are reluctant even to talk to each other – and sport has brought out the best in them in terms of giving them the confidence to know who they are and what they want. And it gives them achievement – sport helps them to achieve little things. They don't have to be great at sports, but that word, 'achiever', it makes them think: 'Well, I achieved that' – it might be throwing the ball – 'What can I achieve if I put my mind to something else'? (Tony Simpson, PE coach at Torridon Primary, London Borough of Lewisham)

While the arts offer unique ways for learning and for developing lifeskills through creativity, expression, or performance, sport offers the opportunity to meet other sorts of individual challenges, and experience teamwork and leadership. Moreover, it has always constituted a high percentage of out of school hours activities, up to 80 per cent in the case of some schools. In the national surveys of study support it remains the most popular choice among both primary and secondary pupils. The ability of sport to reach out and involve the majority of pupils in new learning experiences therefore cannot be underestimated. Along with a high priority given to the arts, *Extending Opportunity* (1998) clearly identified the role that physical education and sport could play in OSHL. Indeed, the three elements of learning implicit in study support interact naturally in sport:

- **Enabling**: 'Physical Education and sport offer a range of exciting activities using a variety of resources and equipment that will challenge young people individually, with a partner or in teams, reinforcing and developing basic and key skills.'
- **Enriching**: 'The great thing about physical education and sport is that there are so many different activities you can do out of school by yourself or with a friend. I'm really into water sports and have just started windsurfing with my friend.'
- **Extending**: 'For years schools across the country have been providing activity clubs that have allowed pupils to develop and build upon

experiences covered during lessons – they are often the backbone of a school's out of hours learning programme.'[12]

The importance of school sport in establishing healthy and active lifestyles was powerfully reinforced by the research finding that, despite the national obsession with football, 'Not only do children not play much sport and not watch much sport on TV but the majority do not go to watch live, professional sporting events either.'[13] At the same time, the majority of parents (and a higher proportion of middle-class parents) recognise that opportunities for participation in sport have increased. The content of delivery has, over the years, become more diverse, ranging from provision for competitive school sports through to innovative programmes integrating sports leadership and family participation.

Its very popularity has therefore placed sport, and to a certain extent the opportunities it offers for children to have a more healthy lifestyle, in an advantageous position in terms of developing a more strategic approach. This approach is represented by the creation and development of a wide range of national agencies with clear investment in and remits to the delivery of physical activity.[14] This proliferation of partners has inevitably meant that there have been some difficulties in partnership development as roles and responsibilities are worked out.

However, while sport has always been valued for its ability to promote lifeskills such as teamwork and lifelong awareness of 'fair play', it is also seen increasingly as a way of engaging and motivating students in the life of the school, and as the Playing for Success initiative shows, of helping students to see the fun as well as the relevance of learning. Using the physical environment of the sports stadium to link work in literacy or numeracy with sports content (whether that is designing a fixture card or calculating goal averages) is a novel development. But the sports environment can be used, equally, to develop an awareness of diet, nutrition, and the elements of what, at a more advanced level, becomes sports science.

Therefore, OSHL can do more than increase physical participation and awareness of the positive nature of a healthy lifestyle. Schools are

[12] Quotes from the Study Support through Physical Education and Sport, School Briefing Pack, published October 2000 by the Youth Sport Trust

[13] Nestlé Family Monitor, ibid p 17

[14] These agencies include: Sport England (formerly the English Sports Council); Sport Scotland (formerly the Scottish Sports Council); The Sports Council for Wales; The Sports Council for Northern Ireland; Central Council for Physical Recreation/British Sports Trust; National Council for School Sport; National Coaching Foundation; British Association of Advisers and Lecturers in Physical Education (Baalpe); and many others. Recently these have been joined by the Youth Sport Trust. All these agencies and organisations have developed partnerships, of some form, with a range of National Governing Bodies of Sport as well as with Local Authority Sports Development Units and LEA Inspectors/Advisers for Physical Education. Work has also occurred with HE and FE

responding to this agenda. Increasingly, they see sport as a powerful agent in their targets for school improvement. The government has targeted areas of high social deprivation within the initiatives Education Action Zones (EAZs), and Excellence in Cities (EiC) as areas where new sports colleges should be located. These will form clear links to existing or soon to be formed Health Action Zones and Sports Action Zones.

Moreover, funding for sport, particularly for attracting young people into sport and supporting excellence, has dramatically increased in the past few years not least through earmarked funding within the current and future programmes of the New Opportunities Fund. This investment in sport has been driven by two overriding concerns. First, declining levels of activity among young people with all its consequences for adult lifestyles, health and mortality rates. Second, the persistent decline in the standards of the performance of British sport – from cricket to athletics. These concerns underlined the perception of the decline in the volume of extra-curricular sporting activities during the 1980s – exemplified by the sale of school playing fields. However, as a national survey found in 1996, this gloomy perception was not entirely accurate:

> 'This decline' is often attributed to a permanent withdrawal of goodwill by teachers during the pay and conditions of service dispute between them and the government in the mid-1980s. Social conditions may have changed, and a return to the traditional dominance of the Saturday games fixtures in secondary schools may not be possible. However, this survey found little to support the notion of irreversible decline. In these schools, the involvement and commitment of most specialist PE staff and many primary teachers were as strong as ever. . . The survey indicated that. . . all the specialist PE staff in the schools visited were deeply involved in the provision of extra-curricular sporting activity.'[15]

Policies for sport have, however, been very inconsistent over the years. Vociferous criticism and complaints about lack of interest or excellence in sport have continued while school playing fields have been sold, leisure centres priced out of range, and coaching opportunities reduced. The 1990s, spurred on by Prime Minister Major's passion for cricket, saw the creation in England of the National Junior Sports Programme, funded by the English Sports Council from lottery money. This, in turn, brought new funding for major agencies to support and develop initiatives that would provide more opportunities to participate, more facilities and eventually more elite performers.

Probably the largest challenge in the development of effective sports strategy has, however, been to get the balance between a 'sports centric'

---

[15] HMSO (1996) *Physical Education and Sport in Schools: A survey of good practice*, quoted in Ofsted/YST (2000) *Sports Colleges: The first two years*, p 22

and a 'school centric' approach. This is reflected on the level of influence and effect made by the government through the Department for Culture, Media and Sport (DCMS) and the Department for Education and Employment (DfEE).

In 1999 Sport England's National Junior Sports Programme was developed into their Active Schools programme. The theme of 'more people, more places, more medals' saw a continued commitment to increased opportunities, facilities and improved performance. This programme has seen the creation of Active Schools Officers within all local authorities. It has also seen the development of two Kitemark awards for schools. Secondary and primary schools can now apply for Sportsmark and Activemark awards. In applying, schools have to clearly show the extent and effect of out of school hours provision within their organisation. Many agencies worked hand in hand with the Qualifications and Curriculum Authority (QCA) and representatives from the PE profession to reshape the new PE curriculum for 2000. These agencies have worked hard to ensure a minimum provision of two hours of PE delivery per week that is supported, complimented and extended by extra out of school hours opportunities

The most significant step in terms of putting sport at the heart of educational excellence, has, however, come with the creation and development of specialist sports colleges, in 1998, assisted by the Youth Sports Trust. The Trust is itself responsible through its TOPS programmes and many others, for training over 100,000 teachers and 25,000 community sports coaches. The Specialist Sports Programme, which has proved to be the forerunner of a new generation of specialist colleges, managed through the YST, has brought a major investment in innovative practices for the development of PE and sport – and has demonstrated the way in which specialist schools can work with other schools, out of school hours, and across the community. 'The Sports Colleges. . . make a valuable contribution to the work of sports clubs, governing bodies of sport, the local community, local health authorities and other adult organisations or initiatives designed to increase participation and establish exit routes for pupils beyond school.'[16]

By 2003, 110 sports colleges are planned, and a recent joint report on the first two years of sports colleges by Ofsted and the YST has shown how out of school hours provision has enriched and expanded the range of opportunities available to the young:

In Sports Colleges the quality and range of curriculum enrichment activities increased strongly and many non-specialist teachers are becoming involved. . . What was the traditional practice in OSHL has changed in many

[16] Ofsted/YST (2000) *Sports Colleges: The first two years*, p 11

schools. In the past, pupils typically took part in practical activity led by their teachers or coaches. Now, however, properly supervised pupils in Sports Colleges are often engaged in the activity as sports leaders, coaches or officials, supporting younger pupils from feeder schools or from their own schools. . .

The following example shows how, in practice, this is working in one outstanding school.

EXTRA

Brookfield High School

In 1997, Brookfield High School, Knowsley,[17] was presented with the Sportsmark Gold Award and in 1998 was designated a specialist Sports College. In 1999, the school developed a pilot project to link PE and sport to raise standards in English, maths and science. This project involves after-school clubs at three primary schools and includes three Saturday workshops. The first focuses on maths (linked to orienteering and cross-country; the second, science (linked to health and fitness monitoring); and the third, football (literacy). The project is supported by Liverpool John Moores University and Knowsley Leisure Services Department and complements the introduction of Top Play and BT Top Sport into local primary schools. Education Extra is a national partner in the work of the school.

Brookfield is also Knowsley's designated link school for physically disabled pupils and a group of students has been working with Springfield Special School pupils to develop sporting skills and support their after-school sessions. Brookfield High School has also developed partnerships with local sports clubs and coaches, putting on Sports Fairs to raise pupils' awareness of the range of sporting activities within the school and at local clubs. As far as the headteacher, Pam Jarvis, is concerned, sport 'has a key role in enriching the quality of lives and enhancing the opportunities of all of our pupils and of our community'.

Opportunities for developing out of school hours sports have continued to increase. In April 2000 came the publication of *A Sporting Future for All*, the government's sport strategy for a new century. Although published by DCMS, it has a heavy emphasis on school-led initiatives and commitment. Its main thrust of Sport in Education, Sport in the Community and Sporting Excellence reflect the improved balance. Probably the biggest initiative to be drawn from the strategy is the creation of 600 school sport coordinators to act as facilitators in creating greater opportunities. These coordinators, backed up by specific training programmes, will be teachers released from

[17] Education Extra (Spring Term, 1999) *Extra Special No 56: After school sports as study support*

schools throughout the year to develop links between schools, clubs and organisations within local communities, creating real partnership for change.

OSHL and sport has therefore developed a clear reputation and a unique position as an initiative that is breathing new life into sport. As *A Sporting Future for All* makes clear: 'out of school hours clubs and activities offer great scope for schools to form partnerships which will broaden and strengthen the range of opportunities available to all young people.'[18] It is one of the main policies that is encouraging effective partnerships between sports agencies and schools as well as making powerful connections to other national arenas such as healthy living, citizenship/leadership, personal and social education, social inclusion and racial harmony.

TARGETED INTERVENTION: NATIONAL INITIATIVES FOR OSHL

So far in this chapter we have looked at the way that OSHL is being developed in different situations, and through different areas of the school curriculum and national life. But OSHL is now moving beyond the single initiative to become a 'given' in the educational landscape and an explicit element in national strategies to raise achievement. The prime target in policies which are focusing on underachievement in inner cities and deprived neighbourhoods, as well as policies to promote social inclusion, is to find ways of re-engaging young people and reinvigorating schools which feel that they are losing the battle against failure. OSHL has a key role to play in that.

Overcoming disadvantage

The Education Action Zone (EAZ) is described in *Meet the Challenge* (1998) as 'a dynamic framework within which schools can work together with parents, businesses, teachers, LEAs and community organisations' to raise standards in areas of underachievement and disadvantage. EAZs are designed to be pathfinder organisations which will test out new ideas and innovations in teaching and learning which might then be available in a tried and tested form for wider dissemination. From the first, study support was highlighted as a way of adding value to other in-school strategies and motivating and energising pupils and schools alike.

By November 1999 there were 66 EAZs across the country from Ashington in Northumberland to Camborne in Cornwall, including an intriguing 'virtual EAZ' linking Kent and Somerset. Most EAZs have within their plan a major commitment to study support, including breakfast clubs, new

---

[18] DCMS (April 2000) *A Sporting Future for All*, p 31

after-school programmes, holiday schemes and summer universities. For example:

- Hackney EAZ aims to resource parent support groups and toy libraries for under-fives, and provide after-school, Saturday and holiday learning opportunities for school-age pupils, in addition to programmes promoting community involvement.
- Newham EAZ has made social inclusion a priority, aiming to develop schools as community learning centres, increasingly available outside normal school hours to provide support to both pupils and their families. Study clubs will grow and there will be Saturday schools for all pupils in Years 5 and 6. Homework clubs and homework packs to primary pupils will also be available.
- Leicester EAZ has made it clear that its New Horizons programme 'will give children the chance to try a whole range of activities – from sports and arts activities to outward bound and enterprise projects. New clubs will be encouraged to start up in the area through offering set-up grants, while existing groups will be given help in expanding their activities. Leicester City Football Club and the Philharmonia Orchestra – both partners to the Zone – are making major contributions of time and expertise'.[19] A Parent Linkworker has also been recruited from each of the four estates which the Zone covers.

The first evaluation of EAZs (Ofsted, March 2001) suggested that the six EAZs inspected were making 'some useful contributions to raising standards in schools, though they are not yet doing so consistently'.

A companion educational initiative, Excellence in Cities, is designed to address low performance specifically in inner city areas by investing £350 million over five years in new models of promoting and sharing excellence.

The initial *Excellence in Cities* report emphasised the need for more targeted support for inner city schools to 'tackle the problems of failure and low aspirations' starting with six large conurbations – Inner London, Birmingham, Manchester/Salford, Liverpool/Knowsley, Leeds/Bradford and Sheffield/Rotherham. The report cited the comparatively poor performance of children in inner city areas at assessment stages and GCSEs, and higher rates of truancy and exclusion. The twin educational strategies (EAZs and EICs) are already confronting, in action, the following facts reported in 1999:

- 33 per cent of inner city pupils get 5+ GCSE grades A–C compared with 46 per cent nationally.
- One quarter of all pupils in some inner city schools get no qualifications.

[19] Leicester EAZ, *Beating the Odds*

- 38 per cent of inner city schools excluded five or more pupils compared with 26 per cent nationally.
- Unauthorised absence rates in inner city schools are 33 per cent higher than the national average.

Well over half of inner city schools have more than 35 per cent of pupils entitled to FSM compared with one in seven nationally.[20]

Significantly, the report observed: 'Learning can and should be about much more than what happens in classrooms; our aim is to develop a wider range of learning opportunities for individuals. We have begun with the provision of study support, summer schools and the implementation of the National Grid for Learning. . .' The report drew attention to the fact that 'Opportunities to learn outside school and engage in wider activities – for example having somewhere to do homework – can be limited'. The implication was clear: part of the strategy would be to take an 'individual rather than an institutional perspective' and would include providing 'access to learning opportunities beyond the classroom and the conventional school day'. The scheme is primarily focused on secondary pupils.

The scheme is designed to ensure that:

- all pupils have good access to a network of educational opportunities beyond the classroom and school;
- all inner city pupils can benefit by ensuring better coordination of activities at local level;
- schools are encouraged to monitor which pupils are accessing these programmes and ensure that all those who need them are benefiting.

The seven programme elements include:

- Learning Mentors for individual pupils who could benefit from individual support;
- Learning Support Units for schools where students can be referred where necessary (eg disruptive students);
- provision for gifted and talented pupils;
- a further 800 specialist schools nationally by 2002–03;
- a target of 1,000 Beacon schools with priority to be given to inner city areas;
- the creation of small EAZs;
- a network of Inner City Learning Centres (ICLC).

Out of school learning should have a role in each of these elements, but specifically in relation to the new Learning Centres which will be funded

---

[20] DfEE (1999) *Excellence in Cities*

for start-up costs to about £1.2 million. These 'centres of excellence' will put a major emphasis on modern ICT facilities, pioneering new approaches to learning and greatly expanding opportunities after school and in the holidays. The first 30 centres may be based at local schools or at FE colleges – which will establish strong links with neighbouring schools, open 12 hours per weekday and 10 hours per weekend day, with 80 Internet-linked work stations and trained staff available for all these hours. The ICLC will run courses/opportunities for individual pupils, cascade good practice and be open to the wider community and network via the National Grid for Learning

The Green Paper on Education, *Building on Success* (February 2001) made it clear that many of these initiatives were seen to be so successful that they would be expanded, particularly the controversial extension of specialist schools to include nearly half of all schools.

LOCAL STRATEGIES FOR OSHL

Learning Plus is about giving children and young people the time, space and support they need to develop their skills, increase their motivation and enhance their self-esteem. It is about enabling children to take control of and make choices about their own learning and it is about enriching and stimulating learning outside of school time. (Essex LEA on Learning Plus in Essex)

None of the initiatives identified, and none of the grand plans for raising achievement or social inclusion, will work unless LEAs have the vision and capacity to make them happen. LEAs are already involved in the single initiatives and with the agencies already identified in this chapter – and many others referred to elsewhere in this book. The challenge facing local authorities, and, indeed, the major challenge to the future of OSHL is to ensure coordination between policies and practice so that each element of policy serves the same end in the most efficient way possible. That, above all, has meant pressures on local authorities to articulate and implement a local strategy for OSHL – and, at the same time, to secure substantial funding for the future.

Some local authorities were already very active in the field of OSHL, often working as partners with the Prince's Trust National Evaluation Programme.[21] Authorities such as Tower Hamlets have had a long tradition of study support for most of the 1990s, running study support centres in all the LEA's secondary schools and undertaking independent evaluation of the benefits. Other innovative learning partnerships, for example in

[21] See, for example, the origins of this programme as described in The Prince's Trust (1997) *Study Support: Learning to Achieve*

Merseyside, brought together several local authorities, voluntary organisations and headteachers' associations in a coherent bid to raise achievement.
Merseyside Study Support Initiatives were part of that strategy and
included opening library access before and after school, homework clubs,
revision classes, paired reading schemes, reading enrichment schemes,
pupil support groups and community projects.

Other LEAs, TECs and EBPs which led the field included Sandwell,
Bedfordshire, Camden, Newham, County Durham, Sheffield, Newcastle,
Cardiff and Birmingham, as well as organisations in the central belt of
Scotland. The concept of Learning Boroughs and Learning Cities provided
a coherent framework in many areas for study support ideas and initiatives.
In Camden, for example, study support was identified in 1997 as having a
key role to play within the five-year strategic plan; while in Cardiff, the
Cardiff Achievement Programme placed a large emphasis on study support
in partnership with the Prince's Trust, the university and business in the
community.

The immediate challenge to local authorities, in 1999, when NOF funding
came on stream and they were already awash with educational policy
initiatives was, however, self-evident. In 1998–1999 fewer than 10 per cent
of LEAs had a written policy for OSHL, but at the same time, 78 per cent
indicated that they intended to include such a policy in their education
development plans. 'It was clear from the policy or consultation documents
received by NFER that these LEAs were tailoring their own policies to
complement the Government's policy on study support.'[22] About three
quarters of LEAs already were involved in study support – under a guise
of other names and initiatives – particularly in supporting homework, skills
activities and literacy. The main groups of students being supported were
low achievers, gifted pupils and ethnic minority pupils. More than a quarter
had already led or supported activities which included the creative and
performing arts, sport and leisure activities, maths, science and ICT,
childcare projects with integrated study support, and summer/children's
universities.

The key role of the LEAs in planning and developing coherent LEA-wide
policies was acknowledged and welcomed – but was also seen as a complex
and challenging task given the 'variety of service providers and a plethora
of funding sources. [It would be] difficult for LEAs to lead/coordinate a
strategic view; partnership working essential'. Other LEAs made the same
point, emphasising the importance of working particularly with the
childcare agencies and developments. Few LEAs had a concept of study
support as a coherent local policy. And few had taken the next steps, which
were: to establish a set of priorities and principles that would guarantee
best value, and enthuse and involve schools and other local learning

---

[22] DfEE (July 1999) *Study Support: A survey of local authorities*, RR 128, pp 2–3

partners; to think through issues such as quality, sustainability and evaluation; and to construct a coherent bid, with the support of local schools, which could be sustained beyond the lifetime of NOF funding.

Significantly, however, the majority of LEAs were keen to develop future plans. Some, for example, were aiming to plan for developing 'greater coherence in study support through a team, school, community curriculum framework. The LEA anticipates study support provision moving beyond the unit of "the school" to encompass a network of learning centres in school and community venues'. The recurring theme of many of the responses seems to have been the importance of partnership and the community benefits which could follow from the creation of a coherent plan.

In 1999, few LEAs had even designated out of school learning officers or understood where decision making in this new area of policy should lie. Vision statements, matched to funding bids and policy outlines, began to appear. For example:

> We recognise that young people are a vital resource and a key force for change in the new millennium and that their skills and potential should be developed through access to both a formal curriculum inside school and an informal curriculum outside school hours.
>
> We believe therefore that study support activities are an opportunity through partnership between schools and others, to make a real difference to the lives and learning of young people and their communities [and] to prepare [young people] for life in a multicultural society through active citizenship. (Leicester City LEA).

Key elements in the process of creating a coherent study support strategy are:

- strong central staff to lead the initiative;
- focused aims and objectives;
- a development strategy across the whole authority, which encompasses the full width of policy initiatives and the range of funding sources.

OSHL/study support can be a separate heading on the EDP or it can 'read across' other priority headings, thereby tying provision to other important aims and showing coherence across policy areas. Above all, OSHL coordinators are mapping OSHL on to the local education development plan, either as a separate aim, or as part of general policies to raise achievement with links across into related policies.

By the end of 2000, nearly all UK local authorities had designated coordinators in place, the majority of whom had already submitted funding bids or were completing bid preparations. Study support coordinators were found mainly within education policy area or community education. As one described it, her job was 'to raise awareness of the potential of study support (across a very remote rural area), write a county strategy, promote the possibilities offered by NOF, and set up some county projects'. (Deborah Duncan, Extra Strategy 6, Summer 2000). In practice this has meant holding advice surgeries, producing a study support handbook with model policies and ideas and contacts, providing a project toolkit, and holding workshops.

Limited time for both officers and schools, and other priorities, slowed things down but by the end of September 1999, the first LEA – Tower Hamlets – had already received its funding (£2 million for a rolling programme).

Tower Hamlets was well placed to get off to a quick start. It already had a study support project in place, involving the EBP, which coordinated study support provision in all the borough's secondary schools, in 24 primary schools, one special school and 16 voluntary centres. 'Thus we had in place, firm foundations for a strategic bid to NOF.'[23] After consulting schools and creating an advisory group of relevant officers from education, early years, library, youth and Inspectorate services, the bid was developed closely in conjunction with local educational strategies. Schools were given the opportunity to join in 1999, 2000 or 2001. The NOF grant will enable 89 schools to provide a broad spectrum of learning activities based on the curriculum, sports and arts activities and learning new skills.

By the middle of 2000 the OSHL coordinator reported 'We now have all secondary schools and well over 90 per cent of primary schools, libraries, community schools and volunteer and partner organisations offering OSHL provision. Most children who wish to access study support can. My job, as I see it, is to embed existing good practice, to move us forward and to create sustainability.'[24]

Another LEA which had taken a very proactive lead, Cardiff, had introduced a School Improvement Programme for secondary schools which promoted a range of homework and revision clubs for pupils at KS4. This was extended in 1998 to the creation of a network of community learning centres linked to the authority's ICT strategy to raise achievement. The first learning centres, established in disadvantaged areas of the city, focused on key skills, study support and out of school hours clubs to develop all-age, all-stage provision. The initiative was managed by a steering group, drawing on education and economic development agencies, and included community representation. Saturday morning clubs, evening opening and even Sunday homework clubs attracted regular and large groups of pupils (200 students at the learning centre during the week).[25]

[23] Jane Leggatt, Study Support coordinator, in *Extra Strategy No 3* (Summer Term 1999) p 1, Education Extra
[24] Andrew Goodman in *Extra Strategy No 6* (Summer 2000) Education Extra
[25] Cardiff Learning Support Centre Strategy – made available to Education Extra

The process was supported centrally by the production of advice and resource materials, training sessions and e-mail networks, which allowed local authority officers to share experience and obtain immediate information about NOF procedures and processes. Education Extra was instrumental in this process, producing an LEA newsletter (*Extra Strategy*) and organising a series of regional seminars at regular intervals.

In post, the new OSHL coordinators are able to show how OSHL provides an ideal opportunity to reinforce existing policies across education, and to make stronger links with other policies for promoting health, ICT access, sport and recreation, and childcare. Local authorities can use the new opportunities in study support to help them to achieve key objectives in raising achievement and reducing social exclusion. For example, to:

- reinforce existing priorities (eg literacy and numeracy support; raise achievement among boys);
- take forward new programmes (eg citizenship);
- extend opportunities for homework provision – enhancing the use of libraries, learning centres and ICT suites;
- improve the transition from primary to secondary stages;
- foster closer youth work/school opportunities;
- make stronger links with family learning and lifelong learning strategies;
- develop holiday provision, possibly linking care and learning;
- build community confidence through neighbourhood renewal;
- support specific disadvantaged communities.

By July 2000, NOF had reached 30 per cent of its target and funds to the value of £61 million had been allocated to 3,289 schools across the UK. The awards for individual schools have varied in size and scope. Standards Funding is also being used to develop and bed down OSHL in many different ways – eg in Norfolk 'with projects as diverse as composing music from the sounds made by a wind turbine, to painting murals on classroom walls, to weekend trips to Derbyshire'.[26]

CONCLUSION

In the UK between 1997 and 2001, the status and visibility of OSHL have been transformed, as have OSHL policy, provision and practice. OSHL has been linked to other areas of priority, there is access to OSHL opportunities across age ranges and abilities and local authorities have been assigned a key role in planning, support, evaluation and sustainability. While NOF funding reaches out across the UK on the same basis, the four UK countries

[26] *Extra Time No 6* (2000) p 5

are also developing different styles and practices which fit with national culture and educational systems – examples (at different stages of development) are the new Community Partnerships in Wales, the new Community schools in Scotland, and the new political settlement in Northern Ireland. Each of the four countries is adopting different forms of research and development to explore, celebrate and develop policy. However, in each of the four countries, as the next section explores, the challenges of developing effective OSHL and making it part of the effective school, are essentially the same. But, so are the opportunities – and, as will become clear – the very positive way that schools have responded.

4

OSHL and improving schools

This chapter takes the analysis of change from the policy level down to the practical level of the school – and from effective learning to effective schools. In this chapter we will look at:

- concepts of 'school improvement' and how OSHL can support the main thrust;
- the range of provision in schools and some of the perceived difficulties to development;
- what is involved in developing successful schemes in terms of the school, the individual learner, and the organisation of the scheme as a whole;
- the different ways in which staff can be involved and can benefit from their involvement;
- how schools can get help for self-improvement and self-evaluation frameworks, concepts of development and 'quality'.

MAKING GOOD PRACTICE COMMON PRACTICE

Many pupils come to the schools in this survey with poor basic skills and the schools give high priority to improving them. Nevertheless, they teach the National Curriculum in full: doing so is part of the commitment to not selling these pupils short. Within this, there is a valuing of cultural diversity and a strong emphasis on the arts and physical education in school and, beyond it, a rich programme of extra-curricular activities.[1]

The learning and policy frameworks discussed in previous chapters face the only test that counts when schools begin to translate them into school policies, and to develop them within the ecology and practice of the whole

[1] Ofsted (2000) *Improving City Schools*, p 28

school. This is where good practice is identified and collected; it is also the test bed for the concepts, aspirations and practical choices which make up the determination to raise achievement through a high-quality OSHL scheme.

OSHL is uniquely inclusive, compared with the competitive and potentially exclusive nature of classroom life; but it is also uniquely sensitive to the spirit, talent and needs of particular students. It is driven by the personal curriculum which every child holds in his or her head. To this extent, therefore, it succeeds by accommodating and influencing that mental map. This chapter looks first at how OSHL is growing and changing at the level of the school, at how it is helping to change schools in relation to school effectiveness and school improvement. It also looks at the individual learner, at how OSHL can provide an effective learning framework and at how individual and institutional needs combine in a successful OSHL programme. Finally, it looks at the passage from bolt-on programmes to built-in provision as schools organise their OSHL provision on a coherent basis in the context of the concept and emerging practice of 'quality'.

This chapter therefore explores the development and the dynamics of good practice within OSHL itself, and at the links between that good practice and whole school development. Knowing about good practice is not, however, the same as operating it. Mapping OSHL/study support on to the school improvement plan is key to understanding how and where it fits into school objectives and why it deserves a high priority when there are so many other pressures on schools.

Above all, because OSHL/study support is different in every school, when it works it does so because it fits the personality of the school, its staff, pupils and community. It cannot be forced but it can be framed in such a way that everyone who can contribute or participate is able to do so, knowing what is in it for them, and why.

OSHL AND THE EFFECTIVE SCHOOL

As MacBeath has observed, 'the quest for the effective school is not only like the quest for the unicorn, but, more practically, has generated many lists'.[2] And study support is, with recurring frequency, appearing on those lists – usually in relationship to the school as learning organisation, and as a way of improving the climate or ethos of the school.[3] In this sense, 'ethos' means the characteristic spirit, as well as the moral nature of the school. MacBeath identified clusters of indicators of the effective school, which sum up the 'school climate' as ones mentioned most often as critical to

[2] MacBeath, J (1999) *Schools must speak for themselves: the case for school self-evaluation*, p 9, Routledge, London

[3] Coleman (1982) *Identified Participation in Extra-curricular Activities as an Element in School Improvement*, quoted in MacBeath, J, ibid p 29

effective schooling by teachers, parents and students. Students, in particular, were very clear about what made 'a happy place to be' and the difference extra-curricular activities could make to the atmosphere and climate of the school. The students themselves put a very high value on extra-curricular activities, mentioning them no fewer than 76 times as important to them and their relationship to the school.[4]

As collective evidence suggests, moreover, that OSHL does help to extend achievement, OSHL should, by any definition, count as one of the elements of an effective school.[5] Clearly, measuring or judging the effectiveness of a school is a complex task, exemplified most recently in the debate over the inclusion of 'value-added' into the equation of league table performance. We saw in Chapter 2 that there has not yet been a thorough research study to evaluate potential links between the quantity or scope of extra-curricular provision and school performance overall. However, OSHL programmes can be linked naturally in practice to the main indicators of school success in ways which will reinforce the ability of schools to deliver their objectives.

Table 4.1 shows the positive parallels between school effectiveness and a well-organised study support programme.

The relationship between effective and improving schools is recognised as complex and highly dynamic. While 'school effectiveness' seems to imply a judgement on practice and performance in the present tense, 'school improvement' indicates a dynamic measure of progress aiming, according to Ofsted, to:

- raise standards;
- enhance quality;
- increase efficiency;
- achieve greater success in promoting the ethos of the school.

In practice, OSHL also fits closely to generic models for school improvement including that outlined in the DfEE publication for governors *From Targets to Action* . The fundamental questions for self-evaluation are equally sound applied to learning in or out of school.

It has been suggested[6] that school improvement itself can mean either a short-term tactical approach targeted at raising attainment, a longer-term strategic approach towards sustaining attainment, or creating extra capacity to meet and implement change. OSHL, whether it takes the form of intensive help with maths in the months before GCSE, a programme of

---

[4] MacBeath, J, op cit note 2, pp 36–38

[5] Andrews *et al* (1996) *Good Policy and Good Practice for the After School Hours*, Pitman Publishing, London, cited the evidence to date, particularly the fact that extra-curricular activity was identified by the National Commission on Education as one of the 10 key features of effective schools, p 8

[6] See John Gray *et al* (1999) *Improving schools: Performance and potential*, OUP, Oxford

Table 4.1 *Mapping study support on to school effectiveness*

Characteristics of school effectiveness	Links to study support
Dynamic and experienced leadership from the head coupled with strong support from the governing body	Opportunity for creative strategies to deal with whole school issues through study support. Links to new professional standards for headship; chance to develop leadership skills in others
High-quality teaching and learning environment (well focused, consistent, purposeful and stable teaching and support staff)	Provides opportunities to improve teaching and learning by extending ideas into the out of hours context and trying out new ideas; actively encouraging use of adults other than teachers
Teaching staff well trained in effective techniques for dealing with more challenging pupils	Provides new learning environments and challenges for the most disaffected/ challenging pupils; includes activities which are not simply school-based; improves teacher/pupil relationships
A well focused curriculum	Broadens coverage of non-core areas, eg arts, sport, citizenship
Close monitoring and effective personal support for pupils (includes monitoring progress)	Can improve quality and breadth of pupil monitoring; provides opportunities for targeted support to specific pupils
Clear communication with parents (includes the home–school partnership, strong parental involvement and support)	Provides opportunities for opening up the school to the community; encourages more parental involvement, eg family literacy
Clarity, intensity and persistence of the school's work (includes shared vision, clear targets and goals)	Builds on areas of ongoing need; raises profile of the school
The rigour with which the school is scrutinised	Is viewed positively by Ofsted; builds on current mechanisms for self-evaluation
High expectations of what pupils can attain (includes positive reinforcement)	Activities – particularly extension and enabling contribute positively to broad definitions of achievement
A positive approach to attainment, behaviour and attitudes (includes pupil rights and responsibilities)	Is directly linked to raised self-esteem, motivation and improved attitudes to learning
Active involvement of local businesses and community organisations (promotion of active support from other bodies, eg youth clubs, careers service, sports clubs)	Draws on a partnership approach to all aspects of provision, ie funding, resourcing and staffing (eg business mentors, Playing for Success scheme with football clubs, involvement of youth workers through NYA work)
Study support activities for young people to support their learning in school hours	Offers a clear rationale and tactics for using extra-curricular activities as a tool for raising achievement

Sources: *Improving Schools: a report of the DfEE/Ofsted conference* (DfEE 1995); *Improving City Schools* (*Ofsted* March 2000); *Schools Plus* (DfEE 2000)

curriculum-led activities linked to science and technology, or bringing in extra partners to enrich the activity programme on offer, can fit within this framework.

What practitioners have long observed as the benefits to teaching and learning has now been validated by inspection bodies. In *Improving City Schools* (2000) Ofsted identified not only curriculum extension activities, but curriculum enrichment activities as two of the elements that set apart improving schools in disadvantaged areas. Key findings showed that: 'Many of the schools put strong emphasis on the arts and sometimes on physical education', 'homework has an important place and is supported in secondary schools by supervised sessions and revision clubs'.

At the same time, in the context of the whole school curriculum the report was emphatic that one of the key features of the most improved secondary schools was: 'A range of curricular and extra curricular activities, for example, in the arts and physical education, to extend the interests of pupils, capture their imagination, and allow them to demonstrate high-level skills.' And, to quote further detail:

Structured support for homework and coursework outside normal hours is often a strong feature of the more effective schools' work in KS4, encouraging pupils to develop a positive attitude to learning and to gain the skills to study alone. At its most basic, a quiet place is provided to study at lunchtime and after school. Important elements of all such programmes are the quality and stability of the staffing by teachers and other adults. Pupils value the opportunity to work with teachers outside normal lessons. Examination results testify to the success of study support, with rises in the number of higher GCSE grades associated with the best programmes.

Aside from study support, many schools provide other out of school opportunities for pupils to extend their experience. Often, with the support of charities and other donors, some schools invest very heavily in these opportunities, which include field trips, visits and residential courses as well as arts and sports activities. The best of them enable pupils to develop interests and skills they otherwise might never have done.[7]

MOTIVATING AND MOBILISING

I didn't do anything at school. I sat at the back and no one took any interest. They didn't know what I was interested in. They never tried to find out. I started to truant and then I tried drugs. I'm now off them but if I had found something that interested me in school I know I wouldn't have dropped out. (Young black teenager speaking at a conference on poverty organised by Queen Mary College, June 2000)

[7] Ofsted (2000) *Improving City Schools*, pp 7, 30, 33

Motivation springs from involvement, absorption and enjoyment. The most powerful evidence for the range of special interests sparked off out of school, and supported by schools assisted by external partners, is provided by the annual entries to the Education Extra Awards. Since 1993, Education Extra has provided over £500,000 to enable students and schools to follow their special interests and enthusiasms. Small sums have been provided for activities and clubs which continually show the breadth and sometimes exotic nature of what will capture the enthusiasm of children and young people. Some examples of activities and clubs supported at primary and secondary schools from A–Z include:

- archaeology and aerobics;
- breakfast clubs, basketball, baroque music and butterfly gardens;
- circus clubs, classic cars, clog dancing and cycling;
- disc jockey clubs and drama productions;
- engineering and e-mail clubs;
- fencing, first aid and flyfishing clubs;
- go-karting and girls' rugby and football;
- Horrible History clubs;
- Indian music clubs;
- jazz dance;
- karaoke clubs;
- lacemaking and library clubs;
- mountaineering and motorbike maintenance;
- newspaper clubs;
- orienteering;
- poetry clubs and pets clubs;
- quiz clubs;
- radio, rocket clubs and reading clubs;
- Story Sacs and science clubs;
- trampolining and short tennis;
- UFO or science fiction clubs;
- violin and visits to the theatre;
- Welsh clubs;
- XYZylophones!

Each of these 'special interests' has mobilised the passion of not just groups of students but teachers and non-teaching staff, parents and grandparents, local experts and enthusiasts, community partners and national organisations. The range of activities provides the antidote to those who say that young people aren't interested in anything – for example, students say:

> I enjoyed the Japanese drumming as it was something I've never done before. . . (Hartcliffe school pupil)

It's great: you do so many things you wouldn't do at home. . . (Boots Family Learning Project)

I have learned how to hold a chisel and hammer without hurting myself. (Pupil involved in Southampton project for the Museums and Galleries project)

We think Drama Club is best! It's creative and even quiet people end up shouting. (Pupil from Church Stretton School in Shropshire)

LINKING TO THE CURRICULUM

Whatever area of interest OSHL champions, as Chapter 2 outlined, it can be linked to the curriculum implicitly or explicitly. At primary level, the links with the curriculum appear to be more diffuse – although reading, number work and ICT are not confined to specialised clubs, they can form part of any structured activity, including sport. At secondary level, however, the curriculum links are deep and diverse.

The closest links between activities and the school curriculum are most explicit with clubs and activities which enable students to practice or reinforce their study skills (preparing for school work and completing homework and project work obviously have direct links across the curriculum). Equally, students can move on from reading clubs or maths clinics which are directly instrumental to the curriculum to all those opportunities to apply and develop what they can do: newspaper clubs (a key opportunity for creative writing or learning about desk-topping); poetry or play reading clubs (an opportunity for performance as well as reading widely); and clubs such as Mathsmania at Invergordon Academy which give pupils an understanding of personal finance, savings, investment and income.

At the level of enrichment, the curriculum links can be attached in different ways. The history curriculum is a fertile area for exploration. Some history clubs open up opportunities for pupils to become local historians, exploring lifestyles and community change in relation to their own and their family's lives; using local resources, oral history, school links with museums, archives, heritage sites. Such clubs can not only entice students towards the history curriculum but give them confidence in applying historical analysis and techniques – including, increasingly, the use of IT. There are many other imaginative ways of developing useful research skills. The Horrible History clubs, the History Backpackers clubs and the archaeology clubs supported by Education Extra, for example, all give students first-hand experience of becoming historians and developing a flair for research and analysis which can go well beyond the GCSE history curriculum.

---EXTRA---

Stephenson Way Primary School

The history club at Stephenson Way Primary school in Durham worked for a year on a History Day centred around the theme of the Second World War, and in particular, the Battle of Arnhem. The pupils split into two groups: British soldiers or Dutch civilians, and every Thursday after school, the hall became 1944 England or Holland or both. Veterans were invited along to help and advise.

All the pupils researched their role (including those who were spies or members of the Resistance) finding out as much as they could about life at the time. On the day, Arnhem was recreated in the hall, with hotels, a café, a garage and a hospital. The day was started by a special assembly. Paratroopers were given their orders and set off, a glider landed on the field and the bridge on the boating area next to the school was eventually 'taken'.

Through this, pupils learnt how to do research, to work cooperatively, and to involve other members of the community. There were also links with geography, arts and creative writing. There is a constant waiting list to join the 50-strong history club, and this year the theme is a medieval day with costumes, dance and medicines from the era.

However, at the third level, clubs and activities can also make the curriculum more accessible by providing the space, time and extra resources outside school to enable pupils to explore and develop for themselves aspects of the curriculum in different ways, often with help and enthusiasm from non-school members.

Science and technology clubs may, for example, focus across one term on making radios or rockets; they may link to the local environment; they may involve a volunteer civil engineer or architect helping students to explore the built environment; or they may focus on the history of science and medicine, reconstructing simple historical experiments or a sustained link with a local museum. One growth area is in the range of after-school engineering clubs and initiatives (eg Young Engineers clubs, Neighbourhood Engineers, or Young Foresight clubs) which help pupils to boost their own creativity and ingenuity and also help to break down some of the negative perceptions of engineering which often obscure the opportunities within a very diverse profession. Such clubs, often supported by professional bodies and local engineers (see Chapter 7), provide an opportunity for practical work, turning an original concept into a practical product. In science and engineering clubs the emphasis is often on teamwork, refining concepts, trying new ideas and practical applications, focusing on a team product. At one extreme, for example, a go-karting or robotics club can lead on to GCSE Design and Technology and even to the next step into A level Technology and a career in one of the many branches of engineering.

Languages (for primary as well as secondary school children) can also be a fertile area for OSHL. For those taught in school, OSHL clubs can make obvious link between the curriculum and the living language – whether that is through language 'cafés' after school where, for example, French food, music, games or films are on offer; or language projects which end up with a residential or day visit; or Internet clubs which take the pupil direct into the heart of schools, homes and communities in other countries. Languages not taught within the curriculum, for example, Chinese and Japanese, Urdu or Hindi, can also be offered in OSHL clubs where the tutors can be parents or members from the community.

DIFFERENT SCHOOLS: DIFFERENT CHALLENGES

In the end, study support only defines a space and a time. There is no curriculum, no guidelines on content, no prescription on how and what you must do. Having defined it, you can fill it in whatever way seems best to you for the good of your pupils. (John Crossman, Education Extra)

By July 2000 it had become clear that government policy and extra funding were making a difference – and that, increasingly, many schools were looking not only to expand their OSHL programmes with NOF and Standards funding, but to improve them. However, this optimism does not disguise wide variations in commitment, resources, scope and quality in schools across the UK at all levels, or the practical difficulties which schools face in realising their ambitions. Indeed, these disparities and difficulties highlight the need for all schools to understand how to put the most appropriate study support in place, linked to school objectives as a whole.

Evidence is accumulating about what constitutes effective study support itself and how schools can be most effectively supported to reach the highest standards. It is important, however, to be realistic. While the speed and scope of change has been dramatic, there are still serious and credible barriers to development in many schools, large and small. The large comprehensive school with a number of senior managers with non-contact time may, in theory, be more capable of putting comprehensive study support programmes in place than the small, rural primary school with the teaching head who has little scope for coordination or even for looking for volunteers to help out. However this is not necessarily so. Large secondary schools are highly complex organisations in which it can take much time and energy to change the current ethos. Smaller primary schools often have a highly cohesive staff who can act rapidly when persuaded of the value of new ideas. Some primary schools indeed have outstanding, comprehensive and well-balanced programmes which offer something for every pupil. Take, for example, St Clement's School in Salford, a school in the most difficult circumstances which sets an outstanding example of involvement in all forms of out of school hours and community learning.

EXTRA

St Clement's Primary School

This exemplary primary school in a heavily deprived inner urban area has, since 1991, reorganised its school day to finish at 3 pm and established no fewer than 22 regular after-school clubs to engage children and parents in greater enjoyment of learning. Some 90 per cent of the pupils are on free school meals; only 3 per cent of the parents are in work. The area offers virtually no provision for children or young people. All pupils attend the clubs; all teachers are involved voluntarily and are trained to run different after-school activities.

School starts with breakfast club at 8 am which is open five days a week, funded by the EAZ. Indoor activities are run every lunchtime by teachers while a PE specialist runs activities outdoors. After-school clubs which run from 3 to 4 pm or from 4 to 5 pm on different nights of the week include structured play, teatime club and science club for the infant classes, and homework, needlework, judo, jazz dance and a cybercafé for the junior classes. Most clubs are free; others, for example, gymnastics, make a small charge. A 7–11 youth club runs twice a week and costs 40p. A family reading club, which runs once a week for all family members, has been funded externally by a national foundation. The school also runs a GCSE English course and an introduction to computers course for parents. Income from small local grants and very modest charges ensure that the after-school budget (in total about £5,000 for materials and resources) is balanced.

St Clements' out of school learning activities have been described as 'excellent' in two recent Ofsted reports and the Diocesan report has praised 'the moral, cultural and community support provided by the school'. The benefits generated by the after-school programme have been marked, for example, in outstanding achievements in gymnastics to raising attainment more generally across the core curriculum. Current plans are to extend the programme with external funding (NOF) to assist pupils at particular risk of social isolation, truancy and apathy.

What is evident is that as school context, structures and curriculum change, OSHL offers not only another way of dealing with some very old problems, but of dealing with relatively new ones as well.

There are many new models of provision (some of which are still in development) which can offer schools ways of improving, for example, what can be the unhappy and traumatic transition between primary and secondary schools.

The Bright Sparks club in Walsall, West Midlands, is one of seven clubs, funded through DfEE and administered by the Community Education Development Centre, which have been designed to address these issues.

EXTRA

The Bright Sparks Club

The programme began in March 1998, with interested schools and clusters encouraged to bid for small grants of £5,000. The Walsall Bright Sparks Club is based in a local secondary school once a week and its aim is to provide creative OSHL opportunities in science, maths and ICT for Year 6 and 7 pupils as well as providing support for parents.

Club members are drawn from Year 7 secondary pupils and Year 6 primary pupils from feeder primary schools. About 20 attend each week. Primary children become familiar with the school site, and are introduced to the curriculum. Students learn to work independently in pairs, small groups or with mentors. Science themes have included, for example, activities around the theme of light. Students have explored the chemical composition of coloured flames as well as cultural and social themes associated with Diwali, the Hindu Festival of Light. Parental involvement is built in with regular, supportive activities devised for pupils to work on at home with parental help.

Funding is used to support the costs of staffing and providing materials for one term's pilot sessions – 14 two-and-a-half hour sessions. Two days of training are also offered, covering for example, recruitment, pupil and parental involvement, target setting, health and safety.

So far evaluations have shown:

- an improved ability by club attenders to solve problems in science and maths using ICT;
- improvements in literacy, numeracy, language, organisation and social skills.[8]

GOOD PRACTICE: THE INDIVIDUAL LEARNER

The OSHL programme, like schools, comes in many different shapes, sizes and characters. But all OSHL has one thing in common – the capacity to help individual students to achieve more.

In terms of learning objectives, the starting point for many intervention schemes like summer literacy and numeracy schools, revision schemes or subject 'clinics', is the simple target of raising attainment in line with national curriculum objectives. However, all forms of OSHL can be framed in terms of the learning needs of the individual without losing either informality or compromising the voluntary premise. The national curriculum covers spiritual, moral, social and cultural development; key skills;

[8] For the full evaluation study of the Bright Sparks project as a whole, see CEDC (2000) *Bright Sparks: An evaluation of a study support programme designed to support the process of transition.* See also the accompanying Good Practice Guide.

financial capability; enterprise education and education for sustainable development, personal, social and health education and (from 2002) citizenship. There is, in addition, a Statement of Values by the National Forum for Values in Education and the Community. In practice, schools and their partners planning activities often state objectives in terms, for example, of raising self-esteem or developing greater motivation and commitment to learning. Each of these areas provides a rich source from which individual learning objectives can be drawn. In addition, there is an increasingly important place for objectives which focus on developing study and learning skills.

But schools may also choose to focus time and resources on certain students who staff feel could benefit in particular ways. Schools have for generations offered extra help, such as special revision classes or Easter revision schools, for specific curriculum purposes, particularly secondary schools with their GCSE pupils. For many younger pupils in primary schools or at KS3, the appropriate use of National Curriculum levels by teachers in assessment means that the pupils' needs can be identified more specifically. This data allows schools to pinpoint aspects of learning and achievement which could be enhanced through study support. This is not only about gaps and weaknesses, but also about extension and enrichment which builds on strengths, for example, with gifted and talented pupils.

PUTTING AN ACE SCHEME IN PLACE

Moving on from the needs of the individual learner to the organisational conditions most likely to create an effective scheme, it is important for practitioners to be able to turn to agreed and shared concepts of good practice – recognising, for example, that successful study support:

- is as much about ethos as organisation;
- depends on energetic leadership and whole school policies;
- recognises the value of voluntary commitment by students and staff;
- does not have to be done just by teachers or schools;
- must fit the ecology of each school and its community.

Making a virtue of the inclusive power of OSHL, schools can also choose to put in place a broad and balanced programme with a coherent set of aims and objectives, which builds on the inclusive nature of OSHL. Table 4.2 gives some examples of how study support can be mapped against some general school aims for development in terms of targeting weaknesses or building on strengths. Both primary and secondary schools may seek, for example, to link their OSHL with a wide variety of different aims and objectives. Building successful and sustainable provision which gives all pupils an opportunity often means starting modestly and building up

Table 4.2 *Linking with other aims and priorities*

Priority	Link to study support/action
To develop partnerships with the community and reduce crime rates, physical/sexual abuse, etc	Investigate partnerships with social services/ youth work/arts service; introduce peer mentoring scheme
To raise achievement in literacy and numeracy	Target KS2 SATs through booster classes/ family numeracy; targeting KS3 literacy through summer learning programme run through LEA
To change attitudes to school	After audit of pupil's needs, introduce kick-boxing, in-line skating, Robot Wars clubs
To develop links with parents	Expand family learning activities, survey parents concerning this year's OSHL programme
Development of speaking and listening skills	Introduce reading club, debating club and an out of school hours transition scheme between the English department and feeder primaries
To ensure that all pupils attain proficiency in ICT	Introduce Internet/computer club, investigate overseas Internet club
Special educational needs	Provide student care, mentoring, personal development/lifeskills
Thinking skills	Pilot learning-to-learn activities; contact UFA for information on accelerated learning techniques; organise OSHL university trip for more able students
To improve attendance	Look for funding for breakfast club; target new entrants through OSHL transition scheme
To increase the relevance of a multi-cultural policy	Introduce traditional Asian dancing, steel band, Owari, Spanish club
Review and revise behaviour policy	Link OSHL programme to strategies of tackling challenging behaviour; plan residential event for target pupils
To investigate potential of further government/other funding	Look for funding through New Opportunities fund, Standards Fund, European Social Fund
To raise the profile of the school	Celebrate through Education Extra award; OSHL activities in local newspapers
Staff/management team training	Use DfEE's Toolkit materials for half-day session on developing OSHL programme
To review use of library/learning resource centre	Extend hours of library before and after school; introduce reading club

capacity steadily, involving students, all school staff, and wherever possible, partners from the voluntary and business community, with the positive support of the LEA.

There are, of course, some fundamental questions which schools will want to ask themselves before starting out. These include questions about:

- **Aims and objectives** – What is the purpose of our plan? Which students do we want to involve and why?
- **The demand** – Do we know what pupils and/ parents want, and why? How will we find out?
- **The activities** – What extra activities can we offer, when and where (inside or outside the school; before school, after school or during the holidays?)
- **Resources** – What will we need to do this? Will we need a budget – and if so, how much? Will we need more people? Partners? More ICT? More materials? More site management?
- **Involvement** – Who can take charge of this? How can we inform and involve staff?
- **Implications** – What are the implications for health and safety? Insurance?

These questions all imply the need for preparation and planning, and, in particular, involving three stages of development which can be summed up as ACE: Audit; Coordinate; Evaluate.

Audit

This means finding out and innovating from what schools know already works. Schools are encouraged, for example, in a wide range of good practice,[9] to:

- Audit the views and skills of all staff – and get their active support. Look for ways of involving personal as well as professional interests in activities.
- Audit the views of potential 'customers' – who is being left out of activities and why? Who could benefit most – and why?
- Audit existing provision and participation in extra-curricular activities and how and where it can be developed. What about weekend arts workshops? Or joint holiday schemes with the local primary?
- Audit the human resources among and beyond the school community – in terms of likely partners and parents. Why not involve the local library or sports clubs? What about a Sports Leadership course for parents?

[9] A wide variety of student and staff questionnaires are available to help schools do this in materials from the Codes of Practice, NNEDP, QISS and Education Extra. For a longer discussion of the issues surrounding evaluation, and achieving good practice, see Education Extra (Summer 2000) *Extra Special No 69: Evaluating the impact*

- Audit the physical resources of the school and what can be put to greater use in out of school hours. What about an (ethnic) cookery club for children and family members where expertise can be shared?
- Audit the interests and enthusiasms of students and what they think they need, would like to do, and would commit to. Line dancing or local history? Duke of Edinburgh's Award or DJ clubs?

Coordinate

This means building on and around the strengths and objectives of the school and giving the programme status as well as focus. The school will need to:

- Appoint a senior manager with responsibility for the overall programme.
- Appoint a coordinator to implement the programme.
- Establish a link between the school development plan and the out of school hours programme.
- Develop a code of conduct which would operate during the OSHL programme;
- Make arrangements for caretaking, cleaning and insurance, building on what already exists and is running well within the school;
- Build on local partnerships and networks to promote and enrich the new programme – eg by getting publicity and local media coverage.

Evaluate

This means finding out what works and why, and how to get maximum value for all concerned. A simple evaluation will look for ways of auditing the 'Three As': Attendance, Attitude, Achievements. This involves:

- Monitoring and analysing attendance patterns; who accesses the activities and why?
- Using questionnaires or 'focus groups' to assess attitudes to an activity, its appeal and how it might be improved; relating attitudes to school in general to participation in clubs, through interviews, classroom observation or feedback from members of staff.
- Comparing the achievements of pupils involved either with their own previous standards (baseline assessment), as may be appropriate for literacy or numeracy schemes, or with similar pupils not taking part in the activities, as may be appropriate when measuring the effects of, for example, revision or library support activity. This approach must be used with caution as educational outcomes are always the results of complex interactions.

At a simple level, looking across the range of potential activities and what they signify there are a range of indicators, both academic and social/emotional which anticipate an organised form of evaluation and which staff involved can begin to detect in the out of school setting. These could include the following outcomes.

Academic-related outcomes:

- attention and concentration;
- capacity to listen, think and remember;
- capacity to learn and make progress;
- motivation and level of interest in learning;
- ability to settle or complete tasks;
- willingness to face work, lessons, school;
- willingness to attend/remain present.

Social, emotional outcomes:

- degree of energy, enthusiasm, equanimity, patience;
- willingness and ability to accept help, advice, criticism;
- independence from adults;
- ability to work in a group/without seeking attention;
- cooperative behaviour – conflict resolution, negotiation, compliance;
- appropriate behaviour in class;
- capacity to develop positive peer relationships;
- ability to cope with others' unpleasantness;
- non-aggressive treatment of and by others;
- involvement/engagement/participation.

This approach obviously represents a 'snapshot' of the possibilities. Not all the factors have to be in place all the time, or even at the same time. In particular, no list does justice to the dynamic quality of study support, or the fact that 'quality' and improvement in study support can mean different things for different schools at different stages, and that the advice and support on offer must reflect that as closely as possible.

While the principles of successful study support may look the same, they represent a very different challenge to the small primary school with only the after-school choir and sports teams to the large secondary school with the senior management team responsible for a whole school programme. As Chapters 5 and 6 illustrate, tasks, time pressures, resources and developmental issues are different between the primary, special and secondary sectors, and this requires some differences in terms of priority, capacity and the type of support.

GOVERNING SUCCESS AND FAILURE

> Healthy schools and their teachers know "their work is never done". There is always the chance that if one put in a little bit more time with that youngster in Year 9 or Year 3 there would be a chance that one would unlock the talent which is the school's main goal.[10]

The pivotal role of the leadership of the head in school is well documented. Nowhere is this more true than in the introduction of OSHL. Schools where there is a high level of activity and considerable staff involvement are almost invariably led by headteachers who:

- articulate a clear vision of the school and its values which encompasses the role of study support;
- provide a framework of effective and efficient management in which staff feel generally supported;
- have systems in place which minimise the considerable pressures on staff, for example by the effective use of the minimum number of meetings, good discipline and reporting systems.

In other words, good OSHL can flourish in good schools as part of a whole school approach. We consider this further when looking at assessing the quality of study support.

For schools to undertake, voluntarily, extra work, staff must not only get pleasure, pride and professional reward from offering extra activities and support, but the school as a whole must be seen to be more effective. Tim Brighouse quotes one example of a headteacher's experience of how the infectious enthusiasm of one teacher can inspire others:

> I asked the teacher would she help. It is her second year in teaching so I asked her what she thought about extra-curricular clubs. She jumped at it – said she could remember in her school how much she enjoyed hockey and such. What if we could really transform the kids' approach to maths – so they could regard it as being fun. She was away after that. Couldn't stop her. Not only has she started the maths – and I gave up two lunchtimes to help – but she has influenced. . . the new historian and he has started a club.[11]

In fact, all the evidence shows that teachers become involved in OSHL activities because they enjoy them, because through them they get to know their pupils and their colleagues better, and because they improve both their own teaching and learning skills. The summer literacy schemes

[10] Brighouse, T and Woods, D (2000) *How to Improve Your School*, p 50, Routledge, London
[11] Ibid pp 50–51

demonstrated this. The national evaluations in England and Wales produced a range of benefits to individual teachers involved which extended from learning about literacy itself, to learning about the needs and potential problems of their new, incoming students. But, above all, teachers discovered something about themselves. As one among many said: 'I have found the entire project to be totally exhilarating. Although I have never worked so hard and with such intensity, I have found the project to be extremely worthwhile.'[12]

In recent years, however, as OSHL activities have developed under different conditions, the professionalism of the commitment made has been encouraged and rewarded in different ways. In many schools, as part of their commitment to developing high-quality study support programmes, interviewing boards and headteachers ask teachers on interview what clubs or activities they can offer, and responsibility payments reflect involvement in extra-curricular activities.

What each school can provide is different, and in each school the organisation and support for OSHL is different. Each school finds its own way of rewarding and supporting staff. The currency is time as well as money. The choices vary but the most common are, in terms of time:

- Directed time. Some schools ask staff to give up a number of hours of directed time per week towards running after-school clubs.
- Redirected time. Staff are invited to commit to OSHL in exchange for reduced commitment to out of school hours meetings or time off-timetable.
- Voluntary time. Staff may choose to maintain a personal voluntary commitment.
- The school day may be restructured to accommodate the extra time for activities.

Staff may negotiate time off in lieu for extra commitments out of school hours and in terms of reward:

- Schools offer responsibility payments for coordinating and organising OSHL activity programmes and designate a post of responsibility for a teacher as School Study Support Coordinator or a similar title. The coordinator may also negotiate a reduced teaching week.
- Schools, sometimes guided by the LEA or acting autonomously, arrange payment based on a range of different salary agreements, including supply rates, youth work and adult education rates.
- Schools may involve a mixture of paid staff and volunteers.
- Schools may bring in staff from outside, eg to run an integrated care club.

[12] Education Extra (1997) *Summer Literacy*

- Schools may support the staff involved by providing additional resources for the department itself – eg for additional ICT equipment or library support.

Each school can find the best way forward for itself even if the choices and circumstances are sometimes difficult. Each choice carries a different significance for internal management as well as future sustainability. Whatever arrangement is used, if OSHL is to be seen as part of a whole school approach, that must be reflected in the responsibilities of senior colleagues, in the leadership of the head and in the role of the governors:

- Senior staff should support the programme directly, enable and support the coordinator and build consideration of OSHL into aspects of all school life, eg records of achievement, departmental meetings.
- The headteacher can celebrate the success and commitment of OSHL, give a lead in playing up its importance and ensure that as many staff as possible are involved, at the same time providing the support and structures necessary for them to do so within a manageable time frame.
- Governors should be aware of the role that OSHL can play in helping the school to meet its targets for achievement, attendance and social inclusion.

The role of coordinator can be an excellent developmental opportunity for a young teacher looking to develop the skills, perceptions and understanding necessary for a promotion to senior post.

SUPPORTING IMPLEMENTATION

The search for appropriate and consistent ways to recognise, incentivise and reward teachers involved in OSHL is matched in many schools by the search for ways to encourage teachers to take part in activities as part of whole school development. In recent years a link between OSHL and professional development has been made and is growing stronger and more persuasive.[13] A key part of the work of the UFA has been, for example, the training of school teachers and others in the principles of the approach which led to the development of teacher fellowships, funded by the Paul Hamlyn Foundation, a long-time supporter of OSHL initiatives. New short courses for the training of teachers in service have been provided in universities such as Manchester, and accredited routes for professional

---

[13] For a range of materials, resources, etc, see the bibliography at the end of DfEE Study Support Toolkit. The production of this Toolkit for study support built on work of the partner organisations, such as the Prince's Trust *Study Support Handbook* and the Education Extra Training Pack *Extra Value*

development have been established, especially through the cooperation of Greenwich, Brighton, Manchester Metropolitan Universities and Goldsmiths.[14]

The opportunities for and in HE are now better understood and we believe that there will be growth in courses and accreditation which offer study support elements:

- In initial teacher training OSHL is being built into courses so that students have an appreciation of its importance and an understanding of the part they can play.
- In CPD courses there is opportunity to use study support as a vehicle for research – this is a field in which there are still many questions to answer. The answers will not only be of great interest but will relate directly to classroom practice.
- In specialised courses for managers or practitioners in the provision and management of OSHL.

An excellent knowledge and experience base has now been created upon which professional development in the area can grow. The next stage might be for the TTA and the DfEE to build a requirement for knowledge and understanding of OSHL into initial teacher training and into serving and potential headteacher training programmes.

Most important, however, is for teachers to realise that the job of providing OSHL is not theirs alone; that there are individuals, experts, mentors, partners and other providers who can and do work with schools to extend and enrich what can be done; that this extra capacity is as good for the school as a whole as it is for the OSHL programme specifically; and that there are many successful models and an increasing wealth of ideas and practice to help schools on their way. Some of these ideas and examples are explored in more detail in Chapters 7 and 8.

CONCEPTS OF QUALITY IN STUDY SUPPORT

Self-evaluation or self-review is an increasingly familiar tool in schools as part of improvement and 'quality' strategies. Schools at every stage of

---

[14] Education Extra, funded by the Esmée Fairbairn Charitable Trust, produced a first training video, *Turned on to Life*, in 1995. Building on the success of this it developed a more complete training package for schools, *Extra Value*, in 1998. This will be further stimulated by a comprehensive pack of materials from the Centre for Education, Leadership and School Improvement at Canterbury Christ Church University College and Education Extra (funded by the DfEE).

For an account of the professional development opportunities available, see Education Extra (Autumn 2000) *Extra Special No 74: Professional development*

development need not be daunted. There are many sources of help and shortcuts to success. The framework documents available are an excellent starting point and provide support and practical guidance for all schools. One example is the Study Support Toolkit, which includes:

- 'Making it Work in Schools': a series of practical modules for school-based coordinators;
- introductory guides for headteachers: a briefing booklet and CD for primary and secondary heads;
- a trainer's pack: activities and materials to photocopy for those training teachers;
- a briefing pack: essential information and resources – at strategic and school level – for LEA study support coordinators.

Also available to support the toolkit are *Study Support: The Code of Practice for Secondary Schools* (1999) and *Study Support: A Code of Practice for the Primary Sector* (1999), both of which are published by the DfEE.

The toolkit materials offer teachers and other practitioners in the field ideas, strategies and practical information to develop their study support programmes. Each publication is aimed at a different audience, although the resources are designed to be adaptable to different scenarios – eg an LEA running a half-day course on study support could take pre-course briefings from the introductory guides for headteachers, agendas from the trainer's pack and generic pupil surveys from the briefing pack. Alternatively a newly appointed coordinator in a primary or secondary school could plan a whole school programme using a module from 'Making it Work in Schools'.

The Codes of Practice are dynamic 'framework' documents, designed to be thorough but very user-friendly. Drawn up by government and voluntary sector bodies in partnership, they are widely applicable and represent distilled good practice. They provide a simple developmental model which any school can use to determine where it is and where it would like to go with study support. The four countries of the UK are preparing models of their own, often sharing key features with the DfEE model. In Scotland the Codes of Practice for primary and secondary schools have been harmonised by adapting the secondary COP to the primary sector. In Northern Ireland a version of the Primary Code of Practice, with examples from across Northern Ireland, is in preparation. Overall the purposes are:

- to identify the dimensions of study support best practice;
- to exemplify each aspect of best practice;
- to demonstrate that ordinary schools doing ordinary things can use study support to make a difference;
- to encourage others to do the same.

Each code offers three levels of development – in the Primary Code these are called 'Laying the Foundations', 'Getting Started' and 'Moving Forward' – and sets out the key questions which schools should ask themselves before taking the next step, for example, in developing a programme or involving staff and students successfully. There are illustrative case studies of good practice for the points being made. The codes can be used for reference purposes (for example the list of external organisations or the potential partners), to assist in future planning or as quality documents to give a framework for self-review.

School can use the codes as very good indicators of the sort of activity they need to undertake and the ways in which a policy and practice can be developed. Full implementation of the codes will lead to quality study support provision.

One example of the use of the Code of Practice is given below: St Aidan's High School in Lanarkshire has a programme with many innovative elements and a strong emphasis on self-evaluation and improvement.

EXTRA

St Aidan's High School

In 1993–1994, the study support programme in St Aidan's High School, a denominational school in North Lanarkshire, began by focusing on the needs of senior students who were preparing to sit national examinations, and who needed skills in order to improve attainment and equip them with lifelong learning and independent skills.

As a result of detailed evaluation, the study support programme has grown and developed each year. Recently, S3 students have reaped the benefits of attending study support, and community links have grown as they embarked on a joint wheelchair dancing programme with special needs students from Stanmore House in Lanark.

The school's large resource centre is well equipped with computer technology and a large range of print and other materials including video and poster resources. Other specialist areas of the school are also used during study support sessions, eg the food and textile technology open area, art department and music rooms. Prominent displays of pupil work, including the students' own painted mural and 'totems', which resulted from the students discussing interesting ways of publicising study support, all help to enhance the ethos of the centre. The school's involvement in The National Evaluation and Development Programme has allowed it to share the programme's work with colleagues nationally – through contribution to the Code of Practice, presentations by the school's coordinating team and by the programme's contribution to the study support CD ROM. The school has also been able to discuss its work in an international forum through the International Network of Innovative Schools run by the Bertelsmann Foundation.

The successful development is heavily influenced by the ethos of the school where, for example, self-evaluation is encouraged – with the views of students and tutors being fully recognised and involved. Target setting and recording skills are also integral parts of all of programmes and have now been included in the Student Planners. Tutors assist younger students with target setting, whereas senior students set targets much more independently, discussing and negotiating targets with tutors.

While the study support programme builds on what is best from the school day, its flexibility allows it to be tailored more directly to the needs of the students. In the junior school programme much of the emphasis is on having fun while they learn, building relationships and confidence, and skills development.

The school places great emphasis on measuring change. It is not enough simply to assume that study support is going well: it has been measuring attainment and attitudes towards study support more closely, and collecting data. As the programme has grown, so has its management team. In 1993–94, there was one coordinator, in 2001 there are five in addition to the overall coordination carried out by one assistant headteacher.[15]

QUALITY AND SUSTAINABILITY

These toolkit materials and Codes of Practice are the threshold to developing concepts of quality for study support. If appropriate, and well supported staff and a clear set of aims and objectives are the key to quality, they also open the door to sustainability. Sustainability is about developing quality of provision, human resources and aspiration as well as planning and resourcing the future. It is as much about proving success as building from it.

As study support has become more strategic and has been funded from central resources, so the demands for assurances of quality have begun to grow. This presents a number of challenges to schools who historically would place OSHL activities outside their normal professional commitment and would not therefore expect it to be subject to the same level of controls and monitoring as the school day. However, the concept of control and quality in provision has already established itself, for example in the case of adventurous outdoor activities, although unfortunately this has usually been in response to highly publicised accidents.

There is a wide range of strategies for developing quality in OSHL. Although the use of the term 'quality' as applied to business and enterprise has only recently become widely applied to schools, with the devolution of funding and responsibility to them, it is gathering speed and refinement. With its arrival there is an opportunity to embed all school activity, including out of school hours activities, within a comprehensive framework.

[15] The Prince's Trust *Study Support Handbook* (hereafter *Study Support Handbook*)

In any enterprise the demand for quality can take different forms depending on the focus. In study support especially, quality is becoming an issue because:

- Success should be recognised and celebrated.
- Pupils need protection – parents and others need guarantees of value and safety.
- The expenditure of money needs to be accounted for and seen to be effective.
- Funders need reassurance to fund further programmes.
- Quality gives a yardstick against which progress can be measured.

Assessing the quality of study support is therefore a way of:

- guaranteeing a good experience for pupils and parents;
- acknowledging and promoting good provision;
- encouraging others to provide to the same high standards;
- building for the future.

However, with the introduction of quality concepts to this area of school life there are challenges as well as opportunities. There is the risk of over-prescription, of undermining the voluntary basis of the work, and of burdening a most creative aspect of education with extra bureaucracy. It is therefore imperative that the quality frameworks provided are simple and flexible as well as robust.

We would identify the following principles in applying quality notions to study support:

- It must be proportionate to the situation. It must strike a balance between the need for quality and the need to nurture the fragile ecology that is voluntary activity.
- It must reflect the essence of study support activity and emphasise celebration and achievement.
- It must be developmental by encouraging further activity and sustainability.
- It must support, approve and improve, not control and direct and discredit.

There is a number of ways in which quality ideas can become part of the provision of OSHL. Schools can start with the statutory need to meet Ofsted requirements, and can then work through the Codes of Practice. They may want to approach OSHL ultimately through the whole school quality frameworks that are available; or they may went to develop a specific framework, as developed in the Quality in Study Support peer appraisal system, developed by the National Evaluation Development Project.[16]

STUDY SUPPORT IN EVERYDAY PRACTICE

The early experience of many vanguard schools was of an inspection service which did not understand and appreciate the key role that study support was providing for them. In a report prepared by Education Extra for Ofsted, one teacher summed up the views of many: 'We did a lot, the inspectors didn't look , the report had one banal sentence.'

In their report to Ofsted, Education Extra identified that in 1996–1997 inspectors tended not to make a link between study support and any wider school aspects such as school improvement or raising achievement; and that, in the absence of any agreed concepts of good practice, reporting lacked consistency, both in the depth of reporting and the application of judgements as to what the inspectors observed. Education Extra made a number of recommendations based on their research and their understanding of the field of study support. These included:

- clear guidelines for inspectors on what to look for and how to report study support;
- exemplar reports;
- identification of the need for further research into the effects of study support on school standards;
- most importantly, the recommendation that inspection should 'positively reflect the voluntary nature of study support'.

The situation is, however, changing fast. It is well known that parents rate OSHL highly when they choose a school and there is an increasing onus on inspectors to ensure that it is thoroughly reported on. The revision of the *Handbooks for Inspecting Schools* in 1999 gave an opportunity for this to be corrected. Study support is now included in the frameworks and guidance for inspectors under the section which deals with the curriculum. At the same time the guidance allows study support to be inspected in a positive way which recognises its voluntary nature. In the secondary framework there was further encouragement for schools which took a strategic approach. In 2000, Ofsted made it clear that:

> The effective school will make arrangements to help all pupils take advantage of opportunities to learn, for example by visits out of school, running after-school homework clubs and extra-curricular activities at different times of

[16] For a comprehensive look at different approaches to quality and applications in terms of study support, and for contact information, see Education Extra (Spring 2001) *Extra Special No 79: Quality and study support*

the day so that all pupils who wish to can attend. Schools often provide a good range of extra-curricular activities including competitive sport, music, drama, community work, foreign exchanges and homework classes. Effective schools will plan this provision and monitor its contribution to attainment and attitudes.[17]

The Ofsted framework does not yet, however, fully recognise the role that these activities, (which Ofsted refers to as 'Extra-curricular activities including study support'), can play in a fully integrated approach to raising achievement. This is especially true in the primary and special school guidance which affords study support a limited role in the overall attainment and attitudes of pupils

The value to schools of the Ofsted approach is that schools remain free to decide on and respond to the need in their area without a complex set of criteria to meet. The inspection of study support is required. There are expectations too that study support will be better assessed and reported on and there is an imperative for inspectors to understand the issues involved. It is anticipated that the next revision of the guidelines will include reference to the voluntary Codes of Practice.

COMPLEMENTARY MODELS FOR QUALITY OSHL

For schools which want to pursue quality in OSHL there are two current ways. The Quality in Study Support (QISS) model developed by the National Evaluation and Development Project is a full quality assessment tool based on the Secondary School Code of Practice. It involves self-assessment and peer mentoring through which accredited school centres will be encouraged to mentor other schools in assessing their state of progress against the COP.

The model encourages schools to develop and provides the materials for them to develop an evidence base which will enable them to get quality accreditation for their work. Schools that do this will be able to claim that they provide quality study support. Accreditation of the school is offered at three levels as defined by the Code of Practice, emerging, established and advanced. The evident strengths and value of this model are that it:

- builds on the Code of Practice;
- provides a very robust and practical guide to development;
- draws on the expertise of other mentor schools;
- is evidence-based.

It is therefore likely to appeal in particular to secondary schools with the commitment to implement the system needed to produce the evidence. In

[17] Ofsted (2000) *Handbook for Inspecting Secondary Schools*

addition the QISS package can provide critical friend support and training for schools and accreditation for those taking part.

The Quality in Education Model is a generic developmental model for promoting quality across the whole school, including OSHL. It was designed by the Quality Management Team at Lloyds TSB as a development of the EFQM Excellence Model for use in schools. The EFQM Excellence Model is well recognised in the business community across Europe, is supported by the Cabinet Office and recommended for government departments. As adapted for education it is spreading rapidly through both primary and secondary sectors as an effective quality tool.

The model identifies nine key elements of any organisation. Around each of these it develops a set of questions any institution can respond to at several depths. The nine key elements are:

- leadership;
- people;
- policy and strategy;
- partnerships and resources;
- processes;
- people results;
- customer results;
- society results;
- key performance results.

Quality in Education offers a series of templates which guide users into self-assessment of their situation based on the nine headings, with the advantage that the model can be applied to the whole school or to individual areas. Schools using the Excellence Model are encouraged to apply it to individual departments and functions in the school, of which OSHL is one. Schools can use the model at very different levels of detail. It can be used to gain a quick overview of the school as a whole, or the highly developed documentation can be used to look in depth at each aspect of the school, using a scoring system if required. Training and support is also provided by Lloyds TSB. Repeated use of the model over time will lead to continuous improvement in all aspects of school life.

In October 2000 Lloyds TSB published a CD ROM offering guidance and tools to schools. It includes the specific study support model Extra Quality developed by Education Extra, building on the primary and secondary codes of practice for study support.

The advantages of this approach are that:

- It embeds study support within a widely recognised and valued quality process.

- It comes with excellent back-up material and support developed by the Quality Management Team at Lloyds TSB in collaboration with hundreds of schools.
- It can be applied very easily and then developed in ways that the school chooses.
- It will lead schools into assessing their OSHL provision in the same way as they assess the rest of their enterprise for quality.
- It leaves the school clear to devise how the criteria are interpreted and applied.
- It is equally applicable to large secondary schools or small primary and special schools.

CONCLUSION

The expectation is that committed members of staff, teachers and support staff alike, contribute in some way to extension, supplementary and enriching activities outside the formal school timetable. It is part of their professionalism. So, chess clubs, dance and drama, debating, computers, vie with each other on a menu that in well run schools owes less to serendipity and more to a coherent recruitment and development policy for staff and pupils alike [ensuring] that learning is not restricted to lessons.[18]

This chapter has looked at the rapid transition in recent years from traditional extra-curricular activities bolted on to school provision, to more coherent and organised provision within the context of changing knowledge about school effectiveness and improvement. The scope of the chapter does not do justice to the distance which has been travelled, or the range of new ideas and provision in this field. The most recent Ofsted report comments that, while the range of study support is good in over 8 out of 10 schools:

there is considerable variation in the quality of the various elements of their programmes. Most schools provide homework clubs but rarely monitor attendance. Those that do so, find that those pupils who might benefit most from participation are likely to attend irregularly, if at all. Provision of subject-based study clubs and support for coursework and revision is good in four out of five schools and is adequate in the rest.

Clearly there is a need to promote good practice and quality across the whole range of OSHL as well as to encourage schools to undertake evaluation as a matter of course in order, not least, to make sure they are reaching those who would benefit most.

[18] Brighouse, T and Woods, D (2000) *How to Improve Your School*, pp 35–36, Routledge, London

All these are relatively new issues for schools and offer a new way of looking at a traditional and, critically, a voluntary commitment. And the speed and scope of change in this area is in itself a challenge to hard-pressed schools looking to support staff and keep them enthusiastic. Part of the challenge, however, is how to put the good practice within the reach of the majority of schools – particularly in view of the difficulties which many face. Above all, the emphasis must remain on what brings students, teachers and other partners into this field in the first place – the chance to do something in a new way, whether that is learning or teaching – and the opportunity to share enthusiasm, and interests, as well as to put the extra time in for examination practice. Schools find different ways of finding time, resources, and the right balance of activities –as explored in the following chapters.

5

Primary and special schools

This chapter looks at:

- the special characteristics of primary schools and special schools in making the most of OSHL;
- the strengths and challenges facing schools;
- participation and patterns of provision;
- the way in which study support can be mapped on to key aspects of the school development plan;
- particular challenges and how primary schools overcome them;
- particular opportunities for OSHL in special schools.

INTRODUCTION

> School, with its songs and stories, and poems and paintings and costumes, with its secure relationships, with its trusted adults, can give children a childhood. Some pupils, buffeted beyond the school walls by cultural dislocation, poverty and ceaseless change, don't have too much of childish things outside school. (*The Times Educational Supplement*, 8 September 2000)

> We are running clubs in this school to allow children to have the very broadest of opportunities to educate themselves and to be turned on to life and to leisure pursuits which are going to be constructive for society and for themselves. (Helen Buchanan, headteacher, St Clements CE School, Salford)

Nowhere has the pace of educational change been more frenetic over the last two decades than in primary schools.

Consider the following: the size of primary schools, the small numbers of staff, the traditional lack of specialisation, the acute issues of safety and supervision, and the speed and vulnerability of development in young children. These issues make it unsurprising that the impact of the National Curriculum and assessment regimes, and the increasing focus on the basic skills of numeracy and literacy, have changed the nature of primary teaching in many respects. One result has been , inevitably, to make the curriculum less flexible and to reduce non-contact time. All this means that a very strong case has to be made for primary schools to expand their out of school hours activities as a matter of priority.

Yet that is what they have done. In the Mori/BMRB poll commissioned by the DfEE in June 2000, 7 out of 10 schools said that they had increased their provision,[1] 55 per cent explaining this as due to the commitment of staff and no fewer than 24 per cent citing the arrival of a new headteacher or staff as the reason. The influence of the individual enthusiast is clear. Primary schools also have other advantages as the starting sites for OSHL. They are, particularly in the rural areas, at the very heart of community. In inner cities they may be the only safe play space. They are places where families meet and where teachers and parents get to know each other. They are well loved, very familiar, and well respected. They are seen to deserve and often get the support of the whole community. They are, above all, the place where habits of learning are laid down and where the habit of social involvement can be so firmly established as to challenge the competing pressures of peer groups and the corrosive effect of negative social pressures. These advantages are all the more important when considering the evidence that after-school activities support these features of the school because they help to:

- establish the habit of active learning outside the school day;
- encourage good study and homework habits;
- encourage and sustain parents' partnerships in learning;
- lay down lifeskills;
- prepare pupils more effectively for transition into secondary school;
- contribute significantly to care provision for younger pupils.

In this chapter we explore the range of special issues which give OSHL a different flavour, edge and purpose in primary schools and special schools. We also look at some of the ways in which schools have responded to the opportunities and overcome the shortages of time, space and resources. Among the unique considerations for primary staff are that additional activities must not overburden children, and focus must be on offering after-school childcare and developing social skills and self-esteem. Moreover, the pressure on primary teacher time means that adults other than teachers may have an important role in the delivery of activities.

[1] See DfEE/NFER (July 2000) *Out of School Hours Learning Activities: Surveys of schools, pupils and parents*

OHSL activities in primary schools by definition are, therefore, different from those on offer in secondary schools. Primary school OSHL can offer a seamless experience combining play and learning. At these early stages of development there is less emphasis on formal academic study support or homework. Indeed, it is only within the past five years that there has been any attempt to introduce homework guidelines and consistent practice for young children and provision still varies from school to school.

Some primary schools have been particularly successful at developing a rich, whole school programme. But the provision of out of school activities varies from school to school and although the resource base is a major issue, the case studies in this chapter show that good programmes are not dependent on size, resources, or situation. The scope and energy of the programme on offer depends, critically, on the leadership of the headteacher, the attitude and involvement of staff and the support of parents.

─ EXTRA ─

St Peter's CE Primary School

St Peter's is an inner city church school in the City of London, with 204 pupils from a variety of backgrounds. Its OSHL activities started when it was helped by Education Extra to set up a gardening club. As Francesca Ingham Thomas, the key teacher, puts it:

> We started running after-school clubs at St Peter's Primary School in September 1996. We have tried to provide a mixture of subjects from sports to arts to languages for both infants and juniors. While trying to achieve a mixture of clubs, they do depend on the staff (and parents) available. And for some sports clubs we have been able to employ local sports coaches.
>
> In Autumn term 2000 the clubs available were choir, infant and junior drama, music and movement, games, art and craft, flute and recorders, fun with music, infant ball skills, sports, infant IT, junior IT and art.
>
> We have tried a number of payment systems. To begin with, all clubs were £1 per session. . . Children could pay half-termly or termly. We found that children on free school meals were not attending clubs and to encourage them we dropped the price to 50p per session for those children. Unfortunately, this did not appear to make any difference to the mix of children joining the club, and so we reverted to the £1 per session. [Significantly, attempts to bring in these children by putting payment on to a daily basis did not work either.]
>
> We have found all clubs to be a great success, with the children achieving things they would not otherwise have achieved. For example, one boy was asked to play basketball in a TV advert; another boy was chosen to play in the Westminster cricket team at Lords; junior drama groups have put on performances and the recorder club and flute club performed in a number of assemblies.

WEIGHING UP THE CHALLENGES

Anything that encourages pupils to attend helps our exam results. (Helen Ridding, St Peter's CE Primary School, London)

National surveys[2] have shown that study support in primary schools is different from that in secondary schools in scope and nature:

- Proportionately more pupils participate in study support at primary school than at secondary school.
- Primary school activities out of school are focused more on enrichment – by raising self-esteem and confidence – than on curriculum extension.
- Activities such as arts and sports are seen as of vital importance.
- A high proportion of activities may be performance-led (ie connected with team sports or drama productions).
- There is a natural enthusiasm for play and learning which blend seamlessly into one another.

These findings have been borne out in a recent survey by Education Extra of primary schools in Hertfordshire and Dudley. More than 40 schools were interviewed in depth across two LEAs and it was found that 'in general schools had more ideas than they were able to implement'. And 'most, but not all headteachers believed that out of school hours activities had benefits for children's learning, not always direct'.

Researchers found, for example, that:

- All schools ran some activities out of school hours and provision had either increased or been sustained in recent years.
- A very great range of activities was provided. Most schools had sports provision, but there was a rich variety of arts, music, drama, environmental activities and 'homework' type clubs.
- Activities ran after school rather than at lunchtime which, in many schools, had been shortened to accommodate pressures on the curriculum (particularly the literacy and numeracy hours).

At the same time, however, some of the strengths of the primary school can also prove to be weaknesses when it comes to planning sustained OSHL activities. The influence and the commitment of the primary headteacher or key teacher, once removed, can spell the end of the programme. This in itself reinforces the argument for a programme of OSHL activities which is expressed both in the ethos of the whole school and school development plan.

[2] Ibid

The key factors which tended to prevent activities starting, or developing, reflected for the most part the scale of provision possible given the pressures of staffing and resource winning; for example, schools frequently mentioned:

- difficulties in finding time to plan;
- reluctance to ask staff to make any further commitments on their time;
- lack of space and appropriate facilities – especially where no additional hall or school playing fields were available;
- staffing changes which meant that activities tended to cease if staff left;
- lack of pupil/parent commitment to activities;
- lack of funding in some places;
- determination not to conflict with community events, eg religious commitments and pupil commitments;
- difficulties in finding local business partners.

On the positive side, however, schools were clear about the benefits which followed. Staff were inspired to offer clubs and activities because of:

- the contribution after-school activities made to the school ethos, school improvement and school rolls;
- the notable increase in pupil motivation;
- job satisfaction, professional development and improving relationships with children and families;
- the additional resources available;
- increasing staff confidence – particularly in relation to dealing with older pupils.

The survey also found, overall, a pattern of informality and improvisation which reflects the reality of life in the primary school as a whole. For example:

- Most schools did not have a formal coordinator. The key organiser was nearly always the headteacher.
- Activities were run by teachers in virtually all cases, supported by brought-in specialists and non-teaching staff.
- Consultation and planning were, in general, not formalised.
- Attendance recording was variable.
- OSHL was usually not mentioned in the school development plan unless it was an explicit part of school improvement.

Where schools were determined to develop schemes they were not aware of major hurdles, but all were aware of the time commitment and the issues raised and were pragmatic in response. They often asked adults from within and outside the school, and parents in particular, to support the after-school programmes in practical ways (eg by providing transport) and by encouraging pupils to commit, for a year or a term, to a regular activity. Some schools had made a deliberate attempt to involve pupils on a sustained basis – targeting groups of pupils, and persuading them to commit for a term a year or for the life of the project.

If this sample of schools is typical, it confirms, however, that few primary schools have as yet been able to put a development plan or structure in place for OSHL. But at the same time, the schools researched also revealed an openness and optimism about what they might be able to do given extra support and resources. For example, all schools were:

- open to alternative models of planning activities, however well developed their own provision;
- frequently keen to involve AOTs, parents/carers, other schools and other community partners with which they were already working;
- keen to have the support and help of external bodies – there was minimal knowledge of funding support for OSHL apart from the NOF, and many schools had never bid for funding;
- interested in improving provision through training and participating in a support system with other schools locally.

Building on these strengths and overcoming difficulties means that the primary school has thrown up a set of key issues to be identified and negotiated in any good quality study support scheme. As Chapter 4 outlined, the new Ofsted Framework gives greater prominence to the role of inspection in promoting quality. Some of those key issues have been identified in the Primary School Code of Practice which steers primary schools towards expansion and improvement of schemes with a minimum of bureaucracy. Above all, however, if primary schools are to make this major extra effort they will want to know that it will help their children to become more successful students overall, and their school to become more effective in achieving that. The following section looks at how study support can do that within the framework of the school development plan.

OSHL AND SCHOOL OBJECTIVES

The effective school will make arrangements to help all pupils take advantage of opportunities to learn, for example by visits out of school, if used well, running after- school homework clubs and extra-curricular activities at different times of the day so that all pupils who wish can attend. The range of extra-curricular opportunities often depends on the skills and availability of staff and parents, but usually encompasses at least some sort of sport and musical activity. **The opportunity to take part and the number of pupils involved will contribute to your evaluation.** (Ofsted Framework for Primary Schools)

The best positioning device for any school, and the tool which informs Ofsted as much as it steers the school itself, is the school development plan. As we saw in Chapter 4, study support can be mapped on to such a school improvement plan in many different ways – either as a separate aim, eg 'the development of coordinated provision for study support' or in support of other aims articulated by the school development plan.

A 'typical' primary school would want as many pupils as possible to reach the national targets in literacy, numeracy and science, and might also aim, in addition, for example:

- to promote the health and well-being of children;
- to develop their fluency and confidence in basic skills;
- to develop their speaking, listening and reasoning skills;
- to help them imagine, invent, create and discover for themselves;
- to respect and cooperate with each other;
- to lead healthy and active lifestyles;
- to enjoy and commit to homework as part of school life;
- to commit to pro-social behaviour.

With this map to hand, the primary school can look for the many different ways in which study support can assist and enhance some of these objectives.

To promote health and well-being

The health and well-being of small children is an implicit duty for the primary school. School meals, school milk, physical education and healthy activities, as well as moral influence, have been part of the developing welfare function of schools since statutory education was introduced. But, today, many schools go far beyond those functions, providing support for parents as well as children, through after-school care clubs, extra sports and clubs which promote exercise and activity (everything from aerobics to first aid clubs). Some of these will be examined in more detail later in this chapter. This section looks at the recent development of breakfast clubs, which offer a positive and highly effective connection between care, learning and social inclusion.

The growing number of breakfast clubs in school is a reflection of growing concern about the practical difficulties facing many parents and children in the early morning. Many parents start work well before 9 am, particularly shift workers. Many children arrive in school early and still hungry, unable to concentrate or even to function well. One school which has made a positive virtue of this and has addressed the needs of children for a calm and nutritious start to the day is Applegarth School in South London which received an 'Excellence' award in the National Breakfast Club Awards 2000 funded by Kelloggs and managed by Education Extra.

EXTRA

Applegarth School

The school shares a site with a nursery and infant school, serving a local community with significant evidence of disadvantage. A high proportion of pupils receive free school meals and almost one third have special educational needs. Home conditions for many pupils are poor and health risk factors are the highest in Croydon. Part of the New Addington EAZ, Applegarth School established a breakfast club in April 1999 as part of an initiative to help with school improvement and raising achievement.

Children from both the junior and infant schools attend, which encourages family groups to eat together and make new friends – contributing to the very warm and friendly atmosphere. The club's objectives are:

- to provide children with food at the beginning of the class and thereby to improve concentration;
- to encourage higher levels of attendance and better punctuality;
- to provide good opportunities for social interaction, supported by skilled adults;
- to provide a warm, friendly beginning to the day;
- to provide opportunities for active play in younger children and study support opportunities for older pupils.

Most children attend the club every day and up to 100 breakfasts are served daily. The children are offered a choice of cereal , toast, yoghurt, baked beans on toast, bacon or sausage in a roll, fruit and a drink.

The effect on individual children has been noted by the headteacher:

> Bernie in Year 6 was constantly in trouble in class and in the playground because of arguments with other children. After one week of sharing breakfast with a group of girls in her class, she was never referred to the headteacher again. She achieved level 4 in her SATs.
>
> Zia was excluded from his previous school and spent nine months in a pupil referral unit. He attended breakfast club when integrated back into the school. He enjoyed helping to set up the club. Three months later all external support was withdrawn because he is coping so well. He still comes in early every day to help get breakfast club ready.

Developing good, supportive relationships between adults and children is one of the key features of the club. Six 'Breakfast Buddies' run the club with a very specific support role. They provide a warm welcome to each individual and spend time talking with pupils. In this way they pick up problems, provide attention and support, and encourage social interaction. They also monitor each individual's attendance at the club and encourage regular participation. They are an important part of the school child's protection monitoring programme, and because the 'buddies' are employed in the school day they offer a seamless link for teachers and parents alike.

Social and learning opportunities are offered to all that attend the club. Older pupils are invited to attend 'Early Bird' sessions in the ICT suite that promotes literacy and numeracy. Others are offered a range of problem-solving activities and some just play games. But many individual success stories are recorded:

15 'Early Bird' certificates were presented in March 2000 to the Year 5 and Year 6 pupils with full attendance for five weeks every day.

Sam, Year 3, attended infrequently throughout the Infant School. Since starting breakfast club his attendance has become regular. One day, he arrived at school at 7.40 am anxious about breakfast club. Nobody woke him up at home, but this was normal. He thought he was late because everywhere was quiet. He got a welcome, and a breakfast!

To promote fluency and confidence

OSHL can promote fluency and confidence in the basic skills of numeracy, literacy and communication.

'I have started to read more books at home because summer school has really shown me that it is important.' (Pupil at Stanney School Summer School, 1997)

The paramount task of the primary school is, of course, to ensure that each child is fully prepared for secondary school with a full set of basic skills and ready to fulfil all his or her potential. The literacy and numeracy hours are already having a major impact on the performance of children against the national targets.[3] However, additional support from out of school opportunities helps to extend their reach and build confidence. The following examples show OSHL can make maths and literacy enjoyable, and different out of school. At Invergordon Academy the school has already established a highly successful after-school maths club.

[3] In 1999 the number of 11-year-olds achieving level 4 at the Key Stage 2 tests rose by 6 per cent to 71 per cent and in 2000 there was another increase of 4 per cent. See the DfEE Standards Web site for the National Literacy Strategy (2 April 2001). The national numeracy tests began in primary schools the following school year, September 1999. In 2000, the Key Stage 2 test results showed an improvement of 3 per cent since 1999 and 13 per cent since 1998. See the DfEE Standards Site (www.standards.dfee.gov.uk) for the National Numeracy Strategy

---

Invergordon Academy

'Maths Mania' – the Invergordon Academy maths club – was formed in late 1999 and has now become a well-established club within the school. It meets every Wednesday lunchtime with an average attendance of 20 to 30 pupils.

The club was named Maths Mania by the pupils and is designed to motivate and enthuse all pupils through a wide range of activities. The club is quite unique compared to other numeracy clubs or puzzle activities designed for more able pupils.

Under the supervision of teacher Michael Aitchison, the club is largely run by an elected pupil committee with members from S2 to S5. The committee takes care of the daily running and management of the club which may include acting as bank managers, checking answers, awarding prize money and drumming up new membership.

The Maths Mania bank is designed to make members rich (in the school's currency!). In joining the club, members are given a bank account and £5,000 of Invergordon money which they can use to speculate on the stock exchange, get interest on savings. They can invest the money they make from consistent attendance and successful puzzle solving, or use it to pay for computer use. At the end of the year, a trophy is awarded to the pupil with the biggest bank balance.

The club recently connected to the Internet through a grant from Education Extra. Using the Internet, pupils access up-to-date stock quotes which they then use to buy and sell stocks and shares through their Maths Mania bank accounts. They can also explore the world of maths on the Net.

Besides the maths club, the school offers chess club, homework clubs in various subjects (languages, art, etc) and a Duke of Edinburgh Award Scheme.

Supporting literacy through out of school activities is becoming increasingly common. The following case study shows how one inner city school in a highly deprived area has undertaken to do it.

Tyne View Community Primary School

This inner city school in Gateshead serves a community with high unemployment and poor health, where over 50 per cent of pupils have special educational needs and almost 80 per cent are eligible for free school meals.

The school has attempted to address these problems through a firm commitment to developing after-school and holiday provision. In 1996, the school formed a partnership with Save the Children Fund, local groups and leisure services. The school had been concerned that children had limited access to books and reading opportunities during their holidays, and that their basic skills were in fact falling behind levels that they had previously reached, in particular after the long summer vacation.

After-school clubs have grown in number, and in particular those with a literacy component, including a breakfast club which runs three times a week where pupils can choose to read in the library or work in the computer suite until school starts. Other clubs in the school include computer courses for pupils and parents, sports clubs, a European club, performing arts clubs including tap dancing, drama, choir and guitar lessons.

However, the main focus for developing and supporting literacy skills is at the Playwrite Club which meets weekly after school, during the Easter and summer vacations. In the club children play games, write plays, design posters, edit recipe books, participate in craft activities, visit theatres, galleries and museums, and through these initial stimuli develop a range of skills in all aspects of literacy. The club is supported by teachers, staff from Leisure Services, volunteers and parents/carers. Since it became apparent that many parents had literacy needs of their own, a complementary family literacy project was set up where children and parents could learn together. Parents and carers have also been able to access training and some have subsequently continued training at the local college or obtained jobs in the community.

These projects have been successful in enhancing the school's work, and over the last three years, pupils' KS2 SATs results have improved. The percentage of pupils attaining level 4 and above in English has increased from 19 per cent in 1997 to 75 per cent in 2000.

To enable young people to imagine, invent and discover

I learnt how to do the wiring up. I couldn't do that before, with batteries and wires. (Pupil, Boots Family Learning Project)

Catching young scientists, technologists and engineers and keeping them, is a major and long-term national challenge. At the primary level there is a major opportunity to involve young children and their families, and build intellectual curiosity and technical competence at the same time. National organisations, and many national initiatives and accreditation schemes, particularly the British Association Youth Section (BAYS), provide many incentives and resources for schools in partnership (see Chapter 8). Many of these are focused on secondary schools but, increasingly, the power of primary science is being recognised.

Some LEAs, such as Blackburn, have given science a high priority. In an exemplary LEA coordinated scheme, 10 primary schools in Blackburn and Darwen are working on a project involving a series of after-school science clubs for KS2 pupils. Topics, created by the school science coordinators, have included making things work, transport and the planets. The activities are being put together into a pack which will be made available to all the borough primary schools.

The coordinator, Terry Wood, is expecting the scheme 'to give science a higher profile, broaden the curriculum and engage parents and communities in the life of the school'. The scheme, which had initial funding from Education Extra, has formed the backbone of a bid to the NOF by the LEA.

Other primary-base examples show a wide range of innovation and imagination, using time and space out of school hours to involve pupils in investigation and discovery.[4]

EXTRA

Middle Street County Primary School

This primary school in Brighton demonstrates the link between science and technology, especially through physics. Run by the IT adviser, Dave Dyer, the project is based on the concept of the television programme *Robot Wars* and includes: controlling vehicles by remote control; using IT to design and manoeuvre robots around specially designed courses; use of a software package 'Droidworks' to construct robots – choosing legs, tracks and battery packs, and solving scenarios using pulleys and levers. The project is run after school and aims to include all pupils in the school – membership is for a 7–8 week period for each form and attracts 17–18 pupils per class.

EXTRA

Brandhall Primary School

This primary school in Sandwell runs activities which show that science can be fun and involve parents as well as the local secondary school pupils. The activities will tie in with the BAYS awards which offer recognition at different levels. Among the practical activities are: the use of a camcorder to record activities which can then be shared with other pupils; dressing up as scientists and explaining things to other pupils, for example how a circuit works (because pupils learn more about concepts when they try to explain them to others).

Coordinator Terry Tromen's advice to those setting out to provide activities is:

- Be single-minded about it.
- Be clear what it is you want for your pupils.
- Make the activity quite distinct from the National Curriculum.

To promote respect and support good behaviour

In many clubs, the rules for behaviour are negotiated with the children, or suggested by them – a practice which encourages maturity and responsibility. For children who live in confined spaces, and who lack opportunities for play outside school, clubs and activities can be a vital part of their personal development as the following case study shows.

[4] See Education Extra (2000) *Extra Special No 64: The excitement of science after school*

EXTRA

Byron Wood Primary School

Ellesmere Club at Byron Wood Primary School, Sheffield, offers pupils aged from 5 to 10 a very wide choice of activities which they are invited to sign up for. Responsibility for planning the activities is shared between several staff.

Activities are run daily from 3 pm until 6 pm. Between 7 and 16 children attend each day. The timetable changes weekly and includes multicultural activities (eg a photographic exhibition of a multicultural festival), music (using handmade instruments) and using computers, for example to produce a newsletter. Other activities include creative and crafts, construction, books and jigsaws and role-play games. There are also outings to libraries weekly and to Pitsmoor Adventure Playground.

Work is displayed and, significantly, certificates are given as rewards not only for specific skills acquired or improved but also for social skills, such as thoughtfulness and sharing. This reinforces the school's behavioural policy which is supported by all the pupils.

To provide space and support for homework

Many primary schools are now looking for ways to help children undertake their homework confidently, and provide after-school homework clubs, in libraries and converted classrooms, as a matter of course. For some young children, however, and for some schools, one option is a community homework centre – often in a local library, but, as the following example, shows, this is not the only option.

EXTRA

Cutteslowe Community Centre

Cutteslowe Unlimited is a project which provides OSHL opportunities for over 50 school-aged children in the Cutteslowe area in Oxfordshire. The activities all take place in the local community centre 'on their territory'. One person involved said: 'They feel safe. There are acceptable boundaries. They feel able to admit that they find things difficult, with no mockery from their peers.'

The project is open each weekday during school terms and has three separate strands:

- a homework club, for up to 15 pupils per session, aged 9–14 years, open three days per week, for pupils in transition from First to Middle School, and from Middle to Upper School;
- contemporary dance sessions, led by a professional dance tutor;
- visual arts, led by professional artists.

The activities are open to boys and girls. The aim is to work in a disadvantaged community to combat the risks of disaffection and disengagement from school. The activities, in particular the homework club, appear to be raising self-esteem, achievement and engagement in the education process by supporting and complementing what is happening at school. Over two thirds of pupils participating have been identified as having special educational needs, at levels 1 to 5.

The homework club was initiated by one pupil who was concerned about the demands of homework. This boy now says 'I invented homework club'. Following a pilot project, a committed group of pupils regularly attend and they make full use of the space, support and resources available to help them with their homework. The club has space both for written work and also for one-to-one reading and there is access to two office computers. The centre is staffed by a club leader and an assistant with at least two trained volunteer supporters, so the staff to pupil ratio is between 1:3 and 1:4.

The pupils' response to the homework club has been very encouraging. They find that the learning side complements the more social and leisure activities including trips, refreshments and celebrations. One girl, aged 12, said in answer to a question in an exercise at another group: 'The thing I hate most about myself is that I can't read.' (This girl attended 51 out of 52 homework club sessions last year.) One of the club's teachers sees it as 'a way of making school more accessible and therefore less baffling or boring'. The school has been very supportive and teachers have given useful, positive feedback. In addition, there has been a good link with families, with parents clearly encouraging their children to come.

To promote a healthy lifestyle

One of the key tasks of the primary school is to lay down those habits and lifestyles which will sustain health and well-being throughout adult lives. Encouraging young children to enjoy sport, outdoor activities, and a concern for personal health and fitness are all part of the challenges facing urban and rural primary schools. The task is much easier when families as a whole are also committed to supporting a healthy lifestyle and when they can help their own children to do that – as the following case study shows.

EXTRA

Sacriston Infant School

The Family Sports, Health and Fitness Scheme at Sacriston Infant School is part of a five-year project funded by the Monument Trust, managed by Education Extra . It works closely with the Youth Sports Trust at local, regional and national levels. The school is also the base for 'Healthy Horizons', one of five such schemes currently funded by the Sainsbury Charitable Foundation.

The Family Sports scheme aims to develop out of school hours opportunities that promote physical activity among all generations. The objective of the scheme is to promote and raise awareness of the importance to families of developing a positive attitude towards their well-being. Two new after-school activities, First Fit, for toddlers aged up to three and their parents, and the Fit Club, for five- to six-year-olds, are already up and running. Further activities, including Tai Chi, Indian head massage, reflexology, aromatherapy and the Fit Family club are planned to involve people of all ages, particularly the activities that involve family participation. Headteacher, Lesley Farnaby, said: 'We already provide a range of extended opportunities for children attending the school and this funding will allow development of additional programmes. We hope to extend partnerships with other agencies in order to fully utilise facilities at the school for the benefit of the whole community.'

The project was launched by former world champion and Olympic athlete Steve Cram, who is also patron of the Youth Sport Trust and who took part in a session of the Fit Club that develops pupils' coordination and ball skills. He felt that the scheme would offer great opportunities for families to develop a positive attitude towards a healthy lifestyle through participation in the planned activities.

Promoting pro-social behaviour

It keeps you busy, out of trouble. (Pupil, quoted in the Education Extra report on arts activities at Hartcliffe School, 1998)

The social benefits of participating in after-school activities are self-evident and well documented, as children and young people learn to share a project, resources, undertake a challenging task, or do something for the school or its community. The links with the citizenship agenda are explored in Chapter 8, but the example which follows shows how OSHL, framed around a school's council, can exemplify the National Citizenship Programme.

EXTRA

St John Fisher Primary School

The citizenship programme at St John Fisher Primary School in Sheffield is part of a much wider programme which sets out to create a national, interactive, debating chamber for children to discuss and exchange opinions and views on citizenship. It also gives children a voice in the democratic process of the school through the election of a school's council. 'Circle Time' has also been introduced, along with a forum for staff and police liaison officers, to develop and share good practice.

The project initially arose out of a study on how primary school children use the Internet to develop their literacy skills, a topic which captured the interest and excitement of children and teachers. The introduction of Circle Time and the election of a school's council proved to be a huge success, improving behaviour and attitude and helping quiet children in particular to feel more confident about speaking out. Other initiatives have included the development of a school newspaper.

Although it has only been running for a short time, the school's council has had a positive effect: children are less unruly and behaviour has improved. Staff observe that self-esteem has been boosted and academic work has improved. Pupils appear to be more controlled and aware of their actions. In response to the 'Toys for Sheffield' Christmas appeal, for example, all children in the school were involved in a public display of their regard for others. One child commented 'I just wanted to help other children who are not as lucky as me.'

TURNING CHALLENGES INTO MORE OPPORTUNITIES

Parallel with the opportunities are the specific challenges facing primary schools in providing OSHL.

The challenges can be briefly summarised as:

- making time for OSHL;
- allocating resources to OSHL – particularly staffing;
- tackling problems with rurality;
- promoting social inclusion – particularly in inner city schools;
- helping pupils make a successful transition to secondary school.

The final section of this chapter looks at some of these issues and how schools have overcome them.

Making time

Primary school teachers are short of time. They have fewer non-contact hours, an intensive curriculum and assessment schedule, an overload of paperwork generated by the National Curriculum, and many other pressures on the school year which range from religious celebrations to school trips.

To compensate for the pressures on time, and the need to safeguard young pupils going home late after school, many schools look to other parts of the day and the school year to provide extra fun. Lunchtime activities come into their own, with, for example, games clubs and gardening clubs taking place. This has the added advantage of offering an alternative to a playground which can often, for many children, be a place more to be feared than enjoyed. Providing lunchtime clubs can offer respite as well as fun. When these clubs are supported, or led, by lunchtime supervisors, classroom assistants, or non-teaching staff, they can also create a vital opportunity for professional development and enjoyable, shared experiences while giving teaching staff much-needed extra breathing space. Partners from outside the school can also be invaluable in making new things happen.

EXTRA

Newport Junior School

The Wildlife Watch Club is held at lunchtime every week and once a month on Saturdays in an off-site nature garden near Newport Junior School in Leyton, East London. The scheme was set up initially as part of a DfEE pilot scheme and sessions were led by a Wildlife Trust staff member.

Each session is attended by 20 pupils from Year 5 and two teachers help run the club. Since pupils were already at the school, attendance is high, with a waiting list for pupils to join. The monthly Saturday meetings involve parents and teaching staff, including the headteacher.

'I like Saturdays, we've got more time so we're not in a rush. . . and we can get dirty and mucky.' (Pupil)

Evaluation of the project revealed that, as members of the club, pupils had gained confidence in exploring the natural area. Many were doing this for a first time and were subsequently learning to make observations independently. They developed a strong sense of ownership over the site which they were keen to maintain (eg by cleaning the pond, or clearing paths). They had also gained many practical and interpersonal skills. Teachers were also able to relax and enjoy the sessions, and to learn to develop different relationships with the pupils. Within the school, the profile of environmental education had been raised and all parts of the school had increasingly become involved with this venture. While the school had previously been in Special Measures, this club, along with other activities out of school hours, was established to help raise levels in numeracy and literacy. This year there are more out of school hours activities for the whole school to share.

Other outcomes from the wildlife project were that pupils from the club were chosen to visit the garden at 10 Downing St regularly to do environmental surveys. The considerable media interest in this has been a great boost for the school.

Successful funding and increased popularity has meant that there are now two clubs running on the same day with 20 pupils in each. The clubs run during lunchtimes for Year 5 pupils and after school for Year 6 pupils. The clubs has also been used as an incentive to reward good behaviour in the school (see DfEE/Wildlife Trust (2000) *Sewing the Seeds of Success*).

Finding extra help can also be part of an answer. As Chapter 7 explores, bringing in individual volunteers, other voluntary organisations, or local partners such as libraries can help to swell what can be done. There are also some prospective accreditation routes available to adults which can enhance and reward their commitment. Parents can be a particular resource for the primary school as the following example shows.

The St Joan of Arc Primary School

The St Joan of Arc Primary School in Sefton metropolitan borough council has a strong commitment to involving volunteers, most of whom are parents. The school is not only concerned with involving parents in their after-school clubs and activities but in raising the skill levels and qualifications of parents in an area where only 1 per cent have a higher qualification and male unemployment is 34 per cent. Over the last eight years, parental involvement has increased in activities, particularly in sport, art and music. The school has worked closely with Merseyside Open College to obtain accreditation for the parents' work, through a 'Parents as Educators' course. During the holiday period the school runs 'Widen your Horizon Days' where children and parents join in subsidised activities organised by the school.[5]

The challenge of resources – or lack of them

In many cases the challenge of making time for OSHL is joined by the challenge of finding resources – and that can mean anything from not having enough IT for the IT club to not having space for the dance group. Local businesses can often be mobilised to provide resources more easily than an open-ended request for money. Paper and art materials, textiles, books, clay for pottery, clogs for clog-dancing, scientific and musical instruments, transport, as well as IT equipment, wood and craft materials, food and drink, local newspapers, have all, to our knowledge, been donated by local businesses to after-school activities throughout the country, along with many different forms of mentoring. This connection between schools and community businesses is essential as partnership rather than philanthropy. Schools have as much to offer businesses, particularly in relation to staff development, community profile, and even their 'market niche' in the community, as businesses have to offer schools in terms of extra resources.

Partnership therefore takes many forms. Partnerships between schools and other partners can add closer fellowship between teachers to an expanded resource base. The following example shows how this has worked very effectively in one rural region.

---

[5] DfEE Code of Practice for Primary Schools

EXTRA

The Odd Socks scheme

OSHL aimed at involving pupils in 'extra arts' can be a very effective way of reducing the disadvantages which stem from social isolation. The Odd Socks scheme is an excellent example of small rural schools working together to make the most of limited resources to promote social and personal development through participation in the arts.

The scheme, which was set up for one year (1998–99), with £3,000 from the Arts for Everyone Lottery, involved three rural primary schools in Lincolnshire, which came together once a week to develop a dance company called Odd Socks. Over three terms, 29 primary children took part. They were chosen either because they were judged to lack confidence (they had little experience of life outside the local village) and/or they showed aptitude for dance. A professional dancer and a choreographer were funded to lead weekly sessions and rehearsals were held at the new South Holland Arts Centre in Spalding. The culmination of commitment and much hard work was a highly successful performance at the Lincolnshire Youth Dance Festival.

The scheme demonstrates the value of rural schools working as a cluster in a collaborative way, and in building community partnerships. Having constituted itself under Articles of Association, which identified clear aims and objectives and administrative roles, the scheme was able to draw in the support of the LEA, the PTA and other community partners. Parents took on some of the administrative tasks, the local arts centre provided studio space free of charge and the local bus company offered a subsidised service.

The scheme was successful in maintaining the support and extending the experience of all the children, many of whom had not been outside their local village before. Practice and performance opportunities built up community and family links between schools, pupils, parents and teachers, as well as teamwork, stamina, and technical abilities. Headteachers at the three schools, with additional funding now anticipated, are planning a local tour for Odd Socks dancers at different venues.[6]

The rural challenge: looking outwards

The future for many rural schools is perilously uncertain, despite government efforts to reduce the rate of closure. The problems of rural schools have become, in recent years, more visible and familiar as concerns about their centrality to the future of the countryside have become more urgent.

As the Odd Socks scheme shows, the issues facing schools in rural areas can be those of isolation, lack of resources and potential partners, and the difficulties of achieving a critical mass of support from children and parents.

[6] For further information on the Odd Socks programme, see DfEE *Insight* (Summer 1999) pp 45–46

Some primary schools overcome these difficulties in innovative and very personal ways, with teachers and heads undertaking to transport children to and from clubs, and arranging 'deals' with local taxi and bus companies.

Some rural schools are turning positively towards after-school provision as a way of providing for the community and thus reinforcing their key position as providers for adults as well as children. In Powys, for example, in mid-Wales, Libanus County Primary School is doing just that.

EXTRA

Libanus County Primary School

This school and the community are described by a teacher as follows:

> On a clear day, the school playground probably has the best view of the three high peaks of the [Brecon Beacons]. It is a typical church school. . . and it still uses the original pupil registers which date from 1870. The school is at the heart of the village and doubles as the community hall. It is the only educational centre in a vast area but Powys has more than its fair share of rural schools and all those with under 28 pupils are under threat. In 1996 the school had 46 pupils but by 1999 the number had shrunk to 15 'and the threat of closure is back'. The school had excellent SAT results with the children taught in classes of 5 and 10 respectively. Pupils are confident, supportive, and caring of each other. . .
>
> Apart from campaigning we are also looking at the services the school provides. We want to build on the excellent curriculum provision by providing 'extras' which will attract more local children to the school. We want to set up five weekly sessions working with artists in art, dance, drama and music activities. The school already hosts a Mother and Toddler group, and we are planning a Summer Holiday scheme, to offer, for example, pony trekking, conservation work, swimming, rugby and cycling. Finally the school is also planning to develop lifelong learning packages for adults from the surrounding community.

The message from this school is that after-school provision which provides wrap-around care and learning, gives it a clear role, and a more cost-effective future at the heart of the community. It is seen as an invaluable resource, a place where adults as well as children can learn to become successful.

Other schools have responded to the rural challenge by recognising that after-school activities, and particularly the use of the Internet, can open up new networks of friendships not merely across the UK but across the world.

Loveston Primary School

In 1998, Loveston Primary School in rural Pembrokeshire ran a Euro-Detectives Club every Tuesday afternoon for all children aged from 4–6. The aim of the club was to give young children the feeling of being young Europeans, and to be aware of differences in languages and culture. The school forged links with Germany and Romania. As one enthusiast put it: 'We sometimes do food tasting – I enjoy that the best because most of the food is delicious. We make games and sometimes people come and talk to us about their countries and we listen to different kinds of music. . . It's brilliant!'

The inner-city challenge: promoting social inclusion

Many of the pressures on inner city schools make for difficulties which, although different, are as complex as those facing their colleagues in rural areas. Inner city poverty and transport difficulties, which make it difficult for pupils to stay after school, can be compounded by the multicultural nature of many inner city schools, the high pupil and staff turnover, and in some areas, a high intake of refugee families.

Again, after-school activities, rather than being an extra burden, are seen by some primary schools as a source of pride and strength, a way of enabling all children, equally, to identify with and commit to the school, and a way of bringing in families, informally, to support teachers. Inner city schools can also call upon a far wider range of potential resource partners and mentors, which can help to enrich the school in different ways and to lift the burden.

Winton School

Winton School in the London borough of Islington is well known for the range of its OSHL and its partnerships. Some of its activities such as country dance have been running for years due to the enthusiasm of an individual teacher, while others are just being set up following requests from children (eg basketball). The clubs are run by teachers, classroom assistants and/or outside experts.

Activities in the school include two chess clubs run for different age groups, country dance and music (including maypole, Morris, sword dances), two groups of football (one of which is run by the school keeper, the other provided by Kings Cross Football), a breakfast club with reading buddies twice a week for two groups, a daily lunchtime art club, and after school, a rock band, drumming, ICT, and a homework club for Years 5 and 6 using the ICT facilities.

The school is also developing a project 'Dance with Words' with The Place using NOF funding. Years 3 and 4 have been selected to develop a programme that focuses on the development of language through dance, also incorporating some elements of accelerated learning. The teachers select the focus. During one term recently, it was science, materials and their properties. The dancers work in the classroom with the teachers on a regular basis to get to know the children but also to work on the ideas and vocabulary being used in the classroom. They then plan with the teachers the dance/ movement element. This includes concepts and specific vocabulary taken from the classroom. This takes place in one lunch hour (for those not able to stay after school) and two groups after school. It will be extended to Years 5 and 6 next year.

Besides the many extra-curricular activities for children, Winton is also developing a programme of learning activities for parents, through their Parent House. This will include ESL, health issues (involving the local health centre), ICT training, parenting and ways of helping children in school.

SUPPORTING THE SPECIAL SCHOOLS SECTOR

I come to after-school club because it gives me my own space for a while, because where I live, I have a load of brothers and sisters, and I sleep in the living room, so I get extra time away from them, and it helps me to improve my reading and exercising. (Pupil, quoted in Education Extra Special Needs report)

Many of the practical challenges facing primary schools are common to special schools – particularly the difficulties of providing OSHL activities for pupils who come from very wide catchment areas and who have to be returned home, safely, after school. Like primary schools, special schools can be relatively small, and despite the high ratios of care and teaching staff to pupils, have relatively small staffs. A survey of 30 special schools (of all types, including EBD schools) conducted by Education Extra in 1998 confirmed the particular difficulties of providing OSHL, but also demonstrated that learning opportunities outside school hours had particular benefits for special needs students, for social and academic reasons. Indeed: 'All the schools said that they thought that the benefits to pupils with special educational needs could be even greater than in mainstream schools, particularly because of the extra opportunities to develop social and personal skills.'[7]

Apart from physical and practical constraints on special schools, there are other more complex challenges which reflect the extra, individual and

[7] See Education Extra (1999) *Study Support in Special Schools: Good practice in special circumstances*

often complex needs and potential of their students. Pupils with special needs often face multiple disadvantages, have fewer choices for both learning and leisure – and face greater barriers to overcome in meeting and making friends. For families also, the challenge of caring for a child with special needs is great. Families may face the difficulties of bringing children up in poverty, with a lack of respite support, as well as managing the conflicting demands of working and caring for other children as well as the disabled child. Social attitudes can also be negative, especially for children with behaviour disorders. In short, as one school observed: 'Pupils often live very sheltered and isolated lives not least because families do not feel it safe or appropriate to allow them much freedom and independence owing to their needs and disability. '

The Education Extra report found that OSHL is especially valuable for students at risk of social isolation. Although many schools offered a wide variety of curriculum extension, including homework and ICT clubs, curriculum and 'enabling activities' and 'enrichment activities' which enhanced leisure and life skills, were particularly popular and seen to be effective by staff. Almost half of all students were participating in OSHL activities and, despite the small size of many schools, and the very wide range of ages, and in some cases, abilities, dedicated staff were investing in OSHL for the benefit of students and school alike. Some 78 per cent of schools were running after-school activities, and, reflecting difficulties with transport, 57 per cent were running lunchtime activities, and 30 per cent organised holiday activities. Of these schools, 78 per cent said that they were providing more, or far more, OSHL activities than five years previously.

Many of the principles of good practice which make for successful schemes in primary and secondary schools also apply to special schools. Schools can aim to audit, coordinate, and evaluate in much the same way as other schools; but, in addition, there is another layer of good practice which puts the emphasis more heavily on the personal curriculum and the partnerships which can be essential for developing the scope and sustainability of the scheme. For example, study support in special schools needs to:

- involve as many pupils as possible;
- allow for demonstrations of individual success;
- be flexible so that interests and skills of staff as well as students can be involved;
- offer creative and expressive schemes which aim to enrich the internal life of the child;
- offer activities which encourage positive behaviour, responsibility and lifeskills;
- offer choices to empower pupils and widen their experience.

Good practice in management means, as in all schools, commitment and long-term planning – and, wherever possible – partnership. Two exemplary schools in very different situations, show how this can be done – and the benefits that follow:

EXTRA

Chesnut Lodge School

This school in the Wirral has a wide range of after-school clubs which are staffed by a voluntary organisation, Halton Crossroads. It is innovative for such a link to be made, in that the traditional role of Crossroads has been to provide care in the community for clients in their own homes.

Currently, there are three after-school clubs, two for pupils aged 7–11, which take the form of an extended school day, and a third which is for pupils aged 12–16 and is organised on a residential basis. All three clubs promote life and social skills and independence training, as well as introducing a range of leisure activities and pursuits. The benefits are immense for the pupils themselves, who gain in self-esteem and learn new skills, and also for their families, who are enabled by means of the clubs to spend quality time with other members of the family. There are plans to create a new club, for pupils aged 5–7.

The youth club at Chesnut Lodge opened at the start of the Autumn term 1999 as an extension to the social development programme. The club meets fortnightly on Tuesdays from 6 pm until 8 pm where all Upper School pupils are encouraged to bring siblings and friends, so that in effect it is a club for both disabled and able-bodied pupils. Between 15 and 20 children come to each session, which is attended by a teacher and at least two parents. The club offers a wide range of activities from socialising to sports and computing.

The school has also been involved with the Duke of Edinburgh Award (Bronze Level) for young people aged 14–25. The award is split into four areas – service, skill, physical recreation and expedition. Young people are expected to give up their own free time to participate in these activities and to achieve some level of improvement in each, gaining new knowledge and skills. The scheme has been running for the past two years with nine pupils to date achieving the award.

For three years the school has hosted a summer literacy scheme involving disabled pupils from Chesnut Lodge and pupils from Simms Cross Primary School. Intensive literacy programmes in the mornings are combined with creative arts programmes in the afternoons. For the creative work, Norton Priory Museum has been used as a resource for poetry, craft or drama. The programme has been very successful year on year in transforming and modifying children's behaviour and attitudes. The school reports that standards were raised, self-esteem blossomed and pupils showed an increased desire to find out more about where they lived.

The following case study shows how an inner city school has also provided extra support through OSHL.

EXTRA

Richard Cloudseley School

Richard Cloudesley is a day school in LB Islington, catering for pupils aged 2–18 with a wide range of physical disabilities and associated learning needs. The majority of the pupils use electric or manual wheelchairs. Several of the pupils use alternative augmentative communication systems while others benefit from Maketon signing. A large proportion of pupils speak English as an additional language and nearly half are eligible for free school meals.

The school has for many years run a Wednesday evening club for two hours. It caters for about 20 pupils and offers IT, music, art and craft, swimming, games and socialising with friends. The club is now a separate organisation from the school.

At the evening club the staff/student ratio is high: the club has one head of centre, a teaching member of staff, two deputies and seven other play workers. All play workers are learning support assistants during the day, paid by Islington Play and Youth Services. Some support also comes from the community for special events and specialist club activities. At present, there is support from the *Guardian* newspaper to help produce a club Web site. Pupils are taken to school by bus daily and the transport is adapted on a Wednesday evening to accommodate the club. Islington Play and Youth Service pays for the transport on a Wednesday evening. The pupils pay a weekly subscription to Islington Play and Youth Service and at time of writing, this was either £2 or £3.

During lunchtimes, there are also clubs for art, games, music, dance, ICT, sensory stimulation and massage. These clubs are organised for two age ranges and run from 12 to 1 pm daily. Finally, on Tuesday evenings, there is a homework club. This is regularly used by 4–6 students who are collected afterwards by their parents.

The staff believe that besides the acquisition of lifeskills such as art and music, many of the benefits lie in the opportunities which are created for pupils to socialise, and providing the space for pupils to sit and talk with friends. The reliability, security and stability of the club is crucial, but the challenge always lies in finding people who can commit the time and who have the experience and knowledge of the many areas of personal need.

THE INDIVIDUAL LEARNER

Good practice in mainstream schools aims to provide a range of options for groups of pupils with different academic and social needs and interests. Special schools are faced with the challenge of meeting specific and individual needs and capabilities, and also of using that extra time to foster greater independence and competence. The schools surveyed aimed to build on pupils' own skills and interests – whether that was through homework or study clubs, dance, drama or music, sports, or ICT. Apart from homework and study clubs, an astonishing range of enrichment activities is provided in the various clubs which special schools offer – dance, drama, drawing and painting, sculpture and ceramics, music in all its forms, computer clubs, outdoor games, trampolining, gymnastics, go-karting, first aid, Braille, snooker, running, sewing, Indian dance, climbing, gardening and cookery.

Many of the schools also offer activities which strengthen personal and social skills.

EXTRA

Sutton School

Sutton School, an MLD school in Dudley, caters for 120 pupils from 11–16 schools, with a range of learning difficulties and emotional and behavioural problems. It was complimented in 1998 by Ofsted for its range and organisation of extra-curricular activities which include first aid and Braille club (led by pupils themselves). Activities take place mainly at lunchtime, and occupy nearly two thirds of pupils. Among the activities are sign language and peer-paired reading involving 40 pupils; many activities – such as stamp collecting – are focused on raising money for charities. The activities are coordinated by the KS3 manager as part of the PHSE role and besides teachers, the community liaison police officer, caretaker, library staff and ICT technicians are all involved in the programme.

The study support forms part of the Dudley Young Person's Charter at KS3 and the Youth Award Scheme at KS4. Some of the activities form part of the Youth Action programme initiated by Dudley Police.

At the top of the list as far as pupils and schools were concerned, are the activities which enable pupils to show what they could do – and which promote personal development and social skills.

EXTRA

Beaumont Hill Technology College and Primary School

Beaumont Hill School in Darlington caters for 225 pupils aged 2–19 across the full range of special educational needs. The school draws from areas of high deprivation where, in total, 60 per cent of pupils are eligible for free school meals.

The school offers a lunchtime and after-school programme for all ages covering sports including a canoeing club after school, and clubs in computing, technology, homework and a youth club. These clubs are determined by age and capacity and pupils have a choice of which club they attend. In addition, there are annual residential experiences, staff-led camps both in the week and over weekends, skiing residentials and participation in

---

activities such as the Great North Run, designed to promote health, fitness and community involvement.

The choice of activities has been influenced by what students want to do and there is an emphasis on giving students a voice, particularly through the student council. On occasions, some pupils have been known to run their own clubs. These additional activities are very popular, although transport problems mean that it is difficult for some pupils to stay after school. The staff enjoy the extra opportunities and value the programme as a way of raising confidence and achievement, and forging close links with parents, volunteers and other local schools. Recently, the school has employed a youth worker to establish partnerships with Community Education and to extend opportunities even further. For example, in 2001, the school plans to run a two-week summer school.

Pupils with special needs whose emotional development may be delayed also benefit from extra opportunities to develop personal and social relationships and lifeskills. Their personal needs increase in relation to the complexity and severity of their disabilities.

EXTRA

Percy Hedley School

This school has many students with cerebral palsy. Lifeskills training is provided in the residential unit and pupils are encouraged to stay after school to enjoy themselves and develop their social skills. They plan and prepare their own tea, learn to plan outings, organise transport, and take part in a wide range of other activities. Lifeskills books, compiled by the students, are a means of recording progress and providing evidence of achievements.

CONCLUSION

In primary schools the investment that is being made in OSHL is producing results. As the Ofsted Annual Report (February 2001) revealed:

About nine in ten schools have satisfactory or good extra-curricular provision. Some rural schools where pupils are bussed to and from their homes find this difficult. Increasingly extra-curricular activities are linked to targets for raising attainment in English and mathematics, and homework clubs and other forms of study support continue to be a significant factor in improving standards. Computer suites are increasingly being used to good effect after school.

The schools cited in this chapter as evidence of good practice are not exceptional but each has made a major commitment to provide for its pupils over and above the statutory requirements. The primary and special schools believe that in doing this they have become more effective and more enjoyable places for both students and staff to learn together. Many of them exemplify the ACE principles of good practice in action:

- *Auditing* the needs of pupils, and the human and physical resources available.
- *Coordinating* the provision, and giving senior management a key role in managing provision and involving staff and partners.
- *Evaluating* the outcome in terms of the individual and the school as a whole.

These schools and the secondary schools that are examined in the following chapter have learnt that OSHL also provides an opportunity for experimentation and use of new ideas in enabling pupil learning and a place where:

- new approaches to learning such as thinking skills and accelerated brain-based techniques can be tried out;
- wider views of intelligence can be explored through activities which use music or modelling to promote learning;
- open-ended, active learning can be encouraged;
- time can be spent talking and thinking about learning;
- tools for thinking and learning, such as memory tools and thinking skills, can be shared;
- partners from within the community can find a new route into the school and new ways of supporting the school.

Many of these schools make a point of:

- involving students and as many staff as possible;
- looking for ways to bring in the potentially marginalised student;
- providing activities which play to the interests and strengths of pupils;
- promoting new ways of learning – using ICT to expand the possibilities, and help pupils to access the curriculum;
- rewarding and accrediting good attendance, commitment and achievement;
- involving teaching and non-teaching staff across the school, and parents wherever possible.

Above all, in these schools OSHL is not seen as a burden, but as a resource for all involved: a way of opening up the school, of ensuring that pupils learn better and more effectively; that they connect with the outside world; that the school itself extends its role in the community. They are greatly helped in many circumstances by the partnerships which are created between schools, between the school and the community, through individuals and organisations, and by the extra resources that flow in through that commitment.

Chapters 7 and 8 look at ways in which partnerships and connections can help, in all sorts of ways, to make OSHL a resource for all involved, and how that can help schools, in particular, to reach those who seem most remote.

6

Secondary schools

Our librarian keeps a newspaper clippings file on teachers and education. While waiting for a consultation evening to begun, I spend two hours trawling through the last year's entries.

I should be teaching boys to be caring, girls to be assertive and everyone to be multicultural. In addition, I should be teaching how to be a good citizen, the importance of voting, healthy eating and being a member of the European Union, the words to the national anthem, lots of English history, the capital cities of all major counties, the complete works of Shakespeare and how to do long division without a calculator. I am also responsible for the failures of the England soccer and cricket teams, the boring play of the English rugby team, the decline of sporting behaviour, and our failure to produce any decent tennis players. Oh yes, and I almost forgot, I have to remember to teach some English as well. (*The Times Educational Supplement*, 4 December 2000, p 13)

This chapter looks at:

- the range of OSHL available in secondary schools;
- how OSHL can motivate students through creativity and activity;
- curriculum extension schemes and higher education achievements;
- enabling students through ICT and reading.

MAKING A DIFFERENCE

As this *cri de coeur* suggests, secondary schools, like primary schools, are staggering under a surfeit of initiatives and issues. Curriculum and assessment changes have put more pressures on the school day and the school year; targets for higher achievement at Key Stages and the introduction of league tables together with the concept of 'failing schools' with the consequent action plans, have intensified those pressures and risk creating a competitive neurosis. Targets now include the reduction of exclusions and truancy. 'Excellence' has now been matched with 'diversity' as an equal goal.

EAZs, EiCs and City Academies have extended local partnerships beyond school, and targeted inner cities as areas where persistent failure and a culture of low aspiration demand radical measures. This has involved freeing up traditional practice, focusing on those who seem doomed to fail for another generation, and creating new opportunities for gifted and talented children at the same time. Funding regimes have changed, leaving school budgets delegated increasingly to schools. Performance management is introducing the idea of excellence and diversity into the concept of teacher performance as well as the structure of schools themselves.

The pace of change has hardly slackened year on year. Current concerns include the need to improve performance, particularly at KS3, and the persistent gap between the performance of boys and girls which now appears to be extending into sixth-form work and beyond.[1] The relative failure of children from some ethnic minority communities gives continuing consistent cause for concern. At the same time, although standards of performance at GCSE and A level continue to rise, and increasing numbers of young people go into higher education, the same, stubbornly uneven patterns of access predominate and there has been very little improvement in the proportion of students from the very poorest homes going on to university.[2]

This is, in part, the context in which secondary schools operate, and these are the demands within which prioritising OSHL activities at school and local authority level has to make its case. This chapter looks at how this can happen, first, in relation to the 'typical' school development plans, and in particular in relation to two related objectives: raising motivation to engage with learning and with school, especially through the arts and sports; and helping students to become more effective learners through 'supported study', linked to the requirements of the curriculum, assessment and examinations.

[1] In the UK, 1998–99, 43.8 per cent of males and 54.6 per cent of females obtained five or more grades A–C at GCSE – a 12 per cent difference compared with 10 per cent in each of the previous years. See DfEE (2000) *Education and Training Statistics for the United Kingdom. 2000* – Table 4.1 At A level the difference is that 59 per cent of boys achieved 59 per cent grades A–C compared with 62 per cent of girls (Table 4.3). In 1998–99, there were 529,451 female first degree students and 472,532 male students. Higher Education Statistics for the UK (1998–99) *Students in Higher Education Institutions*

[2] UCAS figures (on its Web site, Table H2.1) show that the proportion of unskilled males and females accepted for degree courses has remained steady at around 2 per cent of all applicants since 1994 (4,835 students out of a total of 281,809)

The chapter, and the case studies, focus on the design, the content and the curriculum of out of school activities and how, by doing it differently, those involved can make the difference to schools and to students. Because the scope of OSHL in secondary schools is so large, however, this chapter should be read with the two following chapters dealing with complementary issues. Chapter 7 looks in greater detail at how, by involving different people and partners, schools can promote pupils' personal skills and career chances, and their fullest personal development; Chapter 8 looks at the specific challenges facing schools, and society, in finding better ways of engaging with young people who, without additional interest and support, may become disaffected as students and alienated adults.

PATTERNS OF PARTICIPATION

Provision of extra-curriculum activities in primary schools is more variable than in secondary schools, where activities are consistently, although sometimes thinly, provided. In June 2000, for example,[3] 97 per cent of secondary schools offered some OSHL activities – most of them after school but 90 per cent at lunchtime as well; and 65 per cent offered holiday activities. In order of provision are: sport, music, field trips, creative and performing arts and study activities. On average, secondary pupils spent three hours a week participating in activities.

The organisation and provision of extra-curricular activities is also different from primary schools, in terms of scale, scope and priorities. Large schools, with 100-plus teaching and other staff, offer a range of resources, skills and enthusiasms which often go far beyond their traditional teaching roles. Staffing structures allow for additional responsibility which make it possible for senior staff to be given the task of coordinating the OSHL programme. The school itself may have a very wide range of general or specialist partnerships with community, or even national enterprises, from national theatre companies to leading businesses. The school site is likely to be large, well provided for, and flexible in use. Theatres, gyms, music rooms, classrooms, swimming pools and playing fields may be open to the community for learning and leisure. Partnership and mentoring schemes may already be established for the school curriculum itself. Most secondary schools, therefore, may well have a potential capacity for funding, organisation and coordination of OSHL at a senior level.

Also, students present different needs and demands as they negotiate adolescence and adulthood. Their lives are determined by examination and assessment schedules, subject options and career prospects. They are

[3] DfEE/NFER (December 1999) *Out of School Hours Learning Activities: An evaluation of 50 pilot schemes*, RR 178

required to be independent learners; they can support each other's learning in different ways. They are likely to be under increased pressure given the extended sixth-form curriculum. They can be involved in the life of the school in every aspect, from school councils to peer mentoring. They have their own agendas, rituals and rites of passage. They have a life outside the school and they can vote with their feet. Many do not have but do not look for the support of their parents or other adults. At the same time, there are opportunities to record and attribute the achievements of students in many different ways. But, although older, they are exposed to and more vulnerable to intense peer and community pressure to conform, to the hazards of bullying and drug cultures, and, for some, unsafe home lives. Outside the school, the need for extra care, particularly for younger secondary-aged students, during the hours before and after school, and during the holidays, can be very evident.

Given these different sets of conditions, extra-curriculum activities in secondary schools are more complex than in primary schools and differ in organisation and scope, purpose and character. In secondary schools there is a greater urgency to find ways to motivate students, to raise their performance at GCSE and to provide them with the specific skills which they will need to flourish in the outside world. Like primary schools, however, secondary schools will be at different stages of development, each school with a different history of provision, a different culture, and a changing cast of staff and students.

Significantly, a MORI poll in July 2000 found that 7 in 10 schools had increased their OSHL provision in the years 1998–2000 and four-fifths planned to increase their provision in the future. Some 35 per cent of secondary schools, compared with 16 per cent of primary schools, explained these increases by the pressure of raising performance and achievement. Driven by examination imperatives and schedules, targets and school timetables, curriculum extension activities take precedence in many schools. Students and teachers aim to catch up in 'study clubs' 'revision clubs' or examination 'clinics' or simply see the clubs as a place for homework and coursework to be done. Younger pupils in particular are often offered extra help in maths, literacy and access to ICT. Given the concentration on the academic curriculum, and the loss of dance, drama and physical education from the National Curriculum, the secondary school experience risks in some schools adopting the joyless tone of Gradgrind.

While curriculum extension activities reflect the realities of secondary school life, increasing evidence suggests that motivational activities, whether in the arts, sports, special interest clubs, or community activities are valued precisely because they offer a unique opportunity for pupils to engage with school life and learning – and promote personal and social confidence and maturity. In most secondary schools recognising this, curriculum extension and enrichment activities find a balance in the OHSL programmes.

The school itself may prioritise enrichment providing time and space for what cannot be contained within the school day. It might provide:

- more time for arts and sports; for example, giving young artists the chance to try out new materials, to work alongside 'real' artists;
- the opportunity to undertake a sustained music project;
- new activities which push out the boundaries of experience, for example taking part in a One World club which links up regularly with schools in the Indian sub-continent;
- a project bringing in parents to help create and maintain a garden, which might be organic, sensory, or Japanese;
- schemes to explore other cultures through dance, drama or cookery.

The selection of possibilities set out in Chapter 4 shows what a rich menu can be available.

Or the school may prioritise curriculum extension activities – which may range from subject clinics for GCSE candidates; 'Socrates Clubs' to develop thinking and analytical skills; homework clubs over lunchtime or accelerated learning as developed through the UFA and applied in schools such as Westborough HS Bradford. Successful schemes and successful schools can offer a balance of enrichment and extension. And, above all, schools can exploit the great strength of study support – its inclusivity, and its ability to involve all students, no matter what their abilities, in a reassessment of themselves as successful learners.

Finally, as Chapter 7 explores in more detail, all the evidence suggests that participation in after-school activities can create opportunities for, and promote pro-social behaviour in ways which can strengthen social inclusion. Personal and social development can be promoted through peer-mentoring schemes of all kinds; through voluntary action and citizenship schemes; through anti-bullying and crime reduction programmes; and, in special schools, *par excellence*, through a range of activities and opportunities which help pupils to develop their social confidence and abilities.

A balanced programme can often open up the curriculum for many pupils who are less academically able (eg by giving intensive help with reading), but can also devise ways of fostering the lifeskills which can make all the difference. One school, for example, which attempts to balance all these options in a wholly inclusive scheme, is Imberhorne School in West Sussex.

EXTRA

Imberhorne School

The school has developed an extensive after-school programme. It is now offering its students a wide range of activities to enhance the curriculum, enrich learning and extend horizons. Moreover, the school offers the local community access to its facilities for music, sport, art and drama. Recognition as a specialist school (in languages) and the submission of a lottery application for sports opened up opportunities for the creation of ImberExtra – the umbrella under which all extra-curricular activities for students, their families and the local community, are organised.

The school appointed a full-time coordinator for ImberExtra who was charged with the expansion of the programme. She set out to ensure that everyone became involved, by bringing together a team which included senior management, caretakers, teaching staff and governors. A detailed plan was drawn up to ensure the programme met its declared aims and objectives. Support was available for anyone who wanted to offer an 'extra' including training opportunities accredited through Brighton University.

Partnerships with adult education, the university, the TEC and local businesses have helped to sustain progress. Working closely with local organisations and clubs has also allowed the development of a thriving ImberSport Club. Pupils are coached by individuals from local clubs who use the opportunity to inform students about joining their organisations. These clubs in turn use the school's facilities for their meetings, sport practice, etc. Imberhorne also holds Investors in People status and, with partners, offers school and university-based training courses up to NVQ level 5.

Good communication lies at the heart of ImberExtra's success. A newsletter (*ImberNews*) is distributed half-termly and local organisations, clubs and leisure providers also use it to publicise the opportunities they offer. The management team meet weekly to ensure that everyone is kept up to date.

All of this requires time and energy. The Curriculum Development Manager at Imberhorne is not a member of the teaching staff. She is there to increase 'extras', and to give support to those individuals offering them: her commitment and energy have been vital ingredients.

Another example of a school with a systematic and coherent approach to its OSHL activities is Woodlands School in Essex where an extensive extra-curricular programme of activities fitted around the school day and the school year is well integrated into school life and well publicised and supported by parents.

EXTRA

Woodlands School

After a period of falling rolls, Woodlands School in Basildon is now heavily over-subscribed and part of the explanation seems to lie with the explicit commitment made to extra-curricular activities. That commitment ranges across 'experts in residence', an Activities Week (timetable suspended), workshops for parents on helping their children, residentials, weekly bulletins, revision schemes, Saturday morning extension classes and thematic special days.

Many of these activities involve the English department and they publish their own extra leaflet for parents. Activities include a spelling club, a writers' circle, a Shakespeare morning, a book week and a Goosebumps club.

Activities take place in the evening and at the weekends, but there is also a very popular study support group in the library before school, called The Big Breakfast Club. This was featured on the BBC news during the launch of the 1997 summer literacy school's pilot project, of which Woodlands was one of the 50 schools chosen.

Good communication with parents possibly explains why 200 pupils take part in activities on most days at lunchtime and teatime. In addition, many partner primary school pupils join in.

MAPPING OSHL ON TO THE SCHOOL DEVELOPMENT PLAN

Just as the primary school curriculum can map OSHL on to its development plan, so can the secondary school. The core elements of the school development plan in secondary schools will contain, for example, broad policies to raise motivation and achievement. Within this broad headings there may be more detailed targets. Attainment and achievement targets may involve specific learning and teaching strategies, for example:

- raising pupil confidence and self-esteem;
- raising the proportion of A–Cs at GCSE, for example, from 40 per cent to 50 per cent;
- raising completion levels and quality of homework and project work;
- raising numeracy and literacy standards at KS3 and KS4;
- improving thinking, reasoning and study skills;
- raising levels of ICT skills across the curriculum;
- providing opportunities for pupils to express and celebrate their creativity and talent;
- improving the performance of boys at KS3 and GCSE;
- developing skills for employability.

But the targets will also aim to promote policies which deliberately encourage social inclusion, for example, by:

- reducing the number of exclusions;
- reducing the truancy rate;
- reducing disaffection;
- providing additional care and protection for younger pupils;
- developing positive attitudes towards school;
- creating opportunities for pupils to take greater responsibility towards themselves and others.

Chapter 7 explores these strategies in more detail. But before anything can be achieved, students must be motivated to learn. The following sections look at the ways in which motivation can come through curriculum enrichment, how achievement can be raised through curriculum extension, and how pupils with similar needs but different skills can be helped by inclusive strategies and by specific programmes.

MOTIVATING STUDENTS

In particular, this section looks at motivating students by enriching the curriculum through creativity and activity.

> Throughout the term you rehearse each line, each speech, every movement, work on changing the pace, work on memory, on voice, on how to move and how to stand, how to use the stage and how to use your eyes, to control your hands and feet, to keep your head up, to be courageous, to be clear, to be subtle, to be patient, to touch each other, to act natural, to take criticism, to have fun, to do it again and again and again. . . to earn your success and the audience's applause. . . Above all I want to instil in them the value of team work. Never is there a greater chance for self-expression than in drama and never a greater need for self-discipline. For unbounded energy with a sense of wholeness. . . It is extraordinary and sometimes unreasonable to see the level of skill you demand and the mixture of energy and vulnerability you take for granted. . . By the opening night you know almost everything about the strengths and weaknesses of the case. As they do of you. They see the teacher stripped of his classroom act ad style. . . Now I like to see their wild eyed faces, wild at what they have achieved. By not being themselves, by becoming someone else, they have found new limits, they have found out more about life and what it feels to be other people; they have learnt and grown. They deserve the applause. . . What has it all been? In a word, education.[4]

[4] Smith, Jonathan, *The Learning Game*, p 153

Many things can motivate students – not least the company of friends with shared values and interests or working with adults who bring some extra, and valued, expertise, as well as the self-esteem which comes with demonstrating success. Some of the most powerful motivators are the arts – in all their forms. Students put music and creative and performing arts second in the list of most popular choices in both primary and secondary schools.[5] This enthusiasm must be placed against the context of a passionate national debate on the place of the arts in the curriculum, fears for the loss of music teaching in particular, and of the arts being squeezed out, particularly in the primary school, in favour of basic skills. This debate in turn raises questions about whether the arts in the out of school setting are, or are in danger of becoming, the only opportunities for participation and performance.

The essential argument that the arts are vital to the quality, creativity, and effectiveness of education, to the richness and sustainability of personal lives and national culture, and to the wealth of the nation, needs little explanation and no defending. Out of school arts activities should be seen in this context: ie not as a subversive alternative or as a substitute for the National Curriculum but as complementary to what should be available to all pupils during the school day. The case for out of school learning in the arts is reinforced, however, not just by the economic and cultural case as capital investment, but by the wealth of evidence which show how, in this country and elsewhere, inside and outside the school, the arts ignite talent and motivation to learn, and bring pupils and communities together. Putting a value on the arts, and, indeed, evaluating their impact on pupil development, is a complex and often subtle process. The value of the arts to pupils shows up not so much in examination results but in the connection that participation makes with the deepest and most satisfying of individual and school experiences.

> I remember one of our most difficult pupils playing. . . in Ian Serradier's 'The Silver Sound'. It was a most moving portrayal by a very bright pupil who subsequently left school with nothing – but one part of the school and one teacher touched him deeply and reached and developed his potential – would that we had found more of it. (John Crossman, Education Extra)

Both in dance and drama the arts have the potential power for young people to become 'someone else'. End of term plays, musicals, concerts and exhibitions, inspire parents and the community to celebrate what young people can achieve. Indeed, those are the experiences which many adults, and all parents, remember as the most fulfilling and the most lasting memories of schooldays, and of childhood and parenthood respectively.

[5] MORI/BMRB Poll on OSHL activities, July 2000

Significantly, however, research into participation in the arts outside school hours shows that while a causal relationship between participation and academic achievement may be hard to demonstrate,[6] the experience of the arts in performance, or as a curriculum or even career choice, still eludes many children. Recent research has shown that:

- Children from relatively poor homes are less likely to attend music, dance and drama performances.
- Pupils with parents who supported the arts are considerably more likely to take arts options than children whose parents did not.
- Pupils living in inner cities rather than in towns or rural areas have more access to the arts.

The same research suggests that the children most likely to participate were young, non-white girls.

Of older children, figures for those participating 'not at all' ranged from 23 per cent in art to 39 per cent in dance. Music was the most popular area for participation with 16 per cent participating a 'great deal'. Finally, when researchers asked about involvement in relation to what the school itself provided they found that higher proportions of pupils were involved in extra-curricular music where KS3 and 4 music and drama was not provided.

Most significant was the finding which showed 'the substantial impact that the pupils themselves have on the effectiveness of arts teaching. They recognised their own behaviour, motivation to work hard, predispositions towards the arts, their prior involvement and the arts ability, to be key determinants of the number and quality of outcomes they achieved.' Building on this finding, the report emphasised that pupils should be encouraged – through primary education, through parental support, and through extra-curricular provision, to be involved in the arts from an earlier age.[7]

Given the disparities in access and participation, opportunities for extra-curricular arts experiences become more significant. And yet 'the problem remains that some children are quite cut off from the extraordinary potential offered outside school by the people and resources available in the country's first-class cultural institutions and creative industries'.[8] The following examples are just two of the innovative ways in which schools, regional and community arts bodies, national companies and voluntary organisations, are responding to that challenge.

---

[6] NFER/RSA (2000) *Arts Education in Secondary Schools*, the research found that social classes I and II were much more likely to have attended a music concert or drama activity
[7] Ibid p 571. See also pp 537–51
[8] DCMS (2001) *Culture and Creativity: The next ten years*, p 17

┌─── EXTRA ───

The Castle School

The Castle School in Taunton has developed an unprecedented range of extra-curricular activities including several rock bands, two orchestras, a jazz band, a concert band, string and brass ensembles, Renaissance group, percussion groups, chamber choir, SATB choir, barbershop groups, flute choir, keyboard ensemble. . . The secret of success has been in involving both the school's own music staff and visiting instrumental teachers every step of the way and encouraging them to share their skills, interest and passions.

> The extent and range of our musical activities owes a lot to our Head of Music, Sandra Sutton, a finalist in the Music Teacher of the Year Competition, who has motivated so many people to become involved and raise their expectations. Our ethos at the school is very simple. We believe that extra-curricular activities make school more fun. If students enjoy being here, they are more likely to work successfully and achieve even greater success across the curriculum. This is reflected in the results which students have achieved in recent years. (Headteacher)
>
> The creation of a barbershop group was in response to the difficulty in recruiting boys to choral singing. A couple of years later the boys have now been invited to join in workshops and master classes with semi-professional adults group, 'The Rivertones', who, while mentoring the boys, have themselves picked up some points about reading musical scores from the boys. The recent introduction of a new percussion group has brought a similar response and these experiences have been great motivators for the boys. (Sandra Sutton)

It is not only in music that the school excels. The commitment to a wide range of extra-curricular activities extends to many other areas, including drama and sport. Success at area, regional and national level is a regular feature among the school's achievements.

└─────────────────────

One highly successful and systematic initiative designed to involve secondary students in the arts by bringing national and international artists into school on a regular basis is examined in the following case study.

┌─── EXTRA ───

Multi A

Multi A, based in Bristol, is the brainchild of a single teacher, Vic Ecclestone, who for many years worked as a special needs teacher in Hartcliffe Comprehensive School and established an outstanding OSHL programme which grew into an independent charity working with schools across Bristol.

Multi A has been instrumental in setting up a series of workshops which have enabled over 60 young people in schools to work with artists, film makers, animators, musicians, composers, choreographers and a variety of scientific, technical and creative staff. This extensive partnership has resulted in the production of paintings, music, and films, and the acquisition of a wide range of personal skills. It prides itself on being a model of excellence, open to all children and young people.

It began in July 1998, when Tim Rollins and KOS (New York) worked with 20 young people in Bristol (in Hartcliffe, St George and other neighbourhoods) to make their own visual interpretation of the tragedy of Prometheus. After working on the Aeschylus play *Prometheus Bound*, and using images of fire including those in the paintings of De la Tour, Blake, Turner, Siquieros and Marvel Comics' *Human Touch*, each member of the group was inspired to create the beginnings of light in oil pastel. The 20 tiny paintings were collaged on to pages taken from the play and publicly displayed at the Arnolfini Gallery, Bristol.

The project was later extended with members of the nationally known Hartcliffe Boys Dance Company, from Hartcliffe Secondary School, who were working on a new dance piece which focused on the Prometheus myth. A number of company members worked with the composer, Dan Jones, recording blacksmiths at work and a variety of 'fire' sounds. These recordings formed the basis for studio work creating music for the dance performance. Other students worked with a local media company to produce a short computer-animated film. The film incorporated the painted panels and could be used either as 'scenery' for the dance piece or to stand alone, with the music, as a film in its own right. A documentary film exploring attitudes to boys' dance was also made by members of the Dance Company and incorporated both the choreography and music produced.

In all, these arts projects with school pupils have involved a number of different partners including Multi A, Radiodetection, Tim Rollins and KOS, the Arts Council England, View to Learning, Brief Encounters Film Festival and E3 Media.

Overall, Multi A provides a vast range of arts activities weekly every term to 1,800 pupils in 17 primary schools in inner city Bristol. The recent venture between the Cathedral School and Easton Primary School was successful in that the support of the English Chamber Orchestra enabled pupils from both schools with their families to perform together in an orchestra.[9]

The key outcomes from Multi A projects with schools appear to be increased self-confidence, improved academic performance and more self-control. Principally, pupils are given a breadth of educational opportunities in the arts.

But, as the Robinson Report (*All Our Futures: Creativity, culture and education*) made clear, creativity lies at the heart of science and technology as much as the arts. Science and technology activities out of school hours create the space, the time, and the support for highly creative and interactive experiment and design. Research suggests that involvement in science clubs provide the 'little bit extra' that can be the all-important difference between

[9] Information supplied by Vic Ecclestone at MultiA

going on with science or not.[10] There are a wealth of initiatives, schemes, awards and clubs across the UK, supplemented in many schools by the home-grown activities which form a regular feature of school life. Some of these clubs focus on interactive activities which include rockets, robotics, radio stations or astronomy. Others take a broader approach across a discipline, or focused work related to the science curriculum.

EXTRA

Dalriada School

Dalriada School in County Antrim has a lunchtime science club focusing mainly on chemistry, which is run every fortnight by Heather Millar. It has good attendance by female pupils – mainly Years 8 and 9 – and older students from the sixth form help with experiments. Activities have included: making foam fire extinguishers; flame testing products and making fireworks; making fruit pastels; making silly putty; building a butterfly garden and an antworld. Heather views the main aim of the club as 'giving children access to materials and [to] types of experiments which are not usually possible to perform in lesson time.'

EXTRA

Cranford Community College

Cranford Community College, LB Hounslow, is a language college. Ann Marshall, Director of the Faculty of Science, has used the Science Across the World project sponsored by BP to get in touch with schools in other countries. This work is being done by GNVQ students and the intention is to involve them in cascading the ideas to younger pupils. They have taken students to the European Particle Research Centre CERN in Geneva where they worked with students from a Swedish school.

As argued earlier, sport is also seen to have a key role not only in raising self-esteem and confidence, but also in improving health and well-being, enabling leadership and promoting team working, problem solving and lifeskills. The past two years have seen a raft of new funding and initiatives to boost participation, excellence, healthy living and social inclusion. The new coordinators appointed will have a number of key objectives within the out of school hours learning agenda:

---

[10] See Brian Woolnough, Department of Educational Studies, University of Oxford, *The Making of Scientists and Engineers* quoted in Andrews K *et al* (1995) *Good Policy and Practice for the After-School Hours*, p 121, Pitman Publishing, London

- An extension of the curriculum through the establishment of out of school clubs, and in particular an expansion in the range of sports on offer and clubs targeting girls/young women, black and ethnic minorities and young people with special needs.
- Strengthening the links between the school day and out of school hours sport and all aspects of their achievement at school.
- The involvement of new coaches and leaders from outside the school in these programmes.
- The promotion of coaching and officiating awards for school staff, particularly Coaching for Teachers, a national initiative coordinated by the National Coaching Foundation.
- The creation of inter-mural and inter-school competitive opportunities, in liaison with local agencies and existing School Sports Associations.

The following case studies show only a few of the most recent and innovative sports/study support programmes in action which are seeking to link sport with a whole range of achievement strategies, for example, providing opportunities for mentoring and qualification, for addressing performance in terms of gender, and for promoting links with healthy eating and fitness.

EXTRA

Northumberland LEA

Pupils from Richmond Secondary School have completed TOPs training and some went on to complete a Hockey level 1 coaching qualification and umpire courses. These pupils have since supported teachers and coaches providing hockey for younger pupils in out of school hours.

EXTRA

Eastbury School

Eastbury School, LB Barking and Dagenham, is also encouraging more girls to take part in PE and sport through out of school hours clubs. They are participating in the Nike/Youth Sport Trust 'Girls in Sport Project' in partnership with Barking Abbey Sports College. Health and fitness breakfast clubs have also been introduced. The new clubs have meant that many more girls now participate in sport.

EXTRA

Beacon Community College, Crowborough

Beacon College runs extra-curricular sessions for KS4 students, from both the college and other local secondary schools, who excel at sport. The sessions are based around nutrition, analysis of technique, sports psychology, physiology, fitness and training, and putting principles into practice. The sessions are run by the British Association of Sport and Exercise Sciences (BASES) accredited sports scientists from the University of Brighton.

EXTRA

Langdon School

The introduction of a 'Play Well, Eat Well, Look Well' scheme at Langdon School, LB Newham, has encouraged young people, especially girls from ethnic minorities, to take part in out of school hours clubs that link sport with health-related topics such as healthy eating. A steering group involves staff from ICT, PSHE and Food Technology. In addition the school ran a girls-only sports convention at which girls and staff had the opportunity to participate in less traditional forms of PE and sport. Staff and pupils from 12 other secondary schools also attended.

EXTENDING THE CURRICULUM

Motivation is the first step to effective learning, but to be an effective learner requires more help and support along the way. For many students, the practical conditions for effective learning – time, space, resources, skills, simply do not exist, and many secondary schools have not yet made providing those conditions a priority. Yet, OSHL can be defined in a narrower sense as 'supported study' and, linked to the curriculum, can generate not only space but specific and effective support for learning at critical stages of a student's career. It can offer opportunities to address weaknesses and extend skills, provide space and support for homework, or simply demonstrate and celebrate excellence. It is in these areas of OSHL activities that the clearest effects are likely to be found between participation by students and an improvement in examination performance overall.

The learning environment outside school hours can:

- provide the opportunity for students and teachers to work together intensively and voluntarily on diagnosed weaknesses in preparation for Key Stage tests and examinations;

- provide opportunities for students themselves to 'own up to' particular areas of difficulty outside the exposure of the classroom;
- enable students to negotiate individual learning targets and develop their own learning skills and styles;
- enable all students to take some risks with their learning, to read beyond the curriculum, to explore the Internet and to mentor each other.

For teachers, whether involved as tutors in their specialist subject, or as enthusiastic advocates for something quite different (for example the geography teacher who runs the cycle maintenance club), the learning environment offers an equal opportunity to explore different styles of teaching, to develop a different and more equal relationship with the learner, and to become a learner themselves.

The organisation of resources for study support, however, requires management, funding and commitment at the level of school, as well as a clear determination to place the initiative within the whole school context. Providing the space, the resources and the support in different forms is a critical first step. Throughout the UK there are many excellent examples of schools supporting learning and study skills, providing curriculum and revision support, and putting help for homework within the reach of all pupils.[11]

Two examples of inner city schools[12] which have introduced inclusive policies to raise achievement through study support initiatives are Sarah Bonnell School, a single-sex school in Newham, and Oaklands School, Newham. Both schools draw on catchment areas which are impoverished and multicultural, and where the community of the school has to meet a very wide range of complex demands. These case studies show how important it is for schools to create a special time and place for supported study.

EXTRA

Sarah Bonnell School

Sarah Bonnell was designated a Beacon School by the DfEE in September 1999. The school is one of the first of the Prince's Trust Study Support Centres and runs an extended curriculum programme which responded to the students' own assessment of their needs. At the school, the Study Support Centre runs during lunchtimes in the top hall and is staffed by two members of staff for each session. Groups work together on a common topic and communication between students and staff takes place while ensuring an acceptable noise level is not exceeded for those who wish to study silently.

---

[11] Many useful examples are given in the SSNEDP *Study Support Handbook* and in case study series issued in 2000–2001
[12] Ibid

Staff working in the Study Support Centre are expected to take an active role supporting students' learning where possible. Year 10 and 11 students can work in a separate study area if they so choose. Students using the study club games can also be offered a separate classroom to work in where appropriate. There are also Year 11 classes on Sundays, Easter revision classes in the holidays and various other lunchtime and twilight extra-curricular activities.

Students have open access and can arrive at any time from 1.20 to 2.10 pm. They are required to sign in a 'House' folder on arrival and to record with a code the type of work or activity they intend to engage in. Once 25 attendances have been recorded students receive a certificate of attendance in their House colour. There is no limit to the number of certificates that can be obtained.

A further project by the school is the recent NOF project 'Working and Learning Together After School: A Project for Parents and Students' where students and parents will be able to develop ICT skills, word processing skills, use the Internet, improve numeracy and literacy skills or just have time to do homework and coursework all with the help and specialist support of teachers. The school also launched a holiday scheme designed and run by students. Through the scheme, students are encouraged to take more responsibility and their developing maturity and autonomy are valued. The scheme is organised by students aged 13 and 14 and provides a peace of mind for parents. The project is about enhancing the personal development of young women.

EXTRA

Oaklands School[13]

At Oaklands School, LB Newham, study support has grown and is now an integral part of school life. It has contributed greatly to the substantial improvements in the confidence of students, learning ethos and examination results. Study support at the school includes short courses offering a wide range of exciting opportunities and a cybercafé in the early morning where students have a chance to surf the Net. Tutors for study support are either teachers or support staff at the school, and they all receive formal management and monitoring.

When the school opened in 1991, the headteacher decided that all teachers should use half an hour of directed time each week to run a club which provided students with a wealth of activities, though the activities were usually linked to the subject taught by the teacher. A formal study support centre opened in 1995 following consultation with students, parents and staff, running on Wednesdays from 4 to 6 pm. It is not unusual for over 100 students to attend. The centre is based in five classrooms in the school

[13] Ibid

including the library, an ICT room and an art room. The centre also runs GCSE revision and coursework catch-up sessions during the holidays and on Saturdays for Year 11 students. There has been a clear link between attendance at these sessions and improved examination results.

Since 1997, study support has developed even further with Wednesday evening sessions now an established part of the life of the school and around 20 per cent of the student population participate. Short courses have also started where students are offered a range of 10-week programmes of study. These courses are designed in a variety of ways; some are there to respond to pupils' specific needs, others lead to qualifications, others to enhance GCSE programmes, others to reinforce interests or hobbies, others have a community focus while others have a lifelong learning angle.

In Scotland, there are some longstanding and excellent programmes of study support combing extension and enrichment activities with a particular role for study skills.[14]

EXTRA

St Kentigern's School[15]

Over the past five years, St. Kentigern's has consciously developed and advanced a varied study support programme which aims to meet the needs of as many learners as possible. The principle aim of the programme is for pupils to develop a positive attitude towards teaching and learning and through this to raise the attainment of all pupils.

In 1996, the initial aim was to equip pupils with core skills to facilitate their learning across the curriculum. This led to the formation of a cross-curricular study support group with its own subsequent programme which was devised to develop six key transferable skills. The success of the programme was evaluated through a whole school staff and pupil audit. Pupil and staff evaluations are an integral part of each study support programme.

This programme for S1 students has been further developed through the Learning and Thinking Skills pack (You're a Star!) with workshops tackling self-esteem and study skills including mind-mapping skills. The success of this new initiative relies on the informal nature of the workshops, the enthusiasm of tutors involved and also on the pupil ownership (pupils choose to take part in a club or an activity which runs on the same evening).

In addition, the study support programme also allows senior pupils to work closely with subject specialists in tutorial groups, this programme aiming to improve exam performance through study skills and exam technique. Alongside this, a group of 23 S4 boys who have been highlighted by subject departments as underachieving were targeted by SMT to take part in

---

[14] See the *Study Support Handbook* for further details
[15] Ibid and see the Study Support National Evaluation and Development Programme Case Study Series

Successbuilders. This programme was written and implemented specifically to tackle the poor attitude of able but underachieving boys towards school. From this, a mentoring and tracking system evolved to support and manage their studies.

The success of this pilot programme has encouraged the school to extend it to include both underachieving girls and pupils from S3. In addition, the individual tracking programme has been extended to all 400 of S3 and S4 pupils. In partnership with a variety of companies (JABIL and WISDOM IT), the school is piloting an advanced study support programme whereby S3 and S4 pupils use e-mail to correspond with mentors within these companies. The project will help pupils develop core skills in IT and motivate them to develop the skills and attitudes required to be successful in the world of work. Another partnership with NIKON Precision is planned to supplement the study support activities. This partnership will promote teacher placements to foster education for work skills with teaching staff. E-mentoring and site visits will also play a major role in this partnership. This experience will then be fed back to pupils during study support sessions.

Another model of support, often within a broader programme of enrichment and extension activities, is where schools identify students with particular learning needs, then design a diagnostic programme for them in a wide range of curriculum areas. One leading example in Wales is Ysgol Uwchradd Tywyn in Gwynedd:

EXTRA

Ysgol Uwchradd Tywyn

At Ysgol Uwchradd Tywyn, formal lessons end at 2.45 pm, but for many pupils this is not the end of the school day. The school is open until 5.30 pm with most facilities available until this time.

The introduction of Education and Action Plans for pupils on Stages 2 to 5 of the Special Needs Register revealed that pupils of different abilities did tend to share the same problems in certain areas. In response to this the school offers an after-school helpline in addition to a variety of workshops and 'Progress Packs' to cover the core subjects such as English, Welsh, maths and science. Although these are often targeted towards Years 7 to 9, there is always the opportunity for senior pupils to attend or request assistance in any subject that is causing them concern. One pupil commented that 'just know[ing this] makes the lessons seem easier'.

To cater for those pupils who wish to improve other skills, workshops are also offered in art and crafts, drama, handwriting, ICT, problem solving and team-building skills.

These after-school workshops show that pupils of similar ability flourish while working together in small groups. It has been noticed that they are not afraid of making mistakes. Even the quietest of pupils in class will participate enthusiastically. At the end of the course pupils are presented with a certificate recording attendances and achievement. Workshops in Key Skills are also presented across the year group, to help students present work, take notes and revise for exams. For more able pupils, 'reasoning skills' workshops are also organised, to stretch and challenge them through the use of puzzles and problems which encourage them to reason in more unusual ways.

Recent funding (from Barclays New Futures) is for Image 2000 which involves identifying and working with pupils to raise their self-image through team work and support for strategies to develop their self-esteem.

Some schools have put inclusive strategies in place, aimed at improving the academic performance of specific groups of pupils at critical times of the year. Easter revision schemes are particularly timely, intensive, and popular.

── EXTRA ──

Lister Community School[16]

Lister Community School, LB Newham, has an extensive programme of study support activities which both extend and enhance the curriculum in this inner city school. All curriculum areas have study support programmes which operate at KS3 and KS4 and which involve homework clubs, coursework support or activities aimed at specific targeted groups of students. In addition, there is a wide range of activities aimed at improving literacy and numeracy such as the breakfast club literacy sessions for EAL students and after-school numeracy classes for Year 7 and 8 students. Other activities are designed to ease transition from KS2 to KS3 including Saturday school for Year 5 and 6 students. The learning resources area has a library, ICT suite and tutorial rooms and is open from 8.00 am to 5.00 pm. The school also runs a summer literacy and numeracy scheme.

The Easter revision scheme, which has been running for four years with voluntary teacher commitment, aims to give students the opportunity to maintain or improve on their estimated GCSE grades across the curriculum. Advertised from January and starting from February onwards, it takes place on Saturdays and during holiday times, focused around a timetable. Students who are seen to be vulnerable are encouraged to attend – eg those on the C–D borderline. It provides opportunities to complete coursework, practice exam topics and techniques, and practice time and stress management, as well as a forum for teachers and students to meet and agree targets. The borough and the Standards Fund support the programme with funding.

Each year the scheme has been evaluated with very positive results. In 1998–99 for example, 79 per cent of eligible students attended the scheme, with 82 per cent of girls and 68 per cent of boys. Thirty-one teachers took

[16] SSNEDP Case Study Series, June 2000

part, offering 63 classes. Across the school, 26 per cent of students obtained A–C grades. Of those attending the scheme, almost a third obtained A–C grades. Of the 54 students particularly targeted it was estimated that just over 20 per cent would obtain A–C grades. In fact, over 50 per cent did so, more than double the estimate..

Accessing the curriculum, encouraging effective revision, supporting course work completion, and finding out how to use the resources available, are all critical to examination success. But it is vitally important to gain study skills – learning to think and study effectively is a critical skill for all lifelong learners – yet this is an area of the curriculum which has been relatively neglected until recently . Some schools have, however, begun to embrace this new area of skill development enthusiastically, influenced in some cases by the increasing knowledge of brain-based learning. One of the most influential settings for this work has been the UFA's practice of accelerated learning.

EXTRA

Broadgreen Community Comprehensive

This comprehensive school in Liverpool started a study support scheme in 1996, based on the ideas of Gordon Benn. The scheme 'concentrates on mind-mapping and memory-learning techniques' to enhance study. Sessions include developing a personal effectiveness programme, organising revision, developing IT skills, evaluation techniques and language skills.[17]

EXTRA

Holly Lodge School

In 1996–67 Holly Lodge School in Liverpool, a large single-sex comprehensive school for girls, piloted, as one of its study support initiatives, an intensive course in motivational study skills and memory techniques to foster independent learning for a pilot group of Year 10 and 11 pupils. This was designed to tutor students approaching exams in techniques for learning, for memory retention, mind-mapping and visual techniques – and to do so in a way which was comfortable and effective for each pupil. Built into the programme was the opportunity for the 70 students involved to 'cascade' what they had learnt to other pupils and staff through booklets and dissemination days. The students involved were 'very positive' – 'They found revision less stressful [and] it aroused family interest.'[18]

---

[17] See the *Study Support Handbook*
[18] Education Extra (1997) *Succeeding at Study Support*

In many cases, what students need is the encouragement and voluntary help of other people. Teachers themselves willingly provide this in countless instances. (See Chapter 7.) In addition, however, inspiration, information and invaluable help can come from adults or older students. One school which has involved older pupils has been able to improve its homework facilities for all students significantly.

EXTRA

Counthill Secondary School

At Counthill Secondary School in Oldham, a learning resource centre is run by a member of staff with one adult assistant, together with a large team of pupils from Years 9, 10 and 11. The older pupils help with the library resources which include books, careers information, TV/teletext, video and audio equipment, talking books, videos, computers, CD ROMs, the Internet and e-mail. The scheme runs before and after school and at lunchtimes.

The volunteers are given training and learning by shadowing each other. They learn about different forms of information and how to access and use them; they pass their knowledge and experience on to the younger users of the library; they become familiar with state of the art technologies, and there is a marked increase in self-esteem and involvement with the school as a whole.

ENABLING STUDENTS

The final set of case studies in this chapter looks at how specific strategies can work to enhance learning. The first two are, by definition, inclusive. The third is about reaching students who present particular challenges for the school.

ICT – the common factor

In general terms, one common factor in successful OSHL programmes is access to and help with ICT – whether ICT is needed for homework or project work, for Internet and email clubs, for summer learning schemes, or for family learning with parents being tutored by their children in the basic principles of computing, word processing and spread sheets And there is a specific appeal for boys. As one headteacher succinctly put it: 'If you don't make it available, they won't come.'[19] Some schools have been particularly innovative in using different technologies to make information

---

[19] Ibid. Westgate Community School in Newcastle, for example, showed how opening the libraries and computer services at all times around the teaching day would attract consistently large numbers and improved performances

about homework, presentation, and completion more successful. One example is St George College in Bristol.

EXTRA

St George Community College

In 1997, St George Community College, a multicultural inner city community school, pioneered a telephone-based information system known as 'Homework Hotline'. This automated recording system is designed to ensure that all students know what homework is set on a daily basis. Student receptionists are given responsibility for collecting the homework set from teachers and then a member of the administration staff records the details on the system. A simple call to the hotline then allows parents to select the appropriate year group number and hear the homework set for that day.

A homework club for younger children is run to support the hotline facility and other students are offered up to 40 activities as part of the Third Session programme delivered by teachers and community workers. Additional study facilities are provided for students with learning difficulties and a breakfast club has enhanced this provision.

It is difficult to quantify the impact on the homework of the homework hotline and related support facilities but it does enable the college to place the importance of homework at the top of its agenda.[20]

EXTRA

Bishops Stortford High School

Another very exciting model is provided by the Bishops Stortford High School, Hertfordshire, where ICT has been linked to homework, offering benefits to pupils, parents and teachers way beyond the parameters of homework.

A collaborative one-year pilot project with NTL, ensures that all of the homes of the intake of new pupils (Year 8) have access to the school intranet and a pre-filtered service for the Internet. Each pupil and parent/carer has been given an e-mail address for communication with each other and staff. A member of staff is also online to respond to requests for assistance or information from 4 to 6 pm each evening, Sunday through to Friday. A record of the set homework tasks is also available in case pupils miss school.

Pupils either use their own PCs, TV Internet, Digital TV, or are provided with free loan/rental of a PC. Telephone charges are at local rate. However, funding from Education Extra has built in an element of subsidy into phone line costs. Teachers participating in the project have also been provided with Internet access. The aims of the project are:

---

[20] See Education Extra (1997) *Succeeding at Study Support: An evaluation of 12 model projects in primary and secondary schools*

- To improve the quality of support for homework. All homework tasks, with worked examples, are posted on the site. Back-up support from the school's resources is available, including access to 'Know UK' and 'Living Library', suggested CD ROM titles, book lists, revision tasks, etc.
- To increase the use of ICT in the school as a tool for more effective independent learning, as pupils acquire the ability to access and manage resources and information that are vital to their education. The staff's ICT skills will also be enhanced through training, support and practice.
- To enhance parental involvement in their children's education. Parents will have better access to up-to-date information about schemes of work and their children's homework. More parental involvement with homework tasks will be also sought. Information will also be provided on a very wide range of school-related matters, for example, school events, news, sports results, examination dates.
- To demonstrate what the school of the future might look like, where the latest technology used in teaching and learning is available both at school and at home. Learning will also be promoted as a seamless feature of life for pupils and their families, unconstrained by the traditional features of formal schooling.

The project will be continuously monitored, internally and externally, by the University of Cambridge, and at a key stage in the project a decision will be taken to assess whether it should be continued, expanded or converted into a commercial project.

READING THE FUTURE

There are fears that children no longer read and that the appeal of television and computer games is wiping out the appeal of books. These fears may be exaggerated but not unfounded, particularly at the critical age of transition from primary to secondary school. Research also seems to suggest that reading for pleasure can have a significant impact on achievement.[21] In 1999, during the Year of Reading, Education Extra spearheaded a campaign to promote reading for pleasure in secondary schools. By 2000, 140 clubs had been set up involving children, teachers, authors, writers, poets, bookshop and library staff enjoying and contributing to the pleasure and educational effect of reading.

---

[21] See the Education Extra evaluation of the first year of the Book-it Clubs (unpublished, 2001)

┌─── EXTRA ──┐

Haversack School

Haversack School in North London has over 20 Year 7 pupils meeting in the school library on Friday afternoon each week for the Book-it! Club. They are offered a choice of activities, including play reading , paired reading or simply the opportunity to read by themselves. Students from the local university and school staff attend, read themselves, talk about and share their enthusiasm for books.

While the club brings alive the love of reading among many different people, school staff have found that club members' curriculum work has improved by leaps and bounds, and that students' self-confidence in other areas of school life has increased dramatically. 'These factors are particularly critical as club members are now at an age when traditionally pupils tend to lose the reading habit. The "Book-it" clubs have encouraged pupils to maintain a love of books during this critical transitional period'.[22]

└──┘

DIFFERENT STUDENTS, DIFFERENT ABILITIES

The third challenge is how to develop schemes which target the real needs of students of different abilities and requirements. Sedgehill School in South London has a particularly well-balanced programme.[23]

┌─── EXTRA ──┐

Sedgehill School

This is a school of 1,700 students, with a programme of activities which reflects many interests and strategies. Some are open sessions, others are targeted at particular groups of students. The first priority was, according to the responsible teacher, Pat Stack (Senior Teacher for Enrichment and Extension), to provide facilities for students on examination courses and for the development of the library and IT resources. This was followed by provision for all ability groups, including the more able and those with special needs. Staff involved have been offered sessional payments and financial help came, originally from TECs and EBPs, to fund specific projects.

From these beginnings the school developed a series of programmes for students at different stages of development and with different needs and abilities:

- A lunchtime Homework Club for KS3 students to build up good study and learning habits. The Drop In Centre also 'provides a refuge for these

└──┘

---

[22] Education Extra (2000) *Extra Class*, pp 2–3
[23] For further details see the *Study Support Handbook*

students who are too shy or who have difficulties mixing with others at lunchtime'. Staff receive lunchtime supervisors' rates.

- The On Track Club aimed at lower-ability students in Year 9 whose motivation and interest in school was falling away. The funding was provided by the EBP and aimed to promote social and study skills, and group work. The club has run for four years and has been evaluated by student self-assessment, by the teacher in charge and by external evaluation. The club has generally been seen as helping its members to overcome difficulties in the transition from KS3 to KS4. Success is measured by students' continued attendance, improved motivation at school, and, ultimately, some examination success.
- The On Course Club is for students of higher academic ability but who are still underachieving. This club which started in February 1998 is based around projects which challenge the students to cooperate together and solve the problem. Students assess their own progress. This was supported by the Prince's Trust.
- Revision classes in December and Easter holidays. Both are well attended 'and the students attending the revision centre are found to do better at GCSE than those who do not attend'.

At the other end of the spectrum is the fact that OSHL activities offer the opportunity to challenge pupils who are gifted and talented to take their own learning a step further and to set their own challenges. This group of pupils, in the top 5–10 per cent of students, who are also provided for in the EiC initiative, were the focus of an innovative summer scheme in 1999 across England, which aimed to provide learning experiences for incoming Year 7 pupils that they would not have come across in their primary schools. The 50 schemes involved covered all areas of the curriculum defining excellence in terms of the arts, as well as maths and science. One outstanding scheme was that at Ashby Grammar School.

EXTRA

Ashby Grammar School

Ashby Grammar School is a 14–19 Specialist Technology School in Ashby de la Zouch, Leicestershire.

The summer school was thematically structured around a series of focused subject workshops for incoming Year 7 pupils who had, for example, scored level 5 or better in maths and science KS2 SATs which included:

- thinking skills – training memory, mind maps, and increasing reading speeds;
- astro-physics, DNA and chemical changes – including having pupils make their own rocket;
- mathematics – tesselations and Escher diagrams;

- food technology and textiles – including designs for baseball hats and chocolate bars;
- graphics;
- ICT.

Each workshop had specific learning objectives in addition to the general summer school objectives, which included motivating students and raising their achievement in the focus subject areas. A key aim was also to improve curriculum continuity between KS2 and 3. Students were introduced to advanced scientific techniques and how to analyse specific problems and issues, using information from a range of sources, including ICT.

The scheme ran for two weeks, around a carousel of subject areas. The students enjoyed the opportunity to look in depth at different subjects and find out 'new things that I never knew before.' The graphic design focus workshop enabled students to put theoretical knowledge to practice by designing an individualised chocolate bar from start to finish, applying knowledge of colour theory and design techniques in practice. Workshops involved the extensive use of ICT and computer language and programme design. Students were introduced to the mysteries of Web page writing, which they found challenging, but achievable, working on it at home as well as in the summer school. 'This activity brought ICT alive for students and helped them realise that they could use the technology and make it work for them.'

CONCLUSION

Giving young people more time to do more of the same, in the same way, with the same people in the same places, is not going to raise achievement dramatically upward – we need to think about doing some things radically different. (Tim Brighouse, Chief Education Officer, Birmingham Education Service)

Throughout this chapter the links between motivation and achievement have been expressed in a variety of very different examples, drawn from schools across the UK facing many different challenges. The key factor in all these schemes, however, is that what is working outside school hours does so because there is a conscious effort to make it different from the school day, but supportive of it. That is true whether the focus of the activity is the arts, sports or special interests, or whether schools are finding new ways of stretching and supporting children of very different tastes and abilities. Finding ways to make the experience different is, therefore, alongside the raft of organisational good practice outlined in Chapter 4, probably the single most important step on the pathway to successful out of school learning.

The following chapters show how that difference can be expressed not only in the content and the curriculum of out of school learning activities, but in the people, the partners, and the connections which those activities bring with them.

Finally, as the conclusion to Chapter 5 emphasised, the body of good practice evidenced in reports and evaluation shows a consistent approach to success, which all schools can adapt and build on for themselves. These strategies cover the learning environment as well as organisation principles.

7

Study support, school inclusion and social inclusion

In my career as a headteacher there have been moments of utter despair. Occasionally, there are rare moments of immense pride and tonight has been one of them. (Headteacher, West Walton Primary School, comment evoked by the performance and community work of the family choir)

The previous chapters looked at the way OSHL is assuming a key role in the life of the school in relation to raising achievement. This final section of the book explores the ways in which OSHL can promote social inclusion through school policies which:

- support families through family learning;
- support families by providing help with after-school childcare;
- promote improved transition at different stages of education and reintegration into education for children at risk;
- promote the inclusion of pupils who are liable to exclude themselves from the life of the school;
- identify and prevent pupils who are at risk of exclusion from reaching the brink.

OSHL AND SCHOOL INCLUSION

In recent years it has become clear that OSHL can enable schools to address some of the more difficult issues, which, in their solution, contribute to the making of effective schools *and* effective communities. This chapter explores one set of those links – between school inclusion, and social inclusion. At its narrowest point, school inclusion is seen as the antidote to the more familiar term, school exclusion, which marks the exit from school for a small minority of pupils on a temporary or permanent basis. By school inclusion, we mean, however, not only the work which schools do to ensure every pupil has an equal stake in the life and work of the school, but the efforts which schools make outside school hours to involve and include their families so that they too can contribute to that success. School inclusion is also used to express a wider set of relationships which make for a more inclusive set of policies which link school to wider social concerns – specifically, to the range of relationships between schools, families, other services for children, and the wider community in terms of the support schools can give to pupils in terms of their general well-being.[1]

If school inclusion is the foundation of social inclusion – and to individuals feeling that they have a stake in the well-being of society – the opposite, social exclusion, has come to mean those who, for many different personal, social or economic reasons, (whether acute poverty, long-term unemployment, poor skills, family stress, poor housing, low educational achievement or delinquent or criminal behaviour) do not have that feeling.

These are very complex issues and this chapter can only explore them in relation to one aspect of school life – OSHL. However, by definition, OSHL, has a particular capacity for promoting inclusion – a sense of belonging and of being valued – both within the school and within the wider community. No one is excluded from an activity where the only qualification is a commitment to be there, to negotiate what might be on offer, and to enjoy what is being done. Furthermore, it is the one area of school life where teachers can positively encourage involvement safe in the knowledge that they have the freedom to provide what individuals need and will respond to. The selection of case studies and issues has been particularly difficult, given the scope and complexity of the issues, and the serious implications which they have for successful ways of reducing not simply barriers to learning but to quality of life. The examples have been chosen not simply because they are recent and innovative, or in development, but also because they are relatively simple to develop and replicate by schools across the spectrum.

The chapter looks, first, at:

- the role of family learning as a critical element in helping children to learn and succeed – and in helping family members themselves;
- the way in which after-school childcare clubs provide play and learning opportunities within the setting of high-quality childcare for working families and thus provide an essential support for families to play an active role in society;

[1] See Ball, M (1998) *School Inclusion: The school, the family and the community*, Joseph Rowntree Foundation; and Dyson, A and Robson, E (1999) *School, Family, Community: Mapping school inclusion in the UK*, Joseph Rowntree Foundation

- the way in which after-school childcare provision can be extended appropriately for older children in the early years of secondary school when they are still vulnerable and approaching adolescence.

The chapter then looks at points in the school year and the school experience when students can lose confidence and commitment to school, and how OSHL can assist them and maintain their links with school through inclusive strategies. It examines, for example:

- the role of transitional support which helps primary school children to make a success of secondary school transfer;
- some of the ways in which children with disabilities are learning alongside non-disabled children;
- how OSHL can open up more equal opportunities for boys and girls;
- how OSHL can help students who have to deal with very difficult personal circumstances.

The greatest transition of all can be seen as that of exclusion from school. The third set of issues therefore illustrates some ways in which schools are putting in place explicitly inclusive and preventive strategies for students who are identified as at risk and liable to become disaffected or to begin the drift towards exclusion.

HELPING THE PUPIL BY HELPING THE FAMILY

Successful learning starts within, and with, the family. Family life is, after all, the place where the connection between emotional and cognitive learning can meet. As Goleman has put it: 'Family life is our first school for emotional learning; in this intimate cauldron we learn how to feel about ourselves and how others will react to our feelings.'[2] One educationalist recently observed that 'Perhaps the most striking of our findings was the extent to which families rather than institutions seem to make the difference in influencing age ten psychological and behavioural scores. This has clear implications for those who would wish to help people develop the childhood attributes which will help them in later life.'[3] It is self-evident that the child whose parents are interested and supportive of their work in school is more likely to do well than a child whose parents are indifferent or indeed, hostile.[4] Parental negativity about school achievement may

[2] Goleman, D (1996) *Emotional Intelligence: Why it can matter more than IQ*, Bloomsbury London, quoted in Haggart, J (2000) *Learning Legacies: A Guide to Family Learning*, NIACE, p 9
[3] Feinstein, L (2000) *CentrePiece*, LSE, Autumn, p 17
[4] For a review of the literature on parental involvement in learning, and partnership with parents as well as relations between schools, parents and the community, see Dyson, A and Robson, E (1999) op cit

spring from many different sources, not least the failure of adults themselves to succeed. Current figures giving the number of adults in the UK showing dysfunctional adult illiteracy as 7 million suggest that there is still a mountain to climb before every adult becomes a confident reader.

The cluster of initiatives grouped under the term 'family learning' offers a way for families to take a more active role in the process of their children's learning, and, indeed, in their own learning.[5] As well as being learners, 'children and other family members may also take apart as educators themselves'.[6] The SHARE programme, for example, developed by the Community Education Development Centre, is designed to recognise the role parents can play in supporting learning. Materials and resources help the parents to share learning together and to develop their confidence in themselves as educators.

The term family learning is therefore very broad, and can encompass, for example, informal and formal learning within the family as well as family members learning together in educational settings. Family learning aims to promote the benefits of the family unit as a base for learning and to facilitate the three-way connection between children, their parents and teachers. When parents work together with their children, learning outcomes are greatly enhanced. Parents and teachers working together in harmony project a positive role model for children.[7] A recent Ofsted report defined family learning as 'planned activity in which adults and children come together to work and learning collaboratively'. The report found that family learning has a key role in raising achievement, widening participation and countering social exclusion.[8] Increasingly, support for family learning is being built into specific educational initiatives which aim to support families and learning together – starting at the critical early years when communication skills and confidence are laid down. But while there is a wealth of separate and local initiatives and funding streams, there is as yet no coherent policy for family learning as part of the national strategy for education.

For many reasons, not least the fact that family learning offers the possibility of families breaking out of a cycle of deprivation, there is a strong case for more coherence in both its planning and funding. For families who find schools and the school day a forbidding barrier, OSHL offers a second chance to help themselves and their children, in three specific ways by:

[5] A recent MORI poll showed that 68 per cent of children aged 12–16 rate their mothers and fathers as the strongest influences in their learning lives. Campaign for Learning (2000) *A Manifesto for Family Learning*, p 9

[6] See, for example, Haggart, J (2000) *Learning Legacies*, NIACE, p 6

[7] Walton, M (1998) *Family Literacy and Learning*, Folens, Dunstable, p 6

[8] See Ofsted (2000) *Family Learning: a survey of current practice*, p 5

- enabling families to help their own children to learn more effectively;
- providing after-school and holiday care for children while families work;
- providing additional and pastoral support for vulnerable older children in the early years of secondary school (Student Care).

The main element of parental involvement in learning is with literacy and, to a lesser extent, numeracy in the primary years. Literature reviews 'offer evidence that involving parents in their children's learning is likely to enhance the attainments of children, to improve their attitudes to learning and to be welcomed by many parents'. There are many different models now in place.

Recently, the Sure Start programme, for example, has offered some new opportunities for partnership in the development of innovative learning schemes involving families and younger children.

EXTRA

The Playtalk Project

The first Playtalk Project in Woolscote, Dudley, is rooted in the Sure Start initiative and started as one of five family literacy projects funded by Education Extra and Roald Dahl Foundation. The project aims to engage parents in their child's education. The focus is on language development through play with two-year-olds and their parents. A series of eight one-to-one sessions is held with a nursery nurse who provides a model for both parent and child. Resources are available to borrow during and after the course. The course is run three times a year, targeting 24 families, working in English and Punjabi/Urdu. Early in 2000, the school became part of the Dudley Partnership for Achievement, Dudley's EAZ. This provided an opportunity to expand the Playtalk work from which a new project, Playtalk 2, was born.

Playtalk 2 targets children from approximately six months up to three years, aiming to help parents to develop skills for organising play which in turn assists other work in developing children's social and language skills. Sessions take place in the home initially, encouraging parents into school to work individually at first and later in small groups. Parents are also encouraged to attend the open Parent and Toddler sessions which are run by the same staff to aid continuity and nurture parental confidence. These sessions also provide an exit strategy from the project helping parents transfer from specialist to mainstream support.

The project has a current sample of 25 families – which has exceeded the original target number. A significant decrease in the number of children receiving special therapy in the nursery has been achieved in the last year or so due, in part, to the Playtalk projects.

During summer 2000, a new room (the Playtalk room) was built on to the nursery to facilitate the pre-school programmes run. This has allowed more work to be undertaken on site, increasing the number of families attending.

One of the continuing challenges facing the school is to review the support for parents as their children go through school in order to help parental skills develop which are appropriate to the needs of children. In addition to family support for the early years, a wide range of family literacy programmes is run across the UK. These programmes are publicly funded through agencies such as the DfEE's Adult and Community Learning Fund, coordinated by NIACE and the Basic Skills Agency and specifically aimed to help families help their children, and in many cases the adults involved, to read more fluently. The importance of continuing parental support, promoting the right of the child to make his or her own voice heard, and the role of the teacher as friend and mentor are particularly positive responses to this situation. Many schools are now finding funds (for example, from Single Regeneration Budgets or social exclusion funds) to employ home–school liaison workers and other professionals such as youth and social workers, or counsellors, who work within EAZs or EiC areas with students and families who are at risk of failure.

For families with English as a second language or, for example, for refugee families, family learning schemes can make the breakthrough to social as well as school inclusion. But family learning can embrace all aspects of the curriculum. One of the most successful and comprehensive case studies of successful family learning across the curriculum is that in West Walton School, Norfolk – as the following account shows.

EXTRA

West Walton Primary School

West Walton Primary School, Norfolk, is a very ordinary rural school bursting at the seams with 210 pupils aged aged 4–11 years. On entry into school however, over 70 per cent of pupils fall well below national standards in the Bury Infant test, a reflection of the lack of pre-school provision in the village. Very few parents have had access to higher education, indeed, many left school at the earliest opportunity, some feeling that education had failed them or that it had no value for them. In response, and working closely with Education Extra, the school began to build on its open-door policy, gradually bringing in increasing numbers of parents to learn alongside their children and school staff, in an ever-widening range of after-school activities.

The project manager, Maggie Barwell, aims to make the school a more welcoming place where parents and pupils know that they are a valued part of the school community. She wants to encourage parents to recognise their own strengths so that they will value the contribution they can make to their child's learning and to enrich the curriculum. For an hour after school every Tuesday, Wednesday and Thursday, the school is heaving with families full of purpose and optimism; children, parents and staff working to discover new strengths and to achieve success together. Staff often attend clubs as participants and this has been a great leveller. Activities include family French, family band, making maths games, computer club, maypole dancing and pre-school music for babies.

The partnership has moved forward. Next term a parent will run an art club, a grandfather with his grandson will staff a chess club and a deaf mother and her signing daughter will work with a teacher to run a signing choir. The pupil–parent partnership has launched its first publication, the *Partnership News*, a historical record of the achievements of parents and their children, and first time that parents and pupils have genuinely had a voice.

Special needs children have benefited alongside their peers, often finding something they can excel at; perhaps sport, music or a foreign language. Disaffected parents have found that sense of identity and self-worth, at last achieving that feeling of belonging which had always eluded them.

There is clear evidence that the family learning project has been effective in enabling parents to develop new skills and to be receptive to the notion of being learners themselves. Family learning is now embedded in the culture of the school, a reflection of the strength of parental commitment to it.

The project has created a strong sense of community, mutual respect and understanding flourishes where before there might have been disparity and mistrust. The school is a place of warmth and camaraderie, where everyone feels safe and valued as a learner.

In January, the school opens its arms to its community, embracing teenagers and adults as well as children as learners. Working with other agencies, the school hopes to improve employment options for the community by offering qualification routes for the workplace. The school will be training five parents as learning support assistants, providing in-house training as well as supporting their professional development through the GNVQ process. A parenting course will be offered to prospective reception child parents; they will be invited to attend a six-week course with their children to explore issues such as supporting the reception child and enriching the school curriculum.

This project has attracted considerable national and international interest, perhaps because it has found a comfortable juxtaposition between maintaining the professionalism of staff while enabling parents and readily acknowledging the contribution the family can make.

> Pupils say: I never thought I'd be able to play in a band. Now I can read the score, help my friends and manage to play my own part too.
>
> Parents say: What I like most about our club is the way things evolve: we have all been surprised at how we've improved and how much we've achieved.
>
> Teachers say: The family choir has given our pupils a great sense of achievement; the repertoire is much more advanced than anything we could undertake at our own school, but we have had terrific support and the welcome couldn't have been warmer. (Teacher, catchment area school)

Another unusual example of how family learning opportunities can meet community needs is given in the following case study of a rural area in Wales.

EXTRA

Ysgol y Berwyn

The small Gwynedd town of Bala, situated at the southern extremities of Snowdonia, is proud of its rich Welsh heritage and culture. The local secondary school, Ysgol y Berwyn, is an 11–18 predominantly Welsh-speaking co-educational school. It serves a low-economy area, where 90 per cent of the 460 pupils come from a home background served by agriculture and its related industries.

The economy of the community is also reflected in the curriculum through NVQ agricultural studies and construction courses. Both make well-established use of local contractors and farms. These courses are offered to pupils intending to find employment locally. More recently, the school became aware that poor administrative skills were resulting in local farmers not getting grant aid to which they were entitled. After consulting with the two farming unions and the local agricultural college, the response has been twofold. Firstly, a basic ICT evening adult education course has been offered to the local farming community. Secondly and concurrently, parents and pupils are encouraged to jointly attend a Welsh medium ICT course in farm administration. Fifteen families have signed up for the course.

In addition, until the interruption of the lambing season, the school's agricultural department has been running a Sunday morning sheepdog handling course for pupils and parents, with some of the latter being both learners and helpers. This culminated in the participants planning and staging their own sheepdog trial, which attracted an entry of almost 70 handlers and their dogs, from across North Wales – Bala already hosts the largest sheepdog trials in North Wales. Next year, in addition to establishing the school's sheepdog trials as an annual event, it is also proposed to get the pupils and parents playing an active role in planning and staging the town's major event.

Finally, the school, which has its own small farm in its grounds, with a flock that averages around 30 sheep, has set up additional programmes out of school to help develop a range of skills. They include:

- sheep shearing (both hand and mechanical) at a local 'partner' farm;
- a 'lambing care' programme – the school's flock of sheep is sent out to 'partner farms' to ensure 24-hour supervision;
- rearing and preparing sheep for auction at local markets – this includes participation in 'the sales';
- grooming a small number of the flock's 'black sheep' for a series of 'country shows' held during the summer holidays.

This programme demonstrates the purpose of education to those pupils who might not aspire to academic careers that take them away from Bala. It also brings the school, parents and community together to work for the long-term benefit of all concerned.

A £3,000 award from Education Extra has helped to contribute to some of the above initiatives.

AFTER-SCHOOL CHILDCARE AND STUDENT CARE

Extra-curricular activities develop the whole child and make the school seem and feel like a family. (Val Weddel-Hart, headteacher, Franche First School)

Encouraging family support for learning, and providing a welcoming environment for all children through out of school hours activities, is an excellent foundation for building up social confidence and self-efficacy. In recent years, however, one of the most significant changes in public policy has been the importance attached to providing not only pre-school care for children, but also after-school play, care and learning provision for school-age children. The three elements are intimately connected. The provision of play itself as a way of enabling children 'to learn and develop as individuals and as members of the community' cannot be overestimated.

For some years there has been growing concern in the UK not only about the poverty of play opportunities in the general environment and the community, but about preserving children's freedom to play – in the face of competing demands on the child. Without a good range of play opportunities children 'may lose the chance to develop their emotional intelligence, independence, self-esteem and self confidence' and the ability to see tasks through to completion as well as to discover their latent talents. At the same time, play is a major route to learning by providing an opportunity 'to review and absorb and to give personal meaning to what they learn in formal educational settings'.[9]

At the same time, the balance of life and work has changed radically for many families over the past two decades. The difficulty of being there when children come home from school, the loss of safe public spaces for children to meet and play together, without adult interference, and the erosion of the extended family have all conspired to add to the potential social isolation if not exclusion of children. There is, therefore, both a need to expand play opportunities and provision, *per se*, and to provide for play and care for a far greater number of children in principle. While there still needs to be a national strategy for play, there is a National Childcare Strategy in place, implemented by early years development plans in each LEA, which has given a much higher priority to after-school childcare.

The purpose of after-school childcare clubs, whether in school or not, is to provide a high-quality caring environment for pupils aged 5–14. The vast majority of clubs provide for children aged 5–11, and aim to provide an appropriate mixture of play, care and learning. The school featured below has run an outstanding model scheme for many years.

[9] See *Best Play*: partnership publication by NPFA, PLAYLINK and the Children's Play Council

---
EXTRA

Franche First School

Franche First School is a large urban co-educational community first school catering for 487 children aged 3–9. It was opened in 1967 and is situated on the north-west edge of Kidderminster. The school employs over 90 staff working in a broad variety of capacities across the school, both full-time and part-time.

The aims of the school are to educate and develop the children to the very best level of their ability and enable them to achieve their full potential by creating exciting opportunities from within and outside the curriculum.

In 1993 the school launched the pioneering Franche 726 scheme, offering child/playcare facilities and lifelong learning projects for children, parents and members of the community. The school uses its minibuses to transport children to the scheme from 14 schools across the Wyre Forest district. This enables the school to be fully utilised from 7 am to 6 pm for 50 weeks of the year. In order to further support parents of children in the school nursery, an innovative project entitled Wraparound was initiated in September 1999; this provides complementary daytime childcare for children in the 3–5 age range. The school has also recently set up a very popular parent and toddler group.

Franche 726 is proud of its very wide range of term-time and holiday activities, which are planned to stimulate and encourage the children in their creative, artistic and athletic development. In addition to the usual programmes of football, basketball, nature treks, swimming and craftwork, recent activity schedules have also included juggling and clowning work-shops, kite-making, pantomime trips, pond-dipping and the re-creation of Roman costumes and a feast!

The school strongly believes in the values of extra-curricular activities for all pupils. All clubs are free of charge. Children have the opportunity to further their interests and skills in familiar and new activities, which in turn can develop and improve the children's motivation, raising self-esteem at school and beyond. The school has an inclusive policy and is committed to integrating children with special needs into after-school activities.

Franche First School works hard to forge links with both individuals and businesses from the local community. Initiatives including a textile project have enabled children to work alongside parents, managers, governors, and various skilled people. Franche First School places great emphasis on the importance of good home–school links. Many volunteers come into school to support learning and enhance the children's curriculum experience. This includes active involvement in the Better Reading Scheme and the SHARE Project. More recently, the school has become a centre for lifelong learning, promoting computer links for adults.

While providing after-school clubs for primary school children within a care setting is relatively easy, given the willingness of so many primary schools to host schemes, providing for secondary-aged children who have a continuing need for some structure and support after school is more problematic. The transition experience can be particularly difficult for many who have become used to attending after-school clubs in their primary schools and feel the loss of dedicated support very disconcerting. They are, however, not the only clients for extra care. Many young teenagers in Years 7 and 8 of secondary school have few choices after school but to return to an empty home or hang about the streets. Although resistant to any notions of care and resentful of any attempts to patronise them, these young people can be particularly vulnerable to different types of risk, whether that comes from peer pressure or social neglect. Moreover, their needs cannot be entirely met by activity programmes alone which may last for an hour, and then only on one or two nights a week.

Children over the age of 11 need a form of care appropriate to their maturity, as has now been recognised by the National Childcare Strategy, but providing extra pastoral help for this age group is complex. However, in recent years a range of models has emerged which has attempted to combine raising motivation and achievement with a new form of guaranteed care for guaranteed hours and evenings per week which will satisfy the needs of parents in work, training or looking for work. A sum of £20 million was set aside from the NOF to create distinctive 'integrated care and learning' provision designed to:

- enthuse, motivate and support the learning of pupils;
- build their self-esteem and help them to reach higher standards of achievement;
- be linked to particular schools' overall provision and aims;
- request charges no more than necessary to cover the childcare element of the provision.

One successful early scheme, funded through the DfEE and facilitated by Education Extra, is that in Campion Boys High School in Liverpool, in a highly disadvantaged and very challenging area.

EXTRA

Campion Boys High School

The student care scheme provides a range of activities every day with guaranteed pastoral support after school up to 5.30 pm and a breakfast club which runs from 8 am.

Students are consulted about what type of activities they would like to do and the current programme includes golf, electronics, a pet club, toymaking, art, computers and support for homework.

Attendance is good, and the reasons the students give for being involved are to;

- try new activities;
- get help with school work;

- be with friends;
- keep out of trouble;
- do something interesting;
- avoid going home to an empty house;
- avoid hanging around the streets.

There is no charge for the scheme as the school has managed to draw in additional sources of funding (eg from the SRB/Europe). School staff are convinced that the scheme is helping their drive to raise achievement by giving students confidence and improving their self-esteem and motivation. Parents and students fully endorse that. The scheme has recently obtained additional funding from NOF to extend its work.

The Integrated model has now been extended through NOF funding to other schools and other areas. For other examples, see Chapter 8.

PROMOTING INCLUSION

The Student Care schemes represent one relatively novel way to ensure that students in Years 7 and 8 who have just transferred from primary to secondary schools are included in the life of the school successfully. However, there are larger issues. First, as Mog Ball, argues, children in middle childhood have less well developed sources of support than younger and older children, and suggests that 'some supervision is likely to be required but the development of personal interests and skills should give the child a chance to pursue his or her own interests'.[10]

Second, transitional stages of education, no matter at what age they occur, often leave young people feeling confused and vulnerable.[11] It is only

[10] 'Research by educational psychologists in the United States suggests that help at this age is most effective when part of a network that includes peers, pets, parents, hobbies and environmental sources of support. . . Organisations that allow the child to experience autonomy and to master the content of an activity are most appropriate and work better than formal organisations and structured activities.' Ball, M (1998) *School Inclusion: The school, the family and the community*, Joseph Rowntree Foundation, p 21

[11] The DfEE has already responded to the seriousness of the issues raised by transition. The DfEE report 131 *Impact of School Transitions and Transfers on Pupil Progress and Attainment* looked at existing research from UK/the United States, approached schools, LEAs, Ofsted and QCA and concluded that the following three issues are key: giving attention to pupils' accounts of why they disengage or underperform at these critical moments (transfers and transitions); recognising when and how different groups of pupils become 'at risk'; and achieving a better balance between academic and social concerns at various points of transition and transfer.

The report also states that radical approaches are needed which give attention to discontinuities in teaching approaches. Research is still therefore required into gaps in existing knowledge around these areas – for example, to focus on the impact of the strategies on the progress of pupils identified as most at risk. Better baseline information against which various LEA/school-based initiatives can be evaluated will also make for the easier identification of successful strategies.

recently, for example, that research and professional experience have paid particular attention to the often traumatic nature of the transfer to secondary school, and the regression in learning which can follow. As one teacher has observed, having run summer schools for three years running: 'The summer holiday can be quite a long time – it's six and a half weeks for our pupils. . . when they come back to school in September it takes them quite a long time to get back into the habit of learning and to remember a lot of what they learnt the previous year. If they spend some time doing educational activities, not necessarily the same as school, it means they make much faster progress in September.'[12] But there is also a major role for transitional schemes of OSHL across term-time as a way of introducing young people, barely teenagers, to adults and mentors, leisure activities, and learning support. Among the many different transitional initiatives now being developed, the example below is particularly positive. (Other aspects of partnership are explored in Chapter 8).

As pupils mature, the question – What next? – becomes a total pre-occupation for families, students and schools alike. The year 2000 will be remembered not least for the passionate and unresolved debate about what sort of students can expect to be admitted to Oxbridge – and why. For many students the choice is more limited than it need be, and the transition from school to FE or HE or into work can be the most traumatic of all. Some schools have put initiatives in place to build up confidence and expectation of achievement at higher levels of education well in advance.

EXTRA

Little Flower Girls' School

Little Flower Girls' School in Northern Ireland has over 650 students, many of whom come from inner city working-class backgrounds with over 40 per cent of students receiving free school meals. Many of these students have already been 'failed' by a selective education system at the age of 11 and although many of their parents have high expectations of them, these parents often lack the necessary experience to encourage their children to go on to further and higher education. The school staff and parents work hard together to raise aspiration and confidence through a very broad curriculum and access to many extra-curricular activities.

A strong emphasis is put on sharing culture and experience with others in both cross-community and European activities. For students under 16 a wide range of activities is provided designed to raise pupils' self-esteem, for example, issue-based drama and contemporary dance, and to develop their creative thinking skills. In addition, there are outreach media workshops where they can learn and develop technical skills. One example of this is that the pupils are involved in making a video exploring local issues, which may include commentary from senior citizens, and could be used in a history class.

---

[12] Jane Dear, *Woodlands Echo*, 26 July 1999

For pupils over the age of 16, there is the TRAIL project (Transition to Adulthood, Independent and Lifelong Learning) which aims, first, to raise students' aspirations (widening their access to university, offering careers information, building bridges across community divide via residentials with a European dimension). Second, it aims to improve communication skills, through all forms of ICT – including e-mail and videoconferencing, developing the necessary key skills, and undertaking the international enterprise challenge with post-16 students in the United States). Third, it focuses on citizenship – helping others in the community, supporting environmental work, and promoting health and well-being through sport and healthy eating.

Staff and students observe that the TRAIL programme has helped students to value education, to think about future and lifelong learning, to take stock and develop their skills for work and how they can use them, and learn how to become full and active members of society. Overall, the school is also confident that disaffection among young people in the community will be reduced, and that students can become a successful role model for others and an agent of change in their own community.

MAKING FRIENDS WITH SCHOOL AND IN SCHOOL

If transition at different ages is a common experience, other transitions or transfers are specific to individuals or particular groups of children. Failure in school often stems from feeling of being left out, feeling different, or feeling friendless, a feeling which can be reproduced and indeed reinforced in later life. OSHL activities, at their most basic level, can offer all young people a short-circuit into social activities and friendships which can be crucial. Some children move schools frequently, whether they are from Service families, clergy families, travellers' families, or refugee families, and children have to adjust and readjust to new friends, new neighbourhoods and new cultures. For other children, coming back into school after a period of illness or disability, after caring for members of their own family, from care homes or foster homes[13] or after a period of exclusion or truancy, is even more problematic. Low expectations, frequent moves, and inadequate information passed on to schools can contribute to individual failure, despite high levels of ability. Children with limited experience are less likely to bond easily and less likely to share common experiences. These instances present the difficulty that since the children concerned will inevitably be in a minority, they may feel isolated and therefore possibly resentful and

[13] DoH/DfEE guidance seeks to address the key problems faced by looked-after young people, but the provision of OSHL programmes during term time and in the holidays can provide a place where they can mix more easily with other pupils and show what they can do. Looked-after children are particularly isolated, suggests evidence gathered on access to reading and books by the Who Cares Trust and the Paul Hamlyn Foundation (*The Right to Read*, 2001)

even disaffected – or they may opt to suffer in silence. Whether the task is preventing a drift to the margins of school life, or promoting reintegration, OSHL offers the opportunity to build up experiences and to share them with potential friends.

Although figures are unreliable, it is estimated that there are about 16,000 carers between the ages of 16 and 17 who are still in school. The example given below shows how one partnership project, involving two schools and the Swale Young Carers group, is aiming to support young carers by helping them to catch up with their school work and reintegrating them into school.

EXTRA

Swale Young Carers

The Swale Young Carers project, working with Fulston Manor School and Minister College and funded through the DfEE Voluntary Partners project, is based on the Isle of Sheppey, Kent, and is providing dedicated homework clubs for young carers at the schools. Many of these children are caring for family members such as parents or siblings with long-term illness, disability, mental ill health or an addiction to drugs or alcohol. Many have fallen behind with their school work. The homework clubs are seen as a means to identify hidden young carers within the school and also to help raise awareness of the needs of this particular group among staff and pupils. The clubs run for an hour each week in the school libraries, and provide a place of study and specific support for individual carers that may not always be available at home. A worker at Swale Young Carers provides a tutor from within each school and the school librarian supports the students. The group's main asset is the commitment of the parties concerned to supporting young carers.

Besides supporting the educational needs of the young carers, the group also invites young carers to seek support, information and advice from the support workers. The group also allows young carers the opportunity to share their experiences with other young people in similar situations, reducing the feelings of isolation commonly felt. The project's ethos is to encourage young carers to support each other.

As part of the project, a link person (from within pastoral support) exists in each school. The link persons play an important role in supporting project workers and are there to help deal with issues that could arise; for example, concerns over the welfare of a students attending the club. Issues of welfare and protection are of great importance and the project needs someone with knowledge of these issues involved.

The project aims over the next couple of years to encourage other schools in the area to develop similar groups for young carers within their schools.

Other students are traumatised in ways which present a particular challenge to the host school. In particular, refugee children bring with them family histories of loss, torture, death and displacement. Providing opportunities to play together, to learn a new language, to share skills and sorrows, to make new friends, can be critical to successful integration into school and the community as well as to reducing fear and trauma. Here, there is, in particular, an indispensable role for voluntary OSHL activities. The case study below shows how mentoring schemes can play a highly successful role in developing skills and confidence while helping the school to meet its own objective of raising literacy levels across the school.

EXTRA

North Westminster Community School

Since 1998, a paired reading scheme has been in place at Marylebone Lower House at North Westminster Community School. The school has a high percentage of students with English as a second language (ESL) and over half are eligible for free school meals.

The scheme matches a competent reader with a developing reader. Both parties sign a contract stating that they will turn up on time and commit themselves at least to a half-term in the first instance. In 2000, around 12 pupils from Years 7, 8 and 9 have taken part. The scheme works successfully by targeting the more competent readers from Year 9 who are encouraged to take part, both for their own professional development and to help those new to English. Many are very committed and have grown in confidence from the responsibility that comes with participation in the scheme. The younger mentees have also grown in confidence and significantly improved reading ability has been noted by teachers back in the classroom. These children benefit from the small group environment, a personal approach, the positive attitude and support of teachers and peers and from seeing tangible improvement in their work, which in turn raises their self-esteem. Both mentors and mentees receive certificates and credits for their participation. The level of commitment has been high with some outstanding pupils revelling in the extra responsibility.

Initially, the scheme operated as a breakfast club (which the school hopes to restore soon) but has since run in the lunch hour on two days a week. On club days, such students receive a lunch pass so they can have lunch first and then come to the club. The students who are helping the readers receive a short training course which covers ideas on how they can help their partners access the texts, using pictures, non-verbal clues, prediction, and so on. At the end of each session, the reader and partner complete a form which provides a running record of their work.

SPECIAL NEEDS AND SPECIAL NETWORKS

Friendships between students in special schools and 'ordinary' schools are difficult to establish given the few chances there are for meeting together on an equal basis and enjoying similar interests and activities. In recent years, both special schools and maintained schools have found that holiday schemes offer an excellent opportunity to break down some of the physical and emotional barriers.

EXTRA

Chesnut Lodge School

The summer literacy scheme in Chesnut Lodge School, in Halston, Cheshire (referred to in Chapter 1), achieved remarkable success in its summer literacy programmes. In 1998 the school set up a summer literacy scheme which involved 12 low-achieving pupils from a mainstream primary school with problems of attendance and low self-esteem, and 12 pupils from Chesnut Lodge with a wide range of physical and some learning disabilities. The special school provided the staffing. The project focused around the Castle on the Hill at Halston, and pupils produced a fantasy story in the form of a 'Big Book' using different technologies (the Internet, fax, e-mail, etc), and the resources of the Widness Library. A local theatre company worked with pupils to develop drama and story themes.

Attendance was 100 per cent and the two groups of students learnt a great deal about each other. Both schools reported that improvements in confidence and literacy were much in evidence and the special school noted that 'This has been a example of integration at its best, using our excellent facilities. We have seen vast improvements in our own pupils.'[14]

Other models of inclusion draw particular benefit from school partnerships that provide opportunities for pupils of varying abilities to enjoy themselves together.

EXTRA

Fiveways Special School and partners

Fiveways Inclusive Summer Educational Programme Opportunity in Somerset aims to provide two weeks of summer education for socially excluded disabled and non-disabled young people, in a safe, inclusive and accessible learning environment, to have fun and learn together.

The scheme is a partnership between Fiveways Special School, mainstream local primary schools and a local secondary school. The scheme was supported by Barnado's Somerset Inclusion project and the charity's initial involvement was designed to enable the local community to appreciate the benefits of inclusive education and social experiences. The schools jointly ran a week for young people aged 5–11 and a week for young people aged 12–19. This enabled them to differentiate the programme to meet the needs and age appropriateness of each group. The programme included

---

[14] Education Extra (1999) *Study Support in Special Schools: Good practice in special circumstances*

an animation workshop, sports, play, and workshops in percussion and drumming. Significantly, this was one of the first opportunities that the disabled young people, who accessed this provision, had had to learn and have fun alongside their non-disabled peers and vice versa.

The programme was able to offer flexibility and all young people attending had the opportunity to access all that was on offer if they chose to.

Benefits and outcomes were very positive. Over the two weeks, 19 disabled and 60 non-disabled young people accessed the programme. The older students who participated in the first week volunteered to attend the second week as peer educators and enablers – a reflection on the level of enjoyment and learning together that took place during the first week. The special school involved has now become the driving force behind a similarly inclusive summer education programme for next year. The community has taken this project on and is moving forward with plans to run it again.

SELF-EXCLUSION: REDUCING THE BARRIERS

For some vulnerable pupils, liable to exclude themselves, positive strategies must be planned and organised if they are to succeed in school – none more so than those designed to attract and motivate boys. The statistics for OSHL show that, at all three key stages, according to the 1998 NFER survey, more girls than boys participate in after-school activities; that there are more boys than girls in football and computer clubs; and more girls than boys in arts-based activities.[15] OSHL activities can, if planned, not only draw in the reluctant boys, but also break down stereotypical choices. Over the years, for example, Education Extra has funded girls' football and rugby clubs, girls' science and computer clubs, and boys' chefs clubs. Some clubs in kickboxing and martial arts, at Falmer School, for example, have proved that they can attract more girls than boys. At the same time, however, single-sex clubs can attack some of the more stubborn issues in an innovative way.

As Chapter 6 suggested, one of the major challenges is also to provide something irresistible to those students who are at either end of the continuum of achievement – for example to confront in a different way the failure of boys to match the performance of girls. At a deeper level is the challenge that all schools face of motivating adolescent boys for whom the praise of the teacher for work well done is no match for the silent applause of the peer group for distracting and provocative behaviour. The following case studies show how two highly successful schools decided to approach the task, not just by providing for the special interests of boys, but by creating selective schemes to draw out the personal and social skills of male students.

[15] DfEE/NFER (July 1999) *Out of School Learning Activities*, RR 127, p 27

┌─ EXTRA ──┐

Thomas Tallis School

Thomas Tallis School, LB Greenwich, has made a particular effort to involve boys in a variety of specific activities. The school feels that the great range of clubs enables many children to further their interests beyond the National Curriculum. Some, such as reading and handwriting clubs, aim to encourage those less confident in literacy and the numeracy club targets those who need extra input to enable them to cope with the demands of KS3 maths. Others, such as the Connect Only club for Year 8 gifted and talented pupils encourage pupils to make connections in their learning through using the many different sources, for example ICT and reference books.

The school also offers many clubs for Year 7 pupils. In addition, there is also a Year 9–10 boys group, a homework group for KS3 and 4, a newspaper club for Year 8. There are plans to set up further activities through NOF, EiC and Gifted and Talented initiatives. Many clubs are aimed at male students who may be disaffected and underachieving. It was decided that Year 9 was a good time to start since some boys' attitude towards school and learning become negative leading to poor attendance, behaviour problems and underachievement. The scheme uses small group work and team-building exercises to establish a more positive, cooperative ethos among the group.

The newspaper club involves a small group of keen Year 8 boys who have already interviewed new teachers and produced an article for the school newsletter. There is a feeling that gradually the culture in the school is changing with larger numbers of children happy to extend their school day by attending clubs and eager to try out new things and develop new skills. This has raised the confidence of the pupils, which has had a positive effect on their learning and relationships.

└──┘

Another very similar school, identified in 2000 through its GCSE results as the fourth most improved school in England, was Nidderdale School in Harrogate, which set up a specific study support project aiming to increase levels of achievement among boys (the TACKLE project).

┌─ EXTRA ──┐

The Nidderdale School

In 1999, the school set up a working party to look at the gender difference in attainment at the school (which was considerably higher than at any other school in the LEA), and decided to improve the culture of learning among students who were also disadvantaged by rural isolation. The school decided to establish shared objectives and to build a team approach 'giving confidence to teachers to approach business people and people in the community so that they would cross the divide and come into school. Teachers needed to "let go". They did and the benefits have been remarkable.'

The SENCO, working with colleagues and advisers, led a team of boys on a *Changing Rooms* project aimed at creating a suitable environment for study

└──┘

support activities after school. The boys solicited the support of local business which donated fabric for giant cushions and curtains and a 'gloomy classroom' was transformed into a vivid and welcoming study support area. Education Extra and other organisations also contributed funds and support. The boys committed themselves to using the study support area. 'Well over half of all Year 11 students now take part in classes to support GCSEs. Of course, it's not all just about exams. We've extended other provision too – for example, the popular outdoor activity programme which includes wind-surfing is now open to everyone.'

The deputy headteacher observes:

> Our plans seem to have worked. In 1999 the boys' performance improved by 12 per cent with 50 per cent gaining 5 or more A–C grades. This improvement is well above the national average. In 2000, the performance of boys improved again, almost matching that of girls. No boy left the school with fewer than 5 GCSE pass grades. . . The self-esteem of young people involved in TACKLE has increased and evidence of the improved achievement culture within school comes from listening to the conversations of students. Building on these foundations we are ready to move on. A coordinator of basic skills has been appointed and we will be extending support beyond 16. The school also has plans to build on its links with the local business community.

Having appreciated the value of out of hours learning, the school's pro-gramme of staffed after-school sessions continues to increase. The school has also been lucky to take advantage of new ICT facilities.[16]

One of the most negative and depressing features of school life, which may drive pupils to avoid or fear school, is bullying. Most schools have an anti-bullying strategy, often worked out with or by the Schools Council. Apart from the benefit of being able to show excellence in sports or other high value activities, there is also time and scope after school for pupils to learn how to be more assertive and to develop their own personal self-help strategies, but also to learn how through support and mentoring, they can be supported by other pupils.

―― EXTRA ――――――――――――――――――

Canterbury High School

At Canterbury High School, after two Year 11 pupils had been victims of out of school hours bullying, an anti-bullying strategy was developed in 1998, using the school's peer mentoring work. This was extended to other pupils and a group of 12 interested Year 11 students were recruited for a residential course and trained to communicate with and support younger victims. Funding was obtained from the LEA and local sources. In turn, this was extended to a group of students from St Albans who were invited to share

[16] Education Extra (Spring 2000) *Extra Time,* p 6

expertise. The residential was held at The Swattenden Centre in Kent and was highly successful. The following year further training was provided by The Kent Safe Schools Initiative and ongoing support is provided by the school-based counsellor. In the past two years this group has been instrumental in helping approximately 60 students.

A new group of Year 12 students have been identified who will, this term, be working in tandem with the original group. By the end of this term the original group will 'drop out' of the scheme, leaving the new group to carry on.

Besides the peer mentoring, the school has a number of out of hours activities running including a breakfast club and summer school aimed to improve literacy skills of new Year 7 students.

In a very different setting, Kingsmeadow School in Gateshead has found a similar solution.

┌─ EXTRA

Kingsmeadow School

Kingsmeadow School was helped by Education Extra in 2000 to develop an area in the school, accessible each lunchtime, for vulnerable pupil to receive help, support and guidance from other pupils. The school felt that there were certain groups, particularly girls and younger pupils, who needed to be able to take refuge and receive some structured support. The project, staffed by pupil counsellors who have been working with educational psychologists, is designed to offer support and guidance, and an opportunity to be involved in promoting the positive aspects of school. Education Extra helped the school to buy videos on bullying and study skills and provided resources for structured activities during the lunchtime. The facility will, it is hoped, also enable students to develop literacy and communication skills and ICT skills and foster liaison between junior school pupils and secondary pupils.

The pupils who take part are proud to do so. 'It is a really good scheme that can help children who are being bullied at school. . . it helps us to work with people. . . The scheme aims to help people who need help. And it is good for us as it helps us to learn more.'

PROMOTING SCHOOL INCLUSION; PREVENTING EXCLUSION

Excluded from school

No one knows exactly how many children are out of school at any one time because of truancy or exclusion. But each year, at least 1 million children truant and over 100,000 are excluded temporarily. Some 13,000 are excluded permanently. . . There has not been enough work on prevention, particularly through work with families. . . Research shows that where young people have clear and high expectations, trusting relationships with adult role models, participation in out of school activities and in family life, a mentor, and where they have recognition and praise, they thrive.[17]

For some pupils any support available within the school comes too late and is insufficient. School exclusions vary enormously in cause, frequency and duration from school to school. What is consistent, however, is the documented link between exclusion, delinquency and criminality. Young people not attending school are more than three times as likely to offend than those attending school and excluded children commit up to 50 per cent more offences in the year after exclusion than in the year leading up to it.[18] While recent figures for exclusion show a decline, numbers of exclusions increased from 3,830 to 12,300 between 1991–92 and 1997–98. The figures also show a persistent pattern; black pupils are three and a half times more likely than their white peers to be excluded[19] and boys are more likely to be excluded than girls; children with special needs are likely to be more excluded than others.

In summary, as the national charity INCLUDE puts it: 'Research shows that young people out of school experience multiple and complex problems, whose combined effect is to drive them further away from mainstream society. They are more likely to become involved in crime, more likely to need social care, more likely to be unemployed or homeless.' INCLUDE is the largest single provider of services for excluded young people, working with up to 1,000 young people each year in 29 local authorities across England and Wales on a variety of projects designed to develop alternative routes back into education, work and training for older pupils, and preventative and reintegration projects for younger pupils. A companion charity, DIVERT, works with excluded pupils across the UK and is recognised as a leader in introducing mentoring to support, guide and provide positive role models for excluded pupils.[20] Recent research suggests that reintegration rates are rising slightly, but the consensus is that excluded young people still spend too long out of school in inadequate provision; that multi-agency work, although still underdeveloped, holds the promise of more success; and that preventative strategies, 'can resolve problems before exclusion occurs'.[21]

---

[17] School Exclusion Unit (1998) *Truancy and school exclusion*
[18] Audit Commission Report (1996) *Misspent Youth*. Quoted in DIVERT, Annual Report, 1999–2000
[19] From INCLUDE Annual Report, 1999
[20] See DIVERT Annual report, 1999–2000
[21] Parsons, C and Howlett, K (February 2000) *Investigating the Reintegration of Permanently Excluded Young People in England*, INCLUDE

Another major national charity, Crime Concern, which has grown dramatically in recent years, has also developed a range of programmes which emphasises the need for community action to create safer communities, and which enlists the help of many young people in doing so. Providing alternative activities is seen as playing a key role in reducing inner city crime in particular.

It would be simplistic to argue that OSHL activities can make all the difference to preventing school exclusion or reintegrating excluded young people into school. But the evidence of the impact of successful participation outside school hours on activities which can raise self-efficacy[22] and the inclusive nature of the offer, suggests that providing OSHL activities should be part of whole school and whole community strategies for re-inclusion at all levels of school. One way of keeping pupils in touch with the school might be to continue to involve them in OSHL activities in preparation for a return to school. One recent initiative shows how music can offer a bridge back into school for non-attenders.

EXTRA

Community Music East

Since 1998, Community Music East (CME) has run a music programme within the Kerrison Back-to-School Project which offers school non-attenders a way back into the educational system. The young people visit Kerrison and participate in a wide range of activities from IT and crafts to sport and music. CME's music programme provides opportunities for young people to participate in music by learning to write, play and record original popular music. The aim is for participants to develop abilities, self-confidence, knowledge and experience which will encourage them to interact with others and assist them in the future. Staff and external observers have seen that the collaborative group work helps students 'lose the feeling of being exposed and failing' that they had often experienced at school and that the processes of making music helps them to socialise and orient themselves towards the future. The students revealed the benefits they saw to themselves in self-evaluations: 'We became a lot closer when we had to talk and discuss what we do.'[23]

The importance of a holistic approach has also been picked up in a recent Home Office study to prevent young people turning to crime: 'Communities are advised to adopt a strategic approach, combining "early years" initiatives with schools effectiveness programmes and mixing family support services with constructive pursuits for young people.'[24]

---

[22] See the research evidence cited in Chapter 2

[23] Case study quoted in CEDC Network 20 (2) May 2000

[24] Utting, D (1996) *Reducing Criminality Among Young People*, Home Office Research Study, No 161

A harder set of issues are those which cluster around what Michael Barber described as the 'disaffected, disruptive and disappeared'. Breaking this continuum within schools is a crucial contribution to reducing social disaffection and social exclusion itself. The term 'social exclusion' raises a wealth of complex and pejorative issues. At its most acute, social exclusion in practical terms describes the predicament of young people and adults in communities which are devastated by unemployment and poverty, prey to high crime rates and drug cultures, and marked by the poorest housing and public services. These are communities where neither families nor children feel that they have much of a future let alone a stake in education. In such conditions, children can be at risk for many different reasons. They may already be known to the criminal justice system; they may be traumatised by abusive relationships; they may be homeless or in B&Bs; they may be growing up in families where drug or alcohol abuse is common. They may be at greater risk than similar children in other communities.

Schools may be the only secure or safe places in the lives of these children; indeed, it is sometimes only the school which stands between the child and a future of more of the same circumstances. By definition, the schools themselves tend to be those under the greatest pressure, show levels of pupil truancy and exclusion higher than the rest of the country, and levels of staff turnover and pupil achievement significantly lower. It is against this background that £800 million has been allocated to support neighbourhood regeneration through the New Deal for Communities, with the target of reducing truancy and school exclusion by one third by the year 2002.

Government strategies, amidst initiatives to deal with anti-social neighbours, youngsters roaming the streets late at night, and juvenile crime figures which show that the peak age for offending is 18 (with 30 per cent of all arrestees dependent on one or more drugs)[25] have also brought schools and their responsibility for dealing with the disaffected, the disruptive and the disappeared into the frame.

> There should be a full recognition of the protective role of schools and education in respect of individuals at risk of criminal involvement (or increased criminal involvement) and social exclusion. This recognition should encompass the provision of practical support and services which will keep young people who are at risk in school or within education and training full time up to the age of 16 at the minimum. [This] will need to include resources additional to that of the education service as it stands.[26]

[25] Government's *Crime Reduction Strategy*, p 9
[26] Ibid

This judgement reinforces the fact that the motivational force of out of school hours provision can offer positive opportunities to develop personal and social skills – rather than mere in-filling or safekeeping – which can help to allay later difficulties and disaffection.

One successful example of a preventative model is the National Pyramid Trust, begun in 1993 as a way of supporting 7–9-year-olds in primary schools who were already showing signs of difficulty. In 2000 18 local authorities were involved and between September 1999 and July 2000, 930 children attended after-school Pyramid clubs. The clubs – which have a maximum of 10 children and meet for 10 weeks, once a week after school – offer a safe space where children can be heard and have fun. The carefully selected pupils, identified by teachers, with the help of a multi-disciplinary team, are supported by trained club leaders (three per group) who help the children develop confidence, improve social skills and increase self-esteem. The clubs put a high emphasis on activities such as 'circle time' when they are valued and listened to, and can try new activities, working as a group, and develop new skills. The majority of club leaders are volunteers who bring a diversity of experiences; many are students from psychology, education or social work courses. Research and evaluation show that children who attend the Pyramid project tend to make greater progress than the control group, and that their improved social and emotional functioning gives them greater confidence and improved 'risk taking in academic areas'.[27]

However, there is an acid test for OSHL – to develop effective preventative strategies for young people at risk who are bored and inactive in school, disruptive in effect, but perhaps not so seriously that they will directly challenge authority and thus be excluded. They may, however, begin to accumulate penalty points which lead eventually to exclusion. Even in the primary school they have begun to build up a set of strategies for dealing with the intrusions of schooling upon their self-protecting existence.

Finding a way to raise motivation through special interest clubs is clearly one key to involvement – whether through football, motorbike maintenance, or music. In cases where the National Curriculum has failed to engage the interest of individuals or groups of pupils, after-school provision may tap the missing motivation: it provides opportunities to link new areas of learning to outside experience and interests without conceding any principles, or surrendering the substance; it offers opportunities to respond to young people's agendas and to stimulate them without a timetable-and-test regime intervening.

[27] NPT Annual Review 2000, p 12

EXTRA

Rhyl High School

A go-karting club at Rhyl High School in North Wales has helped to motivate a group of potentially disaffected Year 10 pupils who have been provided with an opportunity to be involved in an activity that offers technical expertise, close teamwork, new relationships, a sense of responsibility and helps prepare them for the world of work.

The group meets at lunchtime and after school and races the go-karts at weekends. Pupils have built and raced their own go-kart and have enlisted the support of two local firms to help with parts and with mechanical problems. Further funding from the (then) local TEC enabled them to build two more go-karts.

Initially, girls were reluctant to join in, but increasingly have done so. The teacher involved has noted that 'The group have gelled as a unit and [members] are prepared to help each other... they feel very proud as a group and highly protective of their go-kart'. Other staff have commented on the pupils' increased work rate, improvement in their self-esteem and their attitude towards curriculum subjects. At a recent race which the team took part in, their pupils managed to achieve three first places – 'a great start for the new team!' Finally, the school's whole profile has been raised in the process and other members of staff have become involved.

Another example of a special interest-led club started with the express intention of diverting boredom and building up self-esteem in a rural area with limited social or cultural opportunities, is at Hambridge Primary School.

EXTRA

Hambridge Primary School

In 1997, with funding from Education Extra, Hambridge Primary School in Somerset set up a fly-fishing club on the initiative of a (female) teacher. Starting from small beginnings, the club has gone on to increasing success, as the teacher responsible explains: 'Over the last four years Hambridge School's fly-fishing club has been extended with more children joining each year and moving through the school. Perhaps, the best indicator of the club's popularity and sustainability is that a weekly evening club has been set up for those pupils who have since left the primary school and gone on to secondary school.'

South West School's Fly-Fishing Competition is held every year in May. Hambridge School enters a team every year even though, as a primary, many of the pupils are half the age of the other competitors. In 1999, the Hambridge School team won the competition by beating many older teams. To make the win even more amazing the team was one member short due to illness. In 2000, the school came second, losing first place by two ounces. Two

---

members of this team decided to take part in the qualifying competition for a place in the England Youth Fly-Fishing Team. Although they did not succeed, it was only a trial run.

A further off-shoot of the club is that Sally Pizzi has helped organise four 'Have a Go' days for the Somerset branch of the Salmon and Trout Association, where youngsters from all over the county may try the sport of fly-fishing free of charge and learn about water safety, pond life and fishing knots. The rods have been used to teach the children's parents to fish so that they may take their own children fishing. Overall, the club is a great example of teacher and pupil enthusiasm enriching young people's experience and building up their self-esteem. In the process, the school has developed much stronger relationships with the community including the local fishing club and according to staff, 'it has been marvellous to see relationships forming between some of the members and the children. . .'

Secondary schools, too, are developing inclusive schemes for potentially disaffected pupils in very innovative ways – looking, in the following case, for example, to making provision outside the school.

Such is the nature of much after-school provision, however, that it is likely to have a social agenda, regardless of its overt focus. Family sports schemes may, for example, be about re-integrating small communities; a family literacy scheme may offer the opportunity for work on parenting skills; an arts scheme might provide its participants with opportunities to raise self-esteem as they discover their own talents and potential. Rosehearty Primary School shows how a family-based approach is working in Aberdeenshire, where the school is seeking to involve parents, community members and professionals, and building bridges between SEBD and mainstream work in improving the performance and behaviour of troubled children.

EXTRA

Rosehearty Primary School

In Rosehearty Primary School, children from the Fraserburgh area are referred to Rosehearty Springboard – an exciting new base located within the school – if they have not responded to strategies within their own school or to support at home. They and their families receive a coordinated package, including education, assessment and multi-agency intervention. Existing links between the agencies are exploited and strengthened. Links with the home are actively encouraged, and practical support offered to the families.

After-school activities at the school are already seen as a means of developing social competence, self-esteem and positive behaviour. Cooperative play, together with arts and crafts activities in a structured environment are encouraged, in an effort to boost motivation. It is intended to use after-school provision as an opportunity to foster cooperation between the pupils in the unit and those in the mainstream. This will be reinforced by the involvement of parents in the project.

The explicit aims of Rosehearty Springboard are:

- to provide a learning environment to enable pupils to make the most of their potential;
- to maintain the child's place within his or her peer group;
- to encourage a level of change in behaviour and adjustment which will encourage successful reintegration;
- to understand and support the emotional needs of the children and their families;
- to develop and promote good practice and positive behaviour strategies within the local educational network;
- to look towards the future with optimism and confidence and prepare to meet its challenges.

The unit is a key element in both the school's development plans, and the LEA's strategy. The programme which will run at lunchtimes (although there is also the hope of adding a breakfast-time element) will include sports and games, arts and crafts, and practical activities.

CONCLUSION

This chapter has examined the possibilities that OSHL hold for pupils who might be at risk for different reasons. Just as there is a potential progressive connection which leads from disaffection through disruption to disappearance, so in OSHL there is a spectrum which can lead from proactive strategies for involving young people and their families, to promotional strategies for school inclusion, and to preventative strategies. This chapter has looked at all three elements and at the different ways in which the obstacles placed in the way of young people belonging in school, and wanting to learn, can be reduced with the help of OSHL activities, dedicated teachers and other adults.

It is important, however, to be neither over-simplistic nor over-optimistic about what OSHL itself can do that schools are not doing in this respect. The link between school inclusion and social inclusion is complex. Indeed, it is only very recently that the connection between raising achievement and social inclusion itself has been formally examined in the work of the Social Exclusion Unit. Being successful at school does not guarantee a successful entry into adult society and does not prevent social exclusion, but it is the best start. Self-esteem, skills and successful relationships can passport young people to the next stage, whether that is education, training or work. By enabling pupils to become engaged, to include themselves in the life of the school, to deal with and confront, successfully and collectively, some of the aspects of school life which are most challenging, whether they involve is peer pressure or the individual bully, it gives the young person a positive experience on which to build. Apart from the external success which examination results can bring, being articulate, able to show confidence, aspirations, and achievements – whether they are in sports, in helping others to overcome their problems, or in GCSE grades – brings an expectation of being included in what society has to offer as well. In this respect, reflecting the range of individual achievements and the full contribution to school life which is made by so many pupils in Pupil Records of Achievement and portfolios, is vitally important.

The obverse, as the figures for offending rates among pupils excluded from school show, is only too clear. And the range of initiatives which are already in place reflect how seriously this problem is now being taken by voluntary and statutory agencies. The case studies in this chapter are a partial reflection of the vast range of work and initiatives that are going on inside and outside schools to confront these very complex and urgent matters. The chapter started by examining how by supporting and involving the family the school creates the most powerful lobby group, capable of helping the student to develop and stay motivated; it looked at the ways in which young people at different stages of development, and at different exit and entrance points to education, might never make a successful entry or re-entry, and how OSHL can act as the passport back into school life; at the ways in which young people exclude themselves for different reasons; and how OSHL can provide an acceptable way to be involved. All these are proactive strategies. Moving towards preventative strategies, the chapter examined a selection of initiatives which are targeted at groups of young people who, through disaffection, might move on to the next stage – and become disruptive, and eventually, disappear from school altogether. Finally, it looked at some of the issues around those young people for whom school has appeared to fail and who have become excluded, and it asked the question whether OSHL can act as a bridge back into learning – whether at school or at a later stage.

Broadening the theme, OSHL can give all schools and all pupils a second chance at getting this right – because, critically, it is about:

- valuing young people for what they are good at;
- taking responsibility for each other;
- developing the personal and social skills as well as technical or academic skills;
- valuing the support of families.

What has also emerged in this chapter is the essential role of partnership. Again, starting with the family, this chapter has also shown, by implication, something of the range of personal commitment, support and partnership which has gone into the making of successful OSHL programmes. The next chapter follows this theme by focusing on the people and the partners that make it possible.

8

People and partnerships for OSHL

This chapter looks at the range of partnerships which can help schools to develop the capacity for expanding and improving their provision for OSHL. Possible partners include:

- local authorities and school staff;
- parents, volunteers and experts;
- voluntary partners, for example, from the arts and sports;
- mentors drawn, for example, from education and business;
- learning partners such as libraries and youth services;
- practical partnerships with business.

WHAT PARTNERS CAN BRING

Previous chapters have explored the ways in which study support in school can provide the extension, enrichment and enabling activities which help students to raise and realise their aspirations. Many of the case studies and the issues covered have involved elements of partnership as a logical way forward to achieving the schools' objectives. This chapter looks at a final, but perhaps the newest and most exciting area of development – the partners who can help the schools and students to make that work, and the people and partners who are crucial both to building and, above all, to sustaining the capacity and confidence of the school in this role. Given the wealth of developments in this area, and the significance now attached to partnership for education as a whole, the choice of case studies cannot be comprehensive, but aims to be illustrative of some of the most innovative forms of partnership in place or in development.

Of all the areas of school life, OSHL is one where partnership can flourish well. Whether the potential partner is a business, a library or a parent group, working with the school, coming into school outside school hours can be more comfortable and can offer scope for a more equal relationship. There are no fears of interfering with the curriculum with the relentless demands that the statutory timetable makes upon teachers' and pupils' time. Outside the statutory framework and funding, all things prove possible. And that sense of innovation and mutual responsibility for learning is proving infectious.

Indeed, one of the most impressive developments in recent years in the field of OSHL has been the recognition that the task of education, just as it cannot be confined to the school day, cannot be confined to the single school. It has recently been made clear that: 'Schools have a key role to play in promoting and participating in study support. But schools can often do more and do it more effectively if they have active support from other organisations and from the community. And study support can be provided entirely by people or organisations who are not part of a school.'[1] The document identified the organisations already heavily involved – local and national businesses, volunteers (including parents, other adults, students and older pupils), library services and youth and voluntary organisations – and encouraged more partners to become involved in the new opportunity.

The result has been a wealth of innovative partnerships which have expanded understanding, capacity, resourcefulness and impact. In many instances, local partnerships have also built on success from small beginnings, for example, when individuals and groups have secured additional resources at the right time.

┌─ **EXTRA** ───

Wrexham Homework Clubs Network

The Wrexham Homework Clubs Network in North Wales now organises 25 homework clubs which operate across the borough of Wrexham. It started with one homework club running out of a children's charity based in Wrexham (The Venture Homework Club) which was funded by grant-giving organisations and private donations. Funding from BBC Children in Need, The Welsh Office and the National Charities Lottery Board enabled the club to appoint a full-time development worker and to expand the network across the borough.

Teams of support workers have now been set up to operate as individual units and provide a free, supervised homework service that operates each evening of the week, either in schools, libraries or village halls. Apart from homework, the clubs offer ICT facilities, Internet training and access, help

---

[1] National Assembly of Wales (1999) *Unlocking Potential: A framework for extending out of school learning opportunities in Wales*. See also NEDP Wrexham Homework Clubs, Case Study Series, October 2000

with revision, art projects, animation projects and science projects for students aged from 8–18. The majority of students are under 15. The peripatetic nature of the projects and the sense of partnership generated between all the interested partners – the sessional staff, the young people, the schools, Wrexham Borough Council, the Library Service and the Basic Skills officer – are seen as vital to the project. The clubs are very informal, fostering a caring and sociable attitude with children acting as mentors. Outings, incentives and small prizes are offered within a merit system. Sessional staff are recruited from a variety of backgrounds, including teaching, youth and community work and social work, and access training locally. Communication, not least the network's own newsletter, is seen as essential to good partnership and a close partnership has been established with the library service.

Another example of a very wide range of partners working together to support pupils from a single school is given in the OSHL programme at Haggerston Girls School.

EXTRA

Haggerston Girls School

Haggerston Girls School, LB Hackney, recognises the important part that parents and carers play in their children's achievements and building on that has been a major project for the last year. With funding from the City Fringe Partnership, a family learning project is thriving and developing. During autumn 2000 two parallel evening computer courses for beginners from Year 7 pupils and their parents have been extremely successful. Next term, a Year 7 pupil and mums' Ty-Ga karate self-defence class will be run.

The school is looking to sustain enthusiasm with intermediate, follow-up or repeat courses for others pupils and adults and will monitor the girls who participate in OSHL activities to evaluate their achievement against predicted grades. Other successful and well supported initiatives are the after-school KS3 and KS4 learning clubs recently funded from the NOF. The clubs are run by a rota of staff which includes teachers, the lead learning mentor and the librarian, with the aim of improving personal learning skills.

An exciting chain of events was triggered last summer when the pupils studying GCSE astronomy as an after-school class for the gifted and talented won an essay competition. Their prize was a trip to South America for a rocket launch. This term the astronomy class was invited to Lucerne for an international conference where the girls gave a presentation to all the other delegates.

The school is also particularly proud of its drama production for 2000 – Faust 2000 – a highly challenging and successful performance which involved many different skills and faculties. All the preparation and rehearsal took place after school on two nights a week and some Saturdays and included the creation of a Web site, which gave examples of previous productions.

Local primary schools attended in the mornings and the evening perf-ormances were for parents and friends. The Globe Theatre asked the head of drama to bring the cast back to perform excerpts from this year's play for its students.

In another successful partnership, *The Financial Times*, Bank of Switzerland and Boots plc employees work with Year 10 students to provide support in preparing for the transition from school to the workplace. Liz Veitch, Year 10 head, believes that these sessions are tremendously motivating, especially for 'the more challenging girls. . . who often turn the corner this way'. The school also involves local business in many other ways – both during and after the normal school day. In arts and crafts for example, many local people come into the school – artists, crafts people, silversmiths, stained glass window artists and other specialists who run or support clubs. There are links with the local Geffrye Museum where a project entitled 'Words into Wood' takes place using local crafts people working with Year 7 pupils.

Building extra capacity to sustain OSHL programmes will become even more important over the next few years when NOF funding ceases. However, there are a range of new opportunities beyond that – particularly in forming strong partnerships which can vary in purpose and scope. They may be, for example;

- learning partnerships involving other schools or other members of the 'education family' – from the youth service to local libraries;
- human resources partnerships, involving people as mentors, volunteers, or experts;
- physical or financial partnerships involving other agencies in helping to provide space, additional resources, or experiences.

Some areas, such as the arts and sports communities, offer particularly bold and successful opportunities for partnership. But, additionally, the school's partners may come from different voluntary or statutory sources with different funding regimes and experiences. They can be, for example:

- central government partnerships – funded through DfEE;
- local government partnerships – funded through NOF, SRB, Standards Funding or other local sources;
- voluntary sector partnerships;
- business sector partnerships, providing mentoring, incentives, and direct funding.

This chapter looks at the ways in which people and partners can be involved and at the opportunities they create in terms of staffing and resourcing schemes which stretch opportunities while adding to capacity. The first section of the chapter looks at the people involved and how they can support the staff in the school: parents and mentors; experts and enthusiasts.

The second section of the chapter looks at some of the most innovative learning partnerships in development which add to capacity and wealth of experience: in the arts and sports; involving libraries and the youth services centres; involving museums and art galleries; and involving business.

The final section looks at how additional resources can be found through working in partnership with business and voluntary sector partners.

PEOPLE AS PARTNERS: SCHOOL STAFF

Throughout this book, the commitment of teachers is manifest on every page. Without their voluntary support for the activities that have traditionally existed and their willingness to take that commitment further in terms of time, organisation and evaluation, no extra-curricular activity would ever take place, and the new generation of ideas and schemes would simply not have happened. There would be no school play or sports fixtures, no choirs or orchestras, no summer schools, no regular study support programmes, no Easter revision schemes, no homework clubs, no residential experiences and no school trips. It is to their immense credit that, given the new national and local funding opportunities for expanded and enriched programmes, the majority of schools throughout the four countries of the UK have said 'Yes' to new challenges and opportunities for their pupils.

What each school can provide is different, and, in each school the organisation and support for OSHL is also different. As Chapter 4 discussed, each school finds its own way of rewarding and supporting staff in a situation where the common currency is time as well as money. Whatever the scheme, staff have to be comfortable that it is properly negotiated, fair in principle and consistent with equal opportunities. In addition, however, there are new incentives for staff to participate which go beyond payment and into professional development. In recent years, as Chapter 4 also suggested, new opportunities have arisen for staff to:

- develop their understanding of informal learning as exemplified in study support;
- explore different ways of teaching and learning outside the classroom;
- develop their own special qualifications and interests through study support (particularly in the arts and sports);
- become accredited for this through higher degree qualifications.[2]

It is commonly agreed that the first step towards best practice is the appointment of a school-wide coordinator for after-school activities.

[2] See, for example, *Extra Special No 74: Professional development and training* (Autumn 2000)

Nunthorpe School in Middlesbrough has appointed a full-time coordinator for its Integrated Student Care scheme from among its own staff but the scheme is supported, in addition, by youth workers.

EXTRA

Nunthorpe School

At Nunthorpe School the designated coordinator of the Integrated Student Care scheme, Sharon Carter, Head of Year 7, has created an extensive and flexible programme of activities, which involve sessions for 30 to 120 younger pupils a week, run by some paid and some voluntary staff. To enthuse staff Sharon has run a series of 'WANTED' posters advertising that some paid work is available, but also seeking voluntary contributions from staff, and outlining the benefits to staff and children. It was made clear that involvement in the scheme is seen as positive by senior management, and that staff volunteering will be supported 'in kind' with time off, extra class materials, etc.

Students Enjoying Active Learning (SEAL) runs four nights a week to help to meet the needs of working parents by providing guaranteed student care and learning activities. It is available for Year 7 and 8 students and it is held in the school and at the adjacent Nunthorpe Youth Centre where students can socialise, relax and complete homework. The coordinator emphasises that this enables staff to build very different relationships with the children, who are already signing up not just for the current term but for next term too. Through their chosen activities students will, it is anticipated, increase their skills, motivation and self-esteem, raise their achievements, gain valuable leadership and team-building skills and enhance the home–school relationship. There are also great opportunities to work with a range of people, including adults and other students of a different age group, to develop inter-personal relationships. Monitoring is carried out by course tutors and the scheme coordinator and further evaluation and input comes from the students. Termly meetings are arranged to discuss the progress with the Voluntary Management Committee. Students involved say: 'It's great, we're really enjoying it and getting a lot out of it.'

Current activities are wide ranging and include:

- Toy Sacks – a community interactive reading scheme, where children pick a book and make toys relating to the story which are donated to local community projects.
- Campcraft – part of the Nunthorpe Challenge (a local scheme similar to the Duke of Edinburgh Awards) which encourages transferable skills in camping, survival, outdoors and environmental awareness.
- Health Shop – a discussion space led by a trained counsellor, in which children raise issues of concern (Week 1's topic, for example, was handling relationships).
- *Ready, Steady, Cook* – four children each week bring in ingredients and a youth worker and retired cookery teacher run activities based on the popular programme.

- Sports Tournament – four-week blocks of soccer coaching or pool and snooker skills sessions ending in a tournament. These are very over-subscribed sessions that tap into children's love of competition, run by a soccer coach and two volunteers working on their Duke of Edinburgh Sports Leadership Award.
- Fun with Fabrics – revamp old clothes or turn unwanted items into fashionable accessories, with the course ending an open evening/fashion show.
- Study Skills – learning to love learning, fun methods to boost skills and concentration at school and home.
- ICT course – young people choose the topics and compile a newspaper or Web site for school and community. Run by an ICT teacher who ensures there is no duplication of topics covered in class – keeps ICT fun and accessible.
- Horse Course – six-week session looking at caring for horses and riding skills, and leading to a day out at an Equestrian Centre.

Apart from teaching staff there are many other school staff who can be fully involved in developing OSHL learning: classroom assistants, librarians, laboratory technicians, site supervisors, and lunchtime supervisors. They all play key role in schools in the Education Extra network in every form of OSHL activity from reptile clubs to football. One obvious resource, available in principle to every school, is the lunchtime supervisor.

EXTRA

Parc Lewis Primary School

Parc Lewis Primary School has been in the forefront of training lunchtime supervisors in behaviour management. The training is organised by the Education Support and Inspection Service for Bridgend, Merthyr Tydfil, Caerphilly, and Rhondda Cynon Taff (ESIS), under the supervision of the primary adviser, Chris Morgan. The school was successful in applying for a grant to assist in the purchase of new games equipment and to pay the lunchtime supervisors for their time in training at school which included being trained to listen to pupils read and to offer drama activities (on wet lunchtimes) and activities in the playground. The teacher who trained the supervisors in games activities was a newly qualified PE specialist.

The lunchtime supervisors, who know all the pupils in the school, have grown in status and confidence as they have developed new responsibilities and interests. Two of them now have a job share and assist five out of the six classes at school during classroom hours. One of the lunchtime supervisors has recently become the staff governor for the governing body of the school. They have also lately been trained on a new maths scheme to assist slow learners called 'Numberworks' implemented by the local education authority, Rhondda Cynon Taff. In July 1999, the school achieved the Investors in People award for its development of teaching staff and ancillary staff.

PEOPLE AS PARTNERS: VOLUNTEERS

Supporting teaching staff or staff who are paid for undertaking a variety of extra activities can be a range of volunteers who come into after-school activities in many different ways. Volunteer support for education is hardly new, but OSHL offers a new dimension. In November 2000 the National Centre for Volunteering estimated that 6 million people, almost a tenth of the adult population of the UK, spent on average four hours a week supporting children's education. They included governors, volunteers hearing children read or working in nurseries, PTAs, and helpers at fêtes and sports activities. The value of this extra, unpaid, help has been estimated at £10 billion a year (based on the 1999 minimum wage). Community Service Volunteers and the think tank DEMOS predict that volunteers will play a greater role in the future in terms of citizenship education, mentoring, fighting social exclusion, and helping with learning.[3] Training and support for volunteers is becoming a key issue too, with the concept of 'Time Banks', with volunteers accredited for their time and rewarded in terms of extra resources (such as computers), which were introduced into the United States and Japan over a decade ago now gaining credit in the UK.[4]

Parents make up the majority of volunteers, particularly in primary schools. They bring with them a variety of benefits including:

- provision of good parental role models;
- improved communication between home and school;
- an increased pool of skills.

But there are also benefits for the parent volunteers, who have a second chance to develop their own skills and to look for personal learning opportunities.

Research undertaken by Education Extra in 1998[5] showed that volunteer parents were as likely to be active in secondary schools as in primary

---

[3] See, for example, the 1997 National Survey of Volunteering in the UK. In addition, the DfEE in 1999–2000 was spending £9.6 million on the Millennium Volunteers programme aimed at getting more young people to volunteer. See also, CSV/DEMOS (June 2000) *Giving Time, Volunteering in the 21st Century*. See also the work of Timebank UK

[4] See, for example, the peer-tutoring scheme linked to time banks (the Chicago Time Dollar Peer Tutoring Program). I am indebted to Phil Street, Director of CEDC, for this information. See also, Robert Wood Johnson Foundation (1990) *Service Credit Banking Site Summaries*, University of Maryland, Centre on Ageing, for an account of the 500 programmes running worldwide which are paying time 'credits' to people in recognition of the volunteer efforts they put in

[5] Education Extra (1998) *Schools and Volunteers*

schools. They were also found to bring invaluable extra resources with them – in support of activities as variable as fishing, literacy, dance, philosophy, football, religion, bird watching, local history, or multicultural cuisine. They are involved at all levels with many different types of clubs in administrative, supportive and mentoring roles. Parents are often involved in helping to run reading, library and mentoring clubs, for example.

The three short case studies below show how parent involvement can bring benefits for three very different schools as well as for the parents themselves. The first case study shows how individual parents can expand the opportunities available and complement the skills of teachers.

EXTRA

Weston All Saints Primary School

Weston All Saints Primary School in Bath welcomes parents helping extra-curricular provision. One parent interested in the environment has helped to organise an environmental area in the school grounds. Children are now able to join the after-school environment club helping with planting and general upkeep of the area. Two fathers, both keen footballers, come in weekly to support and help coach the school football club. They have helped to raise the standard of the school team who have been very successful in the local school league. Another parent assists with the ICT club using her expertise to help children further their computing skills. In other areas, such as choreography, acting, music and art/design, parents have worked alongside teaching staff.

Parents offer skills that teachers do not necessarily possess. The school has a record of talented parents who they call upon to complement teachers' expertise. For example, one parent regularly accompanies the school choir at musical events. Last term, they were invited to sing with the Bath Bach choir in the Pump Rooms in Bath.

Mrs Bull, headteacher, refers to the team of parents as an invaluable resource which is greatly appreciated.

'You never know who has ability and one of the things I enjoy is seeing the improvement children can make with just a little bit of coaching.' (Julian Witt, parent football coach)

One headteacher wrote to tell Education Extra about the invaluable contribution one particular parent had made to the development of OSHL activities in her school in Manchester.

┌─── **EXTRA** ─────────────────────────────────┐

Windsor Community High School

In the summer of 1997, Windsor Community High School in Salford ran one of the first summer literacy schools. It was a great success and one of the major factors contributing to that success was the involvement of parents. Janet Simnor was one of those parents who helped. From that initial contact, she became a staunch supporter of Windsor Community High and involved herself in numerous school activities.

After a short period, Janet began to grow in confidence. She approached me with her concerns about those children who are excluded from after-school activities because they are not good enough to be on the school football team or they have not been chosen to take part in drama production. She lived locally and was aware that some of these children returned home at the end of the day to an empty house. So, she began campaigning to set up after-school care activities that were inclusive. As a result, we set up the Windsor Out of School Club (WOOS) which has proved to be a tremendous success. Children are able to take part and succeed in a range of activities.

Janet spends a huge proportion of her time in school – she is there when needed for pupils, acting as mediator between pupil and pupil, pupils and staff. She also helps resolve problems with parents. She is a very quiet, unassuming person, yet has the personality to engage both young and old. She is extremely talented and gives very generously of her time. Windsor pupils are far richer for her time and devotion – she is a wonderful, caring person.[6]

└───┘

At other schools, great efforts have been made to develop and accredit the skills of volunteers, to provide lasting benefit.

┌─── **EXTRA** ─────────────────────────────────┐

St Joan of Arc RC Primary School

This primary school in Merseyside involves a wide range of volunteers, most of whom are parents. Over the last eight years, parents' involvement has increased in activities such as sport, art and music. The school has worked with Merseyside Open College to obtain accreditation for parents' work through a Parents as Educators course; much of this is concerned with raising skills and qualifications of parents and the local community in an area where only 1 per cent of parents have a higher qualification and where male unemployment was as high as 34 per cent in 1998. Many of the pupils' parents have had negative experiences of schooling and this programme engages them in their children's education. The school has an active PTA and a parents group which is involved with management and out of school and community activities and 'even has its own Code of Practice for Parents and Volunteers that was worked out and agreed with wide consultation'.

└───┘

[6] Personal information provided from Bernadette Ahern, headteacher, Windsor Community High School, Manchester

Involving volunteers also crosses age and cultural barriers. Grandparents can be a particularly accessible resource as listeners, mentors and experts. St George's Community School in Bristol, for example, has run a project about the Second World War drawing upon the expertise of the local senior citizens, who worked with the children in constructing a replica Anderson shelter and air-raid warden's office, and developing a soundtrack replicating the experience of life inside the shelter and the office. The children toured with the exhibition after school time to other primary schools and community venues, explaining what they had learnt.

Other schools have developed teams of local volunteers to support students in different ways:

EXTRA

Grangemouth Community School

At Grangemouth Community School, Falkirk, team-building expeditions for senior pupils are organised. On a recent residential expedition, the staff included a parent (local minister), a chaplain and three community policeman (with outdoors activities and mountain leadership qualifications), as well as former and current pupils. They engage in progressive team-building exercises leading to a simulated mountain rescue at the end (pupils are briefed the night before, woken up early, told there is a mountain rescue, allocated into teams with walkie-talkies and given their roles and tasks).

The activities get progressively harder and at the end of each exercise new targets are set for both teams and individuals. The scheme creates a positive climate for community police work and gives the minister an opportunity to work and support young people in a different context.

'The community policeman is perceived differently. Now, they call him Tony and the chaplain Ian.' (Mr Docherty, headteacher)

Parents, carers and grandparents are often artists and experts in their own right – as the following case study powerfully illustrates.

EXTRA

Canonbury Junior School

At Canonbury Junior School, LB Islington, with the assistance of a small grant from the Bridgehouse Trust, two parents have started running an after-school art and design club. One of the parents, Siw Thomas, is an Art, Design and Technology teacher in a London secondary school and the other parent, Mary McKenna, is a painter. Not surprisingly the club reflects the skills of these two parents and the children get a chance to explore ceramics, fabric, painting, design, working mechanisms and woodwork.

Demand for the club has grown over the last year with 26 children now involved and the parents have recently run a two-week arts project during

---

the school holiday. Siw comments: 'The participating children have developed much more confidence, particularly in handling materials and tools. Where they clearly lacked confidence a few months ago, they now walk into the room, pick up a piece of wood or a tool and say "I want to do this!"'.

The increased confidence and ability of the children has been noticed by the parents who have requested that more extra-curricular activity is incorporated into the school. Siw stresses the importance of whole school support for extra-curricular activities and this attitude is reflected in the school's unusual decision to employ two music specialists to work within the school.

However, while they may well also be parents, artists and experts find their way into schools both during the school day and outside school hours in many different roles and situations. Although access can vary enormously depending on location, partnership possibilities, and the willingness of the school to take a few risks, the resident artist – whether a ceramicist, painter, composer, musician, or actor – is no stranger to school life.[7]

In recent years, however, other local experts have also become a feature of the school day, supporting in-school and extra-curricular activities in many different ways. One outstanding example is the network of science and engineering schemes (Young Engineers, Young Foresight and Neighbourhood Engineer's for example) created by the national engineering bodies, which offer opportunities for club and learning activities outside the school day. Neighbourhood Engineers, for example, mobilised 8,000 engineers from various disciplines to assist schools in science and CDT as part of the curriculum.

Education Extra has come across a wealth of individual 'experts' working with schools outside school hours in a variety of different capacities, from archaeologists to artists, photographers to footballers, mathematicians to martial arts experts, poets to policemen – the local policewoman in Falmer, Brighton, leads Fulmer School's line dancing club!

THE POWER OF MENTORING

Many of the adults involved as volunteers and experts in schools become mentors for pupils, and sometimes school staff as well. The power of mentoring is now widely acknowledged across education. Ofsted observed: 'Mentoring, linking pupils with adults for special advice with their work, proves particularly valuable in schools whose pupils tend to lack study skills. Mentoring is widely used to provide guidance to pupils taking

---

[7] See, for example, Education Extra (2000) *Extra Class*

GCSE courses. At best it adds to the network of support, sets targets for improvement and logs progress. Another approach is to promote contact between pupils and adults from the local business or commercial world with the aim of broadening pupils' perspectives. Contact with such adults can have a powerful impact on motivation.'[8] In recent years mentoring schemes have penetrated into many different areas of educational life. As the National Mentoring Network has put it: 'Growing numbers of schools and colleges are using it as a support strategy to raise pupils' achievements, self-esteem, self-confidence and personal and social skills.'[9] Being mentored by another pupil, a student, a volunteer helper or a business counsellor, can have a profound and lasting effect on individual confidence, self-esteem and attitudes to learning. Mentoring schemes take many forms and cross many barriers. They may be internal to the school, or supported by external partnerships. They may be designed so that pupils of the same age can help each other, or so that older pupils can support younger ones. Mentors may listen to a child read, may provide independent counselling for personal difficulties, may enable students to tackle an area of the curriculum they are finding difficult, or support a whole year or curriculum group to develop study skills which will help them to raise their performance. For some children, the attention of an adult on a regular basis may supply what is missing from their own home life.

A growing body of academic research confirms the effectiveness of mentoring, particularly in raising attainment levels among disaffected young people or those at risk for disaffection.[10] For the mentor there are obvious benefits too – the personal reward which follows from helping a friend or a young pupil to do well, the acquisition of skills and experience useful for his or her own personal and career development and, in some cases, an opportunity to accredit the commitment. Giving time also broadens the notion of citizenship. Community Service Volunteers and DEMOS in a recent report, *Giving Time,* anticipate that 'Mentoring will become one of the prime mechanisms of furnishing people with the skills they need to connect with each other and build a moral and social framework for their lives. As mentoring requires a level of independence, volunteers will fill the majority of these new roles.' The introduction of the citizenship curriculum in schools will naturally equip young people with more opportunities to become mentors themselves and acquire the skills of mentoring, whether that is face to face or using the Internet and new technologies.

[8] Ofsted (2000) *Improving City Schools*, p 33

[9] DfEE, *Insight* (Summer 1999) Mentoring raises standards, p 28

[10] See, for example, Fitzgibbon, C (1988) *Peer-tutoring as a teaching strategy*, British Educational Management and Administration Society; *Encyclopedia of Educational Research* (1992) Macmillan, New York

Summer learning schemes have proved a fertile ground for all forms of mentoring and the evaluations reveal that the mentoring aspect has been one of the most popular and successful elements. In 1999, for example, half of the 25 pilot all-curriculum summer learning schemes employed mentors extensively. One of the most powerful forms of peer mentoring is when pupils of the same age, or older, support each other or younger pupils (for example through a paired reading scheme). Some mentoring schemes have aimed to act as a bridge into secondary school for primary school pupils.

EXTRA

Lower Edmonton Secondary School

The secondary school in Lower Edmonton provides a good stream of dedicated mentors who each work with approximately two Year 6 students identified as being 'vulnerable' from the Firs Farm Primary School, LB Enfield. The project is called the Triangle Club. The current system has been mutually beneficial to both the mentors and younger students. The mentors gain great experience and references before going on to further education. The structure of the Triangle Club sessions include literary/academic tasks and practical tasks in addition to the more analytical/mentoring work where the primary school pupils are taught by the mentors to think about the transition to secondary school. It has proved particularly successful in terms of positive role modelling, particularly among those from ethnic backgrounds. Children now look forward to being part of the Triangle Club. It is very much built into the ethos of the school; even when members of staff move on, new teachers come on line to manage the club.

EXTRA

Hexham Middle School

A paired reading scheme at Hexham Middle School in Northumberland involves over 70 children from Year 5 and 8. Vivienne Brown, the teacher in charge, feels that this scheme has made a significant contribution to more positive attitudes to learning and improved self-esteem among the pupils being mentored: 'These children feel less pressure reading to an older pupil than they would reading to an adult. This, coupled with the informal environment in which the scheme operates, has served to encourage children to feel more relaxed about reading out loud and has developed the concept of reading for pleasure.'

The older children have also benefited: 'Their involvement in mentoring has helped them to identify how their own reading has progressed and this has been really motivating for them. . . The school also benefits from the greater interaction between the different year groups. This paired reading scheme has been so successful that we are now expanding it to include students from the local high school.'[11]

[11] Education Extra *Extra Special No 59: Mentoring*

Arts schemes are a potentially very fertile area for mentoring, as the innovative Junior Arts Leadership Award developed in Langley School demonstrates.

EXTRA

Langley School

The Junior Arts Award, piloted at Langley School, Solihull, in March 2000, set out to enable pupils to use their skills in the arts, in order to enhance their peers' and the community's enjoyment of art, music and drama. The course involves facilitating arts for peers, developing skills in the arts, developing social skills, gaining access to arts in the community and informing pupils about career pathways in the arts. Three community projects took place:

- the launch of an arts centre which is attended by 1,000 visitors a week;
- a two-day session helping with an inner city school production working with Shaw Hill School;
- a Christmas celebration involving music and tea for 80 senior citizens.

There are other individual projects taking place including choreography and separate productions.

The outcomes have been wholly positive from the student leaders, the younger pupils, and staff. At the end of the scheme with Shaw Hill School, one 10-year-old student said to the headteacher, 'Can you find me another school to do this?'

Senior citizens wrote thank-you letters and sent Christmas cards following their involvement. One said 'It has given me faith in young people.'

Mentoring for aspiration: FE and HE

While older students from secondary schools can provide a network of friendship and learning support for primary schools, as many case studies have already indicated, students from local colleges and universities can also provide invaluable support as mentors – particularly across the transition into FE or HE. For school pupils who may not have thought that a university or college career could be for them, the chance not only to meet but to form a friendship with a student from the local university may help to raise their aspirations. There are a number of excellent examples of schools taking advantage of this opportunity.

EXTRA
The Dalmuir Learning Support Volunteer Project

In the Glasgow area, the Dalmuir Learning Support Volunteer Project recruits students from local colleges and the university to provide four study and homework clubs in the Clydebank area. The volunteers receive training provided by school learning support staff, educational psychologists and college NVQ staff and, on completion of the training, the volunteer is paired with a pupil. The pupil and volunteer then meet once a week for an average of four to six months. The volunteer works to contribute to the young person's personal and social development as well as academic development and encourages more positive attitudes towards learning.

EXTRA
Leeds University

Leeds University promotes a scheme recruiting students to help set up and participate in after-school and weekend activities in schools throughout Leeds. ICT, music, dance, science, arts, sports and outward bound clubs have been initiated by the students and Margo Hanson, who coordinates the project, has found schools so appreciative that many more clubs are now being planned.

The project helps to promote the idea of continued learning among some of the most disadvantaged pupils in the city. As the headteacher of one of the schools involved says: 'It has provided a model of a world that our kids would otherwise have had little idea of.'

Leeds University now intends to introduce an accredited course unit for all those involved in order to acknowledge the effort that their students put into the scheme and to encourage a wider range of students to become involved.

One recent project demonstrates how well student mentoring in the arts can spark new creativity and enable pupils and mentors alike to discover new art forms and skills, as learners, together.

EXTRA
The London Institute

In 1999, Education Extra and the London Institute – a world-class centre of art and design, made up of five London art colleges – set up a partnership which involved recruiting eight students to work as artists in residence within after-school art clubs in six London secondary schools. They called the scheme ArtOut. The intention was to give pupils an opportunity to work with a practising artist; to give art students an opportunity to develop skills and knowledge as artists in residence; to help schools develop art out of school hours. Teachers attended and supported the sessions. The projects covered

---

using sound as a stimulus for drawing; jewellery and links with other cultures; and connecting performance and visual art, conceptual art enabling students to experiment with new ideas and materials, explore painting and mixed media, and combine visual art and dance. Altogether, 120 students took part and the project was judged to be a great success in terms of creating a really effective and innovative teaching and learning relationship.

'The nature of the learning relationship between student artists and pupils was perhaps one of the most successful aspects of the project. The quality of learning was enhanced by the relationships that blossomed. The project has highlighted the value that pupils put on access to young role models and advisers who can share related and relevant learning experiences, but who at the same time bring new ideas to the learning relationship.'[12]

Mentoring for employability: the role of business

Increasingly, UK companies across all sectors take their corporate and social responsibilities seriously, supporting the work of schools by donating resources (computers and books are particularly popular), but increasingly putting their employees centre stage. Just as corporate responsibility is becoming core business, mentoring is seen as a way of expressing commitment and building up employee skills at the same time. For secondary pupils reaching school-leaving age, guidance from adults in the workplace can be particularly helpful and, since businesses have a vested interest in the next generation of employees, they are often pleased to help pupils at this critical stage in their lives. Providing mentoring support is seen as not only evidence of local corporate responsibility: it is also seen, increasingly, as good for staff development by the company itself – and as a more lasting investment than supporting schools financially.

A number of companies are involved in schemes that provide support for children's key skills. For example, the WH Smith project 'Ready, Steady, Read Aloud' encourages staff members to provide children at their local school with additional support with their reading. BP Amoco runs a Link scheme with schools in the vicinity of its plants. This includes mentoring in OSHL programmes and also site visits and work experience for pupils. They also provide management advice for the schools involved. Pfizer, in 1999, had 45 mentors supporting A level and advanced level GNVQs in five different schools.[13]

'Roots and Wings' is one project promoted through Business in the Community (BiTC) which pairs business mentors with pupils in a scheme which aims to demystify the working environment. Pupils are given a flavour of what is on offer in the world of employment, for example through

[12] Education Extra and the London Institute (2000) *ArtOut: Connecting Art Students with Schools*
[13] DfEE, *Insight* (Summer 1999) op cit p 28

visits to workplaces. As Liz Gooding of BiTC explains: 'The need to enthuse and inspire someone, or to work with a different group of people than usual, is an extremely good way of developing communication skills. The mentor has to ensure that the pupils communicate clearly and listen carefully. And of course, for many companies, it is extremely valuable to have an insight into the world of education for the development of the firm's human resources.'

Templemore School on the outskirts of Londonderry, Northern Ireland, is one of the schools which has put this into practice.

EXTRA

Templemore School

Many pupils from its wide catchment area come from either socially or economically deprived areas of the city. The school is equivalent to a secondary modern school within a selective system, and the headteacher is strongly committed to raising self-belief in the pupils, and what they can achieve. In the midst of a disturbed and sometimes dangerous environment, Templemore School continues to operate a wide variety of out of school activities in order to enhance pupils' education.

The school is very proud of its mentoring scheme linking Year 11 pupils at the school with BT employees which runs on a one-to-one basis throughout the school year. As part of the 'Roots and Wings' venture supported by BITC it aims to promote maturity, self-esteem and confidence, provide strong adult role models, develop links between school and community and to support the transition for pupils between school and working adult life.

Both pupils and mentors are involved in many different activities including outdoor activities and visits. Pupils have helped to design and build a garden in a day centre for people with physical and mental disabilities. Both mentors and mentees have many individual meetings and pupils have the opportunity to share time with the mentors at work. The school has noted that the scheme has made a major difference in terms of personal development. Some pupils have become trusted ambassadors for the school in ways that would not have been imaginable – many have become prefects. The link with BT has also given employees a different perspective on modern school life and promoted the school's links with the community.

Besides the scheme, the school has a programme which aims to offer potentially disaffected pupils a more flexible curriculum. It has also set up a vocational link with the Institute of Further and Higher Education for Year 12 pupils as well as a vocational NVQ course for Year 11 pupils. Other enrichment schemes include a breakfast club, a homework/study club, residential opportunities for Year 8 prefects and sixth-form pupils, cross-community and cross-border activities as well as music, drama and sporting opportunities.

THE ARTS AND SPORTS IN PARTNERSHIP

Of all curriculum areas, the arts and sports offer particular opportunity for partnerships, in the form of local and regional organisations, and a very wide range of professional organisations – especially when linked with social inclusion objectives. Indeed, partnerships, whether large strategic ones, or local and focused on projects or individuals, are seen as 'vital in the rebuilding of communities, as they offer so many opportunities for the development of individuals and groups within the community'.[14]

The drive for partnership is in part due to the realisation within arts organisations themselves that education programmes and long-term partnerships are key to helping them develop relationships with future audiences and visitors. This is reflected at national level in the £5 million funding through the DCMS's New Audience programme, in the announcement of local Creative Partnerships, and at the ability of local organisations to respond to the new opportunities. 'For many years the Arts Council of England has encouraged organisations to work with schools to help develop the arts in the curriculum. The sharing of expertise benefits both schools, through access to the world of professional artists, and arts practitioners through engagement with young people. The major expansion of out of hours activities offers new opportunities to involve arts organisations in developing exciting and valuable experiences for pupils.'[15]

OSHL activities, along with a raft of linked initiatives, has presented arts and cultural organisations with new challenges and opportunities for partnerships to which they have responded with enthusiasm – all the more credible given the loss of arts support services and activity in recent years.[16]

At the same time, however, individual arts organisations and institutions are playing a growing role in developing programmes of learning activity in partnership with local communities and schools. In terms of supporting school-led learning, therefore, the focus for arts education has moved away from local authority managed services, to formal and informal partnership contracts between schools and individual arts organisations.

Indeed, for a growing number of arts and cultural institutions, partnership and education are at the core of their work. This is due in part to government policy – manifest through DCMS and Arts Council conditions of grant support. The Arts Council stated in 1997 that 'high quality,

---

[14] See, Policy Action Team 10 (report to the Social Exclusion Unit), DCMS, Arts and Sports
[15] ACE and QCA publication *From Policy to Partnership: Developing the arts in schools*.This publication, issued to all schools in England, helps schools 'establish partnerships during and out of school hours to meet their own needs and enrich their arts provision'. The preface was signed by David Blunkett, Chris Smith, Gerry Robinson and Sir William Stubbs
[16] See, for example, the Gulbenkian Report, *Crossing the Line* (2000)

innovative educational work should be an intrinsic part of every funded arts organisation's programme'. This intent has been expressed through all subsequent funding policies and has made a dramatic and positive impact on the amount and quality of arts experiences made available through partnerships between arts organisations and schools. In London for example, the number of medium and large-scale arts organisations developing exciting programmes of work with pupils at all key stages has risen dramatically over the last 5–10 years. What was once the exception has already become the norm.

EXTRA

Yorkshire Youth and Music

One outstanding early example of study support partnerships was that coordinated by Yorkshire Youth and Music (YYAM) in 1998–1999. Five professional musicians were commissioned to work with five after-school groups of children for six weeks to produce an original musical composition which was performed at a single event in the Viaduct Theatre in Halifax. The scheme, Sounding Out, allowed children from primary and secondary schools to make music, including electronic music, samba, gospel singing, classical Indian music and Didjeridu and allowed the teachers to work alongside professional musicians within an informal, safe and experimental framework. The scheme received funding from the Calderdale Community Foundation, Nestlé, Yorkshire and Humberside Arts, the Halifax Building Society and Education Extra. YYAM went on to make a successful major bid for NOF funding to develop its partnership music programmes.

The mutual benefits of partnership are self-evident. Arts organisations, despite new funding through the lottery, are still under-funded and are therefore looking for partnerships to stabilise themselves. Schools are becoming increasingly keen to adopt arts activities as a way of tackling specific issues and of motivating groups of disaffected and underachieving pupils. Although there still exists a fundamental gap between what pupils and schools need and what arts and cultural organisations have the potential to deliver, the range of initiatives is impressive – not least in the steady increase in the number of specialist arts colleges with a long waiting list. One innovation in development, for example, is a project recently funded by the Paul Hamlyn Foundation in Croydon which will enable 10 primary school arts teachers to spend 10 days outside the classroom, working on different art forms with an arts partner of their choice – national dance and theatre companies, for example – as a way of enriching their own in-school teaching and developing new out of school arts programmes with the help of their arts mentor.

In addition, however, there are many other signs of vitality in partnership, including an increasing commitment to evaluating the full range of benefits which can follow.[17]

In addition, there are, for example:

- Arts-led EAZs (Arts Council project) in Bristol and Corby.
- The Cape Project in Northern England working with a large and growing cluster of schools to access the curriculum exclusively through the arts.
- Museums and galleries developing ongoing planned relationships with schools.
- The Robinson Report (*All Our Futures: Creativity, culture and education*) which recommends an extension of out of school hours partnerships as a key factor in developing the breadth and quality of formative arts experiences.
- The Society of London Theatres – encompassing the leading theatres of the West End – identified education and linking with schools as one of three vital factors in its continuing existence in *The Wyndham Report* and *After Wyndham*. Key recommendations include 'a new positive partnership with local education authorities' and full implementation of Ken Robinson's NACCCE Report.
- The formation of Youth Music Action Zones to be established by the national foundation for Youth Music, to develop partnerships between music organisations and schools to deliver a wide range of musical activities.

In 1999, new ground was broken by the creation of a national partnership programme between groups of schools across the country and national, regional and local museums and partnerships.[18]

Designed to attract pupils who were not typical visitors, and to build up sustainable relationships between schools and creative artists, curators, and educators, the 17 very different projects were extremely successful in breaking down some of the negative images of museums in particular, and encouraging schools and the museums and galleries to rethink the educational partnerships that were possible. Above all, the projects proved extremely enjoyable, resulted in work of very high quality from students, and were highly valued by everyone taking part – as the following case study illustrates.

---

[17] See Felicity Woolf (October 1999) *Partnerships for Learning: A Guide to Evaluating Arts Education Projects*, DCMS

[18] This programme was particularly timely given the report on the educational purposes of national museums by David Anderson, *A Common Wealth* (1998) (DfEE/DCMS)

EXTRA

The Green Dragon Museum

The Green Dragon Museum in Stockton set up a project with two primary and one secondary school based on the regeneration of the Stockton area. It was designed to attract pupils known to be disadvantaged and in some cases disaffected. Many pupils showed a negative response to previous museum visits. Of the 82 pupils who started the course, 73 finished.

The three aims of the project were to improve the motivation of participants; to develop key skills in communication and oral work, including developing presentational, language and research skills; and to strengthen the museum's links with participating schools. The scheme was based around a mentoring model, whereby Year 10 pupils would work with Year 6 pupils and a local photographer, a local oral history expert and archaeologist. The highlight of the project was an exhibition of photographs and explanations based on a detailed research study of the town; 'the display work was lovingly mounted and both pupils and the museum were terribly proud of what had been achieved.'

> All the children commented that going around with the photographer had been their favourite part. The quality of the photographs taken was so good that in one case the Planning Department of the Council had asked to borrow them. . . Most of the class really enjoyed it and learned a lot about local history, interviewing techniques and taking photos. . . Some of the young people achieved success in all three areas and all of them have achieved success in at least one area. All the pupils involved received a certificate from the Director of Education. Two local papers covered the project and the follow-up work – a CD ROM. And the project was continued with the production of a video.[19]

Chapter 1 looked at the range of sports funding and policy initiatives which have given sport such a high priority and profile in recent years and indicated that sport, too, is characterised by a very diverse and rich source of potential partnerships. Possible partners range from the national bodies, particularly Sport England/Wales/Scotland which run the Active Schools programmes and TOPS programmes, to the professional associations such as the British Association of Advisers and Lecturers in Physical Education, and the national governing bodies of sport. The Playing for Success initiative, featured in Chapter 3, is perhaps the most visible expression of new partnership in study support. Behind all this expansion and experimentation is the conviction, as Smith (2000) states, that:

> Pupils are every bit as likely to succeed in exams, if not likely to do even better, if they take some exercise and enjoy sport. . . The change of scene, the change of focus, the fresh air, the physical exercise, the fun and the

---

[19] Education Extra (1999) *Alive with Learning, Study Support in Museums and Galleries*

face and – above all – the chance to forget themselves. . . And every now and again, you have a game so sensational, so exciting in its gut wrenching involvement, that it makes up for the cold days and the hours of motorway travel and the batting collapses and the dropped catches, and when you come in the front door at 8.30 on a Saturday night and drop your scorebook and punch the air – you're young again and, like all teachers, something of a child at heart. If there wasn't a bit of that in us it wouldn't be much good.[20]

Sports partnerships can, in practice, be set up between schools and local sporting agencies, funding and professional bodies, or with a host of further and higher education specialists – to say nothing of family links. The following examples show some of these possibilities in practice.

EXTRA

Heston Community School

Heston Community School lies within the London borough of Hounslow, a diverse, multicultural authority. The secondary school has over 1,300 pupils, and a high percentage are of Asian descent. The coordinator and head of PE, Peter Lammas, aims to help pupils with ESL, and a reluctance to take part in physical activities, by offering sports activities to many of the parents that come and wait on Saturday mornings.

The Family Sports, Health and Fitness Scheme has been developed over 18 months in partnership with Education Extra, with funding provided over three years by The Monument Trust, a Sainsbury's Family Charitable Trust. Initial Teacher Training students from Brunel University are able to develop their skills in delivering Physical Education and Sport while at the same time providing cost-effective provision for the school. The coordinator has also nurtured an improved partnership with the providers of adult and community education within the borough.

On a wider scale, the scheme is also integral to the borough's programme for the Youth Sport Trust's TOPS programmes and also runs Junior Sports Leaders Awards through the Central Council for Physical Recreation. The scheme therefore aims to:

- provide opportunities within the school community to promote sports activities for the whole family;
- raise awareness of the importance of fitness and a healthy lifestyle;
- enable parents to support their children's learning as well as developing their own;
- forge links with the national curriculum and develop strategies for the promotion of specific areas.

---

[20] Smith, J (2000) *The Learning Game* pp 162–64

The four areas of activity originally included:

- family sports clubs – for the whole family on Saturday mornings;
- Tumbling Tots – for children aged 4–6 on Tuesday afternoons;
- breakfast fitness clubs – for children aged 11–16 on Wednesday mornings;
- Fizz Kids – for children aged 7–10 on Thursday afternoons.

But the programme soon expanded to include a range of new activities that included:

- trampolining, aerobics and yoga;
- family fun days;
- family health and fitness awareness days;
- ICT and sports club;
- expansion of projects to feeder schools;
- development to whole community involvement.

In the third and final year of the scheme the school will team up with a local special school. Heston will deliver activities for its pupils on its own premises and on the site of the special school that will touch the lives of both sets of students.

Another, very different, partnership was that set up in the summer of 1999 between the Wright Robinson Sports College in Gorton, Manchester, the Brian Johnston Memorial Trust and Education Extra, supported by Lancashire CCC, the Youth Sport Trust and Manchester LEA. This partnership was designed to bolster and extend the cricketing opportunities of the youth of Manchester, and will provide an all-year-round programme for cricket. The school will work closely with the Cricket Development Officer for Greater Manchester, to offer extended cricket opportunities for children from the sports college and primary schools that surround it.

Through a planned structured scheme of coaching sessions, indoor practice at Old Trafford, matches, competitions and increased resources, the project will offer access to children aged 8–16. Adults will also get involved through plans to develop coaches from the local area in collaboration with the local schools and cricket clubs. The provision will take place out of curriculum time at breakfast clubs, during lunchtimes, after school, at weekends and during holiday periods, building on and enriching the curriculum-time delivery of the sport. Both boys and girls will be involved in the project, which runs for three years, and it is hoped that new young cricketing stars will emerge from it.

This transitional programme of extra-curricular cricket provision has many unique components and with the support of all parties involved and with the backing of the England and Wales Cricket Board, it is hoped that

'EXTRA JOHNNERS' will be repeated in other locations starved of cricketing opportunities.

EXPANDING SKILLS AND RESOURCES: THE YOUTH SERVICE AND LIBRARY SERVICES

Given that the challenge for OSHL is to bring into the extra learning day young people who are particularly hard to reach, one of the most likely and relevant partners in OSHL is the Youth Service. In terms of its traditional role and its developing work in study support, the Youth Service has worked with some of the most disadvantaged groups of young people and with young people whose relationship to school was seriously compromised or non-existent. The National Youth Agency (NYA), on the basis of evidence collected by the *Schools Plus* report has observed, for example: 'On this basis the youth service has almost certainly helped to broaden the profile of young people involved in study support.'[21]

While the context and skills offered by youth workers, whether working inside schools or out reach, are different from those offered by schools, there is a wealth of evidence to show that the contribution of youth work knowledge and experience can be particularly effective for young people, particularly in terms of personal development – and for those whose hold on education is tenuous. Evidence suggests that at the moment, 40 per cent of the Youth Service involvement in study support is focused on exclusion rather than directly on achievement, but that there are many examples of good practice where the service is providing free-standing study support centres for young people – evidence of growing commitment and good practice in this area.[22]

'What appears to be changing,' observes NYA, 'is that the priority of study support and the exclusion agenda are helping to give a clearer shape and priority to the work of the youth service in this area. This appears to be broadening the range of young people engaged in study support and not simply through the work on school exclusion.'[23]

The following example shows how OSHL programmes, set up in partnership with the Youth Service, can help to deliver key skills and promote personal development in key ways, involving the skills and scope of youth workers.

[21] NYA (September 2000) *Study Support: The youth work contribution – setting the scene*, p 19. A new Code of Practice for Study Support and the Youth Service was nearing completion at the time of writing.

[22] See NYA, ibid, for examples of different models and the current range of issues developing around youth work and study support

[23] NYA, ibid, p 19

```
┌─── EXTRA ─────────────────────────────────────────────────┐
```

Archway School

Archway School in Gloucestershire developed a scheme in partnership with a local youth project called the Painswick Inn Project (PIP). This scheme targets young people who have left school without many qualifications and who could benefit from the acquisition of vocational skills. The partnership aims to encourage students at Years 10 and 11 who are at risk of achieving little at GCSE to consider taking up training places or employment with training when they leave school. PIP trainers who are studying for NVQs are asked to act as mentors for the school students.

The school runs a programme of elective activities with PIP one afternoon a week in which the students are paired with PIP trainees and together they are taught skills such as landscaping, design, bricklaying, etc. One of the activities which really caught the imagination of some of the young people involved was the reclamation of a plot of derelict land on a council estate. The young people took charge of the planning, labour and publicity, and turned the plot into a 'pocket park' for community use.[24]

```
┌─── EXTRA ─────────────────────────────────────────────────┐
```

Neville Lovett Community School

At Neville Lovett Community School in Hampshire, an Education Extra Easter project (the Triple E Project) focusing on personal development for young people aged 14–19 ran during the Easter holidays. The activities took place at a purpose-built youth centre which proved to be an ideal location. The pupils participating in the scheme had been previously identified by the head of year as being vulnerable, isolated or disaffected members of the school community. The scheme employed two youth workers for the eight-day programme, both with the necessary skills. These included sensitivity, creativity, youth work skills, besides the more practical issues such as having a driving licence.

Essentially, the Triple E Project was an outreach programme which encouraged the students to confront the potential common issues that affected them as a group. It also aimed to raise students' awareness of how they could contribute to the school community and how links could be built between community-based activities and the school.

After initial meetings with the young people involved it was agreed to focus on those areas that they felt were important in their lives: these being generic life/employability skills, such as self-esteem, leadership, artistic and creative skills. Following this meeting, a programme was drawn up which took into consideration the need to combine activities that were attractive to teenagers with a structured educational experience. Nevertheless, once

[24] Education Extra (2000) *Extra Class*

> the programme was up and running, the teenagers were still able to adapt it to meet their needs.
>
> At the end of the project, Triple E was evaluated and the final programme reflected the participants' own hopes and aims for the two-week scheme. The pupils, staff and wider community were all committed and involved in it. The only negative side of the project was the reporting in the press where some sensationalism and misquoting of pupils caused difficulties and had a profound effect on their feelings.

Public libraries are playing an increasingly vital role in providing an alternative and neutral space for young people to study after school. In 1998, a Library Association survey found that almost a quarter of all UK library authorities have developed homework-centre provision. Many libraries have developed innovative ways of boosting achievement through study support, particularly through the provision of ICT and through activities such as holiday reading games. Recent research into the value and impact of homework clubs in public libraries based on a national survey concluded that:

> a structured homework club service works extremely well in public libraries, providing a wide range of study support resources, in a neutral and welcoming environment. Half of all the clubs involved public library staff, but many staff were employed from a variety of professional backgrounds. In addition to the obvious educational focus of homework clubs, their benefits to children and young people had far wider implications, for example: easing the transition from primary to secondary education; helping young people to assert their individuality; and providing support and pastoral care which is frequently unavailable in the home or school environments.[25]

Recent support for libraries includes a new Code of Practice for Public Libraries in study support which shows how libraries can develop and improve their study support provision in the same way as schools can.[26]

Some local authorities have been particularly proactive and have developed multi-agency partnerships built around the library.

[25] Train, B et al (2000) *The Value and Impact of Homework Clubs in Public Libraries*, Library and information Commission Research Report, 32

[26] See DfEE/DCMS/NYA/Library Association (1999) *The Code of Practice for Public Libraries: Study Support*

EXTRA

Sandwell Library and Information Service

In Sandwell, the Library and Information Service has developed partnerships linking 19 separate venues, all libraries, each of which has its own homework club operating 1–3 sessions a week for students aged 9–16. Although standards in school have risen steadily in recent years in an area which is the seventh most deprived district in England, Sandwell still ranks towards the bottom of the league tables. The homework clubs, which have the support of a dedicated linkworker, free photocopying, access to ICT, homework collections and fax machines, are part of a general commitment to school improvement.

The impetus for partnership came not only from the young people identifying their own needs, but from 'a quite unexpected quarter' – Sandwell Safer Cities initiative which was looking for projects 'which gave a fresh slant to crime prevention – not purely locks and chains'. The lifelong learning librarian at Sandwell Library and Information Service responded. 'The more I listened the more I was convinced that the homework club fitted the bill.' The library put in a bid with a group of local schools, Social Services and the Youth Service – and the first homework club, 'Time Out', was started. Safer Cities went on to fund a second homework club and more clubs evolved, with support from the Prince's Trust, the local Rotary Club and other partners. In summary,

> Sandwell Safer Cities gave us the chance to build on what we knew young people wanted. It gave us an excellent grounding in monitoring and evaluation which has been of lasting value. We gave them a model for a scheme which raised enormous interest nationally. Petty vandalism and crime has decreased in our area. . . Fortunately, homework clubs are a core service and their future is secure.[27]

EXTRA

The Peartree Homework and Study Support Centre

Study support is provided in Derby by The Peartree Homework and Study Support Centre, in partnership with the LEA, the city library and youth services. In an inner-city area with a high proportion of families who speak English as a second language, low ability levels, and low aspirations, the study centre provides pupils from Years 5–9 with a quiet place to study within easy reach of home – but within their own community. The project offers additional help in terms of technology, books and people, access to the Internet, books related to homework and the National Curriculum subjects. Staff are drawn from the library and youth service. Informal peer mentoring takes place all the time, and pupils 'bring all sorts of different things to do.

[27] NNEDP case study series, January 2000

These could be homework or word processing or finding information. . . we have helped them to understand how the library is arranged and given them confidence to branch out in their learning. . .' All the anecdotal evidence points to this having been hugely successful – and the library has 'a much more positive image within the community, a greater sense of being owned by local people.'[28]

EXTRA

OnLine@Leeds

As part of its Single Regeneration Budget (SRB) programme, Leeds launched OnLine@Leeds in 1998. This project was set up in partnership with the education service to provide ICT facilities at five libraries and four schools. Centred in inner city wards, with high levels of deprivation and social exclusion, its effect has been dramatic. Ten 'Learning Librarians' were recruited to work across all nine sites, offering a friendly, supportive and informal approach to learning, and giving the personal attention that young people have responded to enthusiastically. The sites are open after school hours, early evenings and on Saturdays, and span the 7–25 age range.

Most take-up has been from school-age children – 2,000 joined in the first six weeks, and membership is currently over 4,500. Young people see this as an exciting and fun way to learn, and feel a real sense of ownership of the project. As a result of consultation with them, a breakfast club is going to be piloted soon.

EXTRA

Lancing Library Homework Club

One other example, from the other end of the country, shows why the library can prove to be so successful. In West Sussex the homework club at Lancing Library is held on Tuesday and Thursday nights and staffed by two homework helpers, one with a background in youth work, the other a library assistant. The homework club provides a quiet place to study, with access to the whole library stock, including multimedia. As the librarian recently described it:

> It's 3.30 pm and already a flurry of kids has rushed in the doors of the library asking for the homework helper. Children from the local school get in first, followed by those bussed home from further-flung schools. Those with a good understanding of the library head purposely for the resources they need. Others gather round the homework club study table signing themselves in, sharing ideas noisily and trying to grab a seat near the homework helper. Well-organised children will already have booked some time on the PC to interrogate the CD ROMs or browse the Internet. Others have come without paper or pen.

[28] DfEE (Summer 1999) *Insight*, p 5

> Soon an atmosphere of relative calm takes over. A student from a local secondary school is helping out and is very popular with the younger children, helping them to find the books they need. A few children are making good use of the adult library, in particular the reference section. Parents occasionally pop in and peer into the homework zone with a look of vague amazement that children should enjoy homework so much. . .

PRACTICAL PARTNERSHIPS WITH BUSINESS

Corporate support for OSHL is growing and changing continually. The summer learning schemes gave local companies the opportunity to offer specific and invaluable help, for example, in providing food and drink for pupils, outings and trips to local places of interest, basic materials for learning activities and transport. On a more sustained level there are many outstanding examples of continuing commitment for initiatives which take place out of school hours – Barclays New Futures, for example, or the initiative of Radio Rentals in South Wales in supporting homework clubs. Some companies, such as Kellogg's, make an extended commitment to a particular initiative – in this case a national Breakfast Award Scheme for school breakfast clubs; or make a professional link with school objectives – for example, WH Smith's reading schemes.

Less common, however, are projects which involve the company in sustained and evaluated project development. One example, however, is the Boots Family Learning scheme, based in Nottingham.

EXTRA

The Boots Family Learning project
The Boots Family Learning project was launched in 1998. The Boots Company has a long history of community involvement, working in partnership with local and national organisations on projects relating to education, health, environment and safer communities. The project is based on the Clifton estate in Nottingham where there are pockets of extreme poverty and a prevailing sense of low aspirations. Five local primary schools have been involved in working with Education Extra to develop a family learning project focused around CDT. An outstanding project leader was appointed in July 1998 to be responsible for content and organisation of the scheme, to train voluntary helpers and manage resources. The schools committed themselves to work closely with the project, to develop a whole school approach to family learning, to ensure that at least one member of staff was present at each workshop, and to agree the project aims which were essentially:

- to raise standards of achievement, self-esteem and confidence through family learning;

- to support parents as children's first and natural teachers and to encourage parental involvement in their children's learning;
- to support the school curriculum through an after-school programme of design and technology;
- to foster the participation of business and other partners in the education of young people and their families;
- to develop a sustainable model of good family learning practice;
- to create fun, collaborative learning opportunities in a relaxed atmosphere.

The scheme was named The FEATHERS workshops – Family Evening Activities That Help Everyone Relax Socially. Workshops were focused on specific tasks – eg to extend problem solving and language skills; and on aspects of design and technology – eg using simple circuits, gears and pulleys, story sacks, wheels. The experimental workshops, with high-quality resources and materials, were supported by booklets for families to try activities at home.

There were grades and different levels of challenge. Student mentors were recruited from Nottingham Trent University. All participating families receive Special Award certificates and the scheme has expanded to include holiday 'finding out' initiatives.

The outcomes, measured in consistent and high attendance, and the response of pupils and parents, have been very positive. Attendance figures have 'exceeded any previous initiatives involving parents' and have ranged between 466 and 200; with 50–90 people in each workshop. Parents and pupils say that the workshops are 'enormous fun' which give 'an insight into the school curriculum and a clearer picture of how they can contribute to their children's learning. . . Understanding of how and what children are taught in schools. . . [and] a considerable enrichment and extension of the school curriculum. . .'[29]

Some schools are adept at bringing in not only business, but the voluntary sector too.

EXTRA

Heathfield Community School

This school in Somerset has had an Education Business Development Group for the last three years, and people from 26 different firms have become involved with the school. The group meets each month to discuss areas of interest such as training, education, the curriculum and ICT.

Business mentoring is also part of the school's programme and individuals from both the public and private sectors offer students interviews and add a new perspective for them on their careers and further study. This is part of the national COMPACT programme and has been adapted and incorporated into the school's own structure, adding in facets such as police checks, training and counselling.

---

[29] *The Boots Family Learning Scheme: Evaluation of Year 1* (2000)

> The school has also worked with voluntary agencies such as the Red Cross who provide volunteers whom they have trained. A Red Cross volunteer runs a baby-sitting course, for example, with an ex-nurse. With Taunton Interagency Group (TIGA), they help produce a useful transition handbook for young people in the last year of secondary and first year of college. The group is a joint collaboration between the Citizens Advice Bureau, Heathfield Community College and Richard Huish College.

CONCLUSION

There is much more scope for partnership – and many new initiatives under consideration by faith groups such as the Salvation Army; national children's charities; and local organisations. As proof of where partnership can lead, in 1999 the most extensive and challenging national pilot scheme involving voluntary and other partners was set up by the DfEE to test out the extent and quality of potential partnerships.

EXTRA

The Partners for Study Support Grant scheme

This scheme involves 200 partnership projects with schools working with an enormous range of voluntary partners – drawn from the arts, voluntary organisations, museums, libraries, trade and professional associations, business, the police, libraries, museums, galleries, local theatres, and many others. The partnerships include such imaginative schemes as:

- Age Concern volunteers – working with local schools in Brighton on a story-telling and reading project;
- Arrow Valley Brass – working with Warwickshire schools to establish a brass ensemble;
- Black Families Education Support Group and Media Arts Development – working with St Gregory's School, Years 9–11 black and ethnic minority young people on ICT, media arts, photography, video and Web page design;
- British Federation of Young Choirs – working in partnership with 150 students in Leeds schools, February 2001–02, on 'Keep them singing';
- British Film Institute – working October 2000–March 2002, with Devon EA and SW Media Development Agency and Devon schools to enhance access to and understanding of films from different cultures and periods;
- Centre of the Earth Wildlife Trust for Birmingham and the Black Country – working with James Watt Junior School and Mathew Bolton Community School on themes relating to the environment, sustainable development and citizenship;
- English Table Tennis Association and Stowmarket Table Tennis Club working with two schools (Stow Upland High School and Becton Community

> Middle School) from 2000 until March 2002 to develop an innovative and sustainable school–club link to engage young people in cross-curricular activities;
> - Haymarket Theatre Leisure – working with Eyes Monsell Primary School producing plays, workshops, etc;
> - Leicestershire Libraries and Information Service working with Leicester schools to increase long-term library usage; involving 30 male and female children, 50 per cent of whom are at risk of exclusion;
> - Middlesborough *Evening Gazette* – working with local schools, aiming to give 35 GT children in Years 6–9 the opportunity to experience production of a real newspaper;
> - Neighbourhood engineers, working in partnership with Church Stratton School to design, make and test buggies.

From 2001, the Welsh Assembly will be funding 16 new partnership projects in Wales, involving for example:

- The National Museums and Galleries of Wales in a project which will look at sustainable development, technology and responsible citizenship;
- The National Trust in a holiday project: Splashout Stacpole;
- The Powys Pyramid Trust project which will work with young children in Welshpool, Machynlleth, Llandrindod Wells, Brecon, Llanidloes, and Ystradgynlais;
- The Welsh National Opera and Family Days in North Wales.

These new schemes are planned to run, typically, for two years and will show the way forward for many more schools and local communities who want not only to explore and audit the potential resources available for OSHL but who want to ensure that OSHL activities are here to stay because all the learning partners have a stake in making them work.

This is one way forward for the future. The final chapter looks at some of the other possibilities.

9

Conclusion: extra connections

. . . so much is expected of you and you are being measured up against such objective standards, then of course there won't be any time to discuss the ills of the world, to take an interest in politics, and even less chance to sit around listening to music, discussing poetry and attending lectures in other disciplines. . . They will be set fair, most of them, for a course that will train them to be good employees – but will they actually be 'educated'? (Professor Susan Greenfield, Director of the Royal Institution, on the 2000 student intake)

This book has charted the radical and rapid change across the UK in policy and practice in the field of OSHL. The challenges facing the UK educational system within which these changes have taken place are hardly unique. They include the need to promote the rights and improve the protection of children;[1] to educate young people for a lifetime of unpredictability; to achieve the right balance between knowledge and competence; to connect children with the integrity of a national culture as well as international citizenship; to offer all citizens an equal chance of prosperity and equality on the basis of effective education – and they are all challenges shared by developing and underdeveloped countries alike.

While the speed and focus of this change is unique to the UK, the same desire to find ways of rethinking the place of school in relation to the learning needs of pupils and the community is taking place in many other parts of the world. In the UK this is being done within the exceptional context of a history of voluntarism and a relatively short school day. In other countries, other initiatives have been taken which illustrate the different cultures and constraints of national policy. In France, for example,

[1] See, for example, as evidence of this, the creation of the Children's Commissioner for Wales, under the Care Standards Act 2000. His is the first such appointment in the UK

recent years have seen a high emphasis on decentralisation of education, closer partnerships between schools and cultural organisations, and more flexible timetables so that more extra-curricular activities take place in the early afternoon, followed by formal teaching towards the end of the school day. Significantly, however, in addition to aiming to provide all children 'with an introduction to sporting and cultural activities which they may continue in local clubs and associations', reception centres are being set up in Zones of Educational Priority to help children with their school work. Most projects 'can be traced back to a request from parents' rather than to government or school initiative.[2] Other countries with different school structures have adapted different systems, Sweden, for example, having an outstanding record in providing care and learning on an integrated basis. Schools are now becoming, according to one authority, 'a community institution, complex and potentially potent, which functions as a local network and a site for different modes of learning by professionals, parents and children'. At its heart is 'a learning child within a learning community, rather than the recipient of already processed knowledge handed down from adults'. The participation of the child in the life of the school is increasingly valued and extended.

In the United States, within a very different tradition, the Carnegie Council noted in 1994 that 'though educators have, in the main, not endorsed. . . nonschool learning opportunities as vital to academic support and career development, economists, civic leaders and juvenile justice professionals are increasingly taking up this idea. As they do they speak out directly on the matter of the potential of the hours from 3–8 pm in the lives of students, for expanding, complementing and supplementing formal classroom learning.'[3] The community education tradition has recently fused with greater concern to involve parents as a necessary condition of successful learning, and federal programmes to encourage family–schools and schools–community links. Under the 21st Century Community Centre Learning Programme, for example, US$200 million has been awarded to 90 schools in 300 communities to support activities such as longer opening hours, safer places to do homework, mentoring in basic skills, drug and violence prevention counselling, recreational activities and technology education.[4] Other initiatives are beginning to flag up the increasing

---

[2] Moss, P, Petrie, P and Poland, G (1999) *Rethinking School*, Joseph Rowntree Foundation, pp 11–12

[3] Carnegie Council on Adolescent Development, *A Matter of Time: Risk and Opportunity in the Out of School Hours*

[4] Among the chief agencies for leaving behind the classroom is the Chevlen Stewart Mott Foundation, which has a particular commitment to reducing disadvantage by raising achievement, and supports many different out of school learning programmes and community educational enterprises

importance given to OSHL – from national organisations for research and development, to city-based initiatives to campaign for public funding.[5]

The intention of these recent programmes is very close to the motivation for the UK policy initiatives.

> This is partly about enhancing educational achievement and personal development. . . But it is also about preventing juvenile delinquency, vandalism and other anti social behaviour. . . Overall the most cited purpose of these programmes is providing adult supervision. . . in the context of an increasingly dangerous environment, increasing parental employment and the evidence that at least 1.6 million 5–14-year-olds (1991 figures) are unsupervised while their parents are in work.

The result has been, according to Moss, Petrie and Poland, 'a new and unprecedented wave of school community initiatives has appeared over the last decade and grown exponentially'. The concept of Full Service schools – which provide for the full community needs of the local community – is one such development.

We have seen that developing countries are rethinking when and where learning takes place, and how to provide beyond the school day, the school year and the school structure, for the needs of learners young and old. The developing countries, too, have reason to be interested in all of the following: putting scarce physical resources in the community to greater use; examples of partnership, identifying and building on voluntary commitment and personal interests to raise self-esteem and confidence; involving parents and other adults as tutors and mentors in supporting teachers.[6] From China to Latin America, new models and new ideas are taking root as the search for a more effective education system moves up a gear.

What the countries cited have in common is the conviction that out of school learning activities have a fundamental role to play in modernising education and social provision, and in connecting the two. But in the UK we now have an imperative to move on. This final chapter reviews some of the newer ways in which OSHL is connecting to the educational and social agenda, and hazards some hopes for the future. Significant changes will, for example, follow from modernising local government itself, with its new emphasis on partnership structures involving all elements of the community. In this context, not least, informal learning is increasingly seen as a way of enabling individuals across a lifetime of learning, and that this

[5] See US example, the New York-based After School Corporation, and the Out of School Learning Web site

[6] China, for example, is beginning to explore ways of funding after-school programmes in Beijing, following exchanges between the UK and Chinese educationalists on lifetime learning issues in 1999 and 2000

will certainly have implications for the shape and role of the school of the future. There is also the fact that OSHL is seen to have a key role in helping to build stronger, more inclusive and more successful communities.

The advent of OSHL is also part of a trend away from the highly mechanistic and prescriptive functional view of education which has its origins in the mid-1980s. Since then a more reflective and inclusive approach has developed, with a greater perception that what young people will need in 20 years' time is unforeseeable and that they should be encouraged to see learning as exciting, fun, and essential for their future. This prescriptive model grew at a time when there was rightly a concern to ensure common access to a quality experience for all school pupils, but became a prescription based on a particular political philosophy within which wider society had little place. Although OSHL has been and is presented, especially at government and policy level, in terms of its utility in affecting achievement and improving skills and experience, it also, in many subtle ways, encompasses and taps into much wider, holistic views of education. It offers also the opportunity to compensate for the lack of breadth and opportunity in individual experience. It offers some effective ways of energising both teaching and learning within the school curriculum itself.

In OSHL there can be a focus on the needs of the individual, on the making of the key links to enable each person to move forward, often to an agenda determined by him- or herself rather than 'the system'. It accepts the importance of enthusiasm, creativity and serendipity – both for the learner and the provider. It redefines, in challenging and exciting ways, the roles of all those engaged within it.

Finally, as specialist schools are predicted to grow in number, as EAZs and EiCs begin to explore the scope for doing things in different ways and with different partners, the fixed point of the school structure cannot be taken for granted. Changes are being made to the structure of the school day and the school year. Many schools (for example, the highly successful Thomas Telford School in Staffordshire) are moving over to continental school days with longer afternoon timetables for activities. Others, such as Brookfield School, Knowsley, are setting aside two afternoons a week for extra-curricular activities, with appropriate adjustment to the rest of the week. Debates are starting about the form of the school year. The six-term year, for example, has been debated, involving parents as well as teachers and educators.

However, the main challenge in the UK, as far as OSHL is concerned, is to ensure that the progress made over the past few years is not only sustained, but is *embedded in* the life and ethos of every school and every neighbourhood. That is the only way to ensure that OSHL will not be just another temporary innovation which withers away with a change of fashion or government. The many examples of partnership in place and in development already cited in this book show how far the idea and practice has spread, enthusing and sweeping up statutory, voluntary and professional organisations and agencies in its progress. As OSHL becomes part of the portfolio of public services, stretching from libraries and leisure centres to soccer clubs and cyber cafés, the out of school hours club can become the most outward and visible expression of the learning community in action. Realising the promise which this holds means consistently giving priority to this new area of public policy so that the entitlement of every young person is realised. This will be investigated later in the chapter – along with the major challenges that exist alongside the opportunities.

BUILDING INCLUSIVE COMMUNITIES

One of the challenges of the new curriculum is to make a reality of the new citizenship curriculum from 2002 – a highly significant development, and not just in terms of education. For the first time, when the country is undergoing radical constitutional change in terms of devolution, changing institutions and voting habits, and against the continuing debate over our place in Europe and our global responsibilities, children and young people will learn what it means to be a 'citizen' and to practice 'citizenship' in a plural, global and fast-changing society. Complex questions will be raised about the values and practices of democracy, about rights and duties, and the role of the individual in society. It is, for schools, largely uncharted territory.

The new curriculum will create many more opportunities not only for young people to participate but to design, develop and deliver projects which enable them to demonstrate their contribution to a changing community as citizens. The three strands (KS1–4) cover:

- social and moral responsibility – learning self-confidence and social and morally responsible behaviour both in and beyond the classroom;
- community involvement – learning how to become helpfully involved in the life and concerns of the neighbourhood, including learning through community involvement and service;
- political literacy – learning about the institutions, issues, problems and practices of democracy and how citizens can make themselves effective in public life through skills, values and knowledge.

Both at primary and secondary levels, by definition , success in promoting the citizenship curriculum can only be fully achieved by maximising the involvement of the young people concerned. In practice this is already happening both within the curriculum and beyond. By its very nature, OSHL brings a particular vision and a set of values to the curriculum agenda which is already being implemented both within school hours and outside because:

- OSHL is by definition active and inclusive;
- it enables children and young people to demonstrate many of the concepts, values and skills which lie at the heart of the citizenship agenda;
- it creates opportunity for the practice of citizenship outside school hours, as individuals and groups of pupils, expressing moral and social responsibility, which is required of the citizenship curriculum;
- it creates the optimum conditions for the full involvement of pupils of all ages and abilities.

The essential elements to be reached by the end of compulsory schooling set out very clearly the interrelated range of key concepts, values and dispositions, skills and attitudes, knowledge and understanding. At KS3 and 4, in particular, OSHL can create the time, space and environment lacking in the classroom for sustained debate about a range of complex issues, and provide first-hand experience. The citizenship curriculum at primary and secondary level can, in its simplest form, be promoted by such activities as:

- schools councils, debating societies, newspaper clubs – activities which enable young people to understand and explore the political context of citizenship;
- school activities with and on behalf of the community – environmental protection schemes, community radio clubs, signing clubs, or creating a garden for local residents; schemes which enable young people to work together to identify charitable causes and raise money to meet the needs of others;
- activities which extend pupils' knowledge of other countries through development education, Internet clubs which connect pupils across the globe;
- activities which encourage volunteering, and which connect schools and pupils up with national initiatives such as the Millennium Volunteers, etc.

In this context a whole series of complex and sensitive issues also begins to be raised – about tolerance, discrimination, censorship, freedom of speech and expression, equal opportunities, human rights and issues relating to sustainable development.

Some of the values of the citizenship curriculum lend themselves particularly well to OSHL. One is 'a disposition to work with and for others' demonstrated, to give one example, by a school in Yorkshire catering for hearing and hearing-impaired children which runs a signing choir. Both hearing and hearing-impaired children perform in the choir, signing the words to the music. Children from Holywell Green and Savile Park primary schools participate and the choir is tremendously popular.

Practical citizenship must replicate the voluntary nature of the actions and involvement it is trying to encourage in young adults. For this reason volunteering and mentoring schemes are obvious ways that students demonstrate active citizenship. For example:

EXTRA

Hirst High School

One initiative which Education Extra recently supported was at Hirst High School in Ashington, which is designed to encourage young people in Ashington and the surrounding area to participate in volunteering in a project 'to challenge the myths and stereotypes surrounding young people with disabilities and disaffected young people. Not only will this positively affect the community's perception of these groups but will also aim to demystify the school as an institution, raising awareness of training and reskilling opportunities'.

The project's aim is to design a programme working with young people with disabilities in Hirst High Schools's Riverbank Special Needs Department. After a training programme surrounding issues such as communication, listening, teamwork and programme planning, the department will offer a wide range of activities, designed to further the personal and social development skills of the young pupils. These activities may include outdoor education or gardening, IT or a community project.

The school is working in partnership with the Choysey Project which is designed to attract socially excluded or 'hard to reach' young people. The project organisers work with the Education Welfare and Employment Services. The school will act as the venue and administration centre while the project will design and deliver the face-to-face work in conjunction with the school's Community Department. Education Extra provided a digital camera to support the work.[7]

Finally, for some schools the community and citizenship agenda come together in perfect harmony. The Ashley Special School in Stoke-on-Trent is one such example.

EXTRA

Ashley Special School

This school's mission is to develop a sense of community by putting a great emphasis on individuals' interaction with communities varying in size from the family or form groups to global membership. Moreover, the school has agreed that a community-based curriculum should allow its pupils to explore their values and attitudes in order to develop their sense of identity and self-esteem. Crucial to enabling pupils, staff, governors and parents to

---

[7] See *Extra Special* (Autumn 2000) *Study Support and the Citizenship Curriculum*

contribute to the decision-making process is the School Council and the supporting committees.

All members of the school community, together with its wider community, have a stake in the council/committee-led achievements, all of which have implications for the school's learning objectives. Examples of the school's many successes are that Ashley was the first school in the North West and the first special school in the UK to gain the Eco-schools Award from the Tidy Britain Group. In addition, it received the Anne Frank Educational Trust's Merit Award for an outstanding community entry (drawing up a school charter). The Newspaper Committee produced a newspaper which in 1998 became a regional winner in the *Daily Telegraph* Newspaper Awards. In June 2000, the school received the Schools Curriculum 2000 Award.

The out of hours activities of individuals and groups are not seen as an 'add on' but as central to the curriculum delivery with planned extensions. Students are also taught the skills necessary to be active in their communities. For example, the school is involved in many ventures, including rehearsing a new play about homelessness and a student surgery with the local MP.

Elected pupils on the Sport and Leisure Committee investigate different ways in which sport and leisure activities after school can enrich the lives of pupils. They work in partnership with health promotion, arts and sports development personnel to involve pupils and families in events, trips and activities with the aim of maturing lifelong healthy involvement in the community.

Finally, since citizenship is essentially local in practice, OSHL offers communities in each of the four UK countries a way of linking with the particular concerns and characteristics of their schools – while OSHL itself provides a framework in which local and therefore more efficacious responses can be made.

Making policy inclusive

The task is. . . to enthuse young people to seize opportunities for learning. (National Assembly for Wales, 2000, *Extending Entitlement: Supporting young people*)

There is a whole range of new ways in which OSHL will be able to connect with initiatives in development which could bring about a more genuinely inclusive approach to education as well as reinforce the place of education at the heart of social and economic objectives. Many of the case studies in this book show the way forward in different ways, while meeting the needs of different groups of pupils. Much of this excellent work can be replicated and can help to make a reality of many of the new education and social policies which are currently being developed. For example:

- OSHL can link with the development of the concept of the healthy school – with increasing emphasis being placed on healthy activities, health education, safety, sport, fitness and nutrition as an antidote to fears of increasing obesity, passivity and lack of physical exercise among children. The Healthy School Standard is already pioneering exciting work in this area – particularly in building partnerships – and will be able to put a high emphasis on promoting the emotional and mental health as well as the physical health of young people. There is an obvious need, as part of this policy, to develop new activity programmes, more programmes which educate pupils about food, nutrition and diet – and which enable schools to offer more programmes which can assist development of personal and lifeskills such as cooking.[8]
- There could, for example, be links between programmes which provide OSHL activities to motivate and challenge young people and protect communities/promote citizenship. The new initiatives to reduce street crime and divert young people who are both the leading exponents and victims will surely depend for their effectiveness on putting something in place of terminal boredom and routine exclusion. The excellent programmes cited in the book, together with systematic provision for OSHL activities, can provide the foundation for a different future for many young people.
- In the area of new technology, The National Grid for Learning and the growing familiarity with new technologies as part of the curriculum and as a way of accessing the curriculum as a whole, bring great promise, but also threaten to strand some pupils and families in the information have-not ghetto. Positive action will be needed if this disability gap is not to widen. One possibility would be to ensure that each school develops an integrated learning centre, based around the library and ICT, which is open all hours, available to pupils and their families, with access to the Internet as well as to all other research and communication possibilities.
- Another relevant issue is the increased integration of children with special educational needs and disabilities into mainstream schools. From 2001, for the first time, children with disabilities will have a positive right to be educated in mainstream schools, and access will be widened for those parents who want their children who are identified as having special needs, to be educated in the local school. The challenge of greater integration will not merely be one of new resources, but of finding ways in which children with disabilities become part of the whole life of the school. OSHL activities can play a key role in this.
- OSHL can also play a role in the increased efforts to promote higher aspirations and greater confidence among young people who might not

[8] See, for example, DH/DfEE support materials on the National Healthy School Standard on Partnership (July 2000)

have considered higher education. It could provide more transitional support for students aged 14–16 to introduce them to FE and HE to accompany more systematic development of transition programmes at earlier stages, particularly aimed at young students with the disadvantage of an interrupted school career. More programmes which are geared, without stigmatising those children, to providing targeted social and academic support for young carers, travellers' children, and refugees, for example, would be very helpful.

In addition, however, there is a whole range of emerging connections which will give OSHL a key role in realising economic and social objectives. Some might, for example, involve:

- More systematic provision for family learning as part of the drive to raise adult skill levels – not just in literacy but in numeracy and ICT as well.
- More systematic attempts to prepare young people for the world of work, using time out of school for creating opportunities to:
  - get to know local and national employers;
  - introduce primary children to the range of modern careers;
  - explore with older pupils some of the choices they might not otherwise consider, such as the new careers in engineering and technology, and their links with the creative industries;
  - explore with older pupils the FE or HE curriculum or get them to audit their own skills developed outside school hours.
- More opportunities to connect culture and creativity with education by opening up schools 'to the exciting opportunities available in the wider world' of the arts and culture. This includes a 'cultural pledge' that 'in time, every pupil will have the chance to work with creative professionals and organisations and thereby enrich their learning across the whole curriculum'.[9]
- More opportunities under the proposed new funding strands for the NOF, including community development and environmental awareness and action.
- More opportunities to use OSHL as a vehicle for building learning communities.

That we can make this case exemplifies the immense value of the recent policy initiatives in demonstrating the broad value of OSHL so that it has now become a well-understood vehicle for delivery of other policies rather than just a policy in its own right.

[9] This, plus the concept of culture online, was set out in *Culture and Creativity: The next ten years* (DCMS, 2001)

REASONS TO BE CHEERFUL

There are many reasons to be cheerful.

First, there is the growing priority given within education itself to enabling individual and lifelong learning – and to all the connections between them, and to the conviction that individual learning in the future can and must cross formal and informal boundaries. This can be seen, for example, in the emergence of ideas and new institutions such as individual learning accounts and the University for Industry. OSHL gives shape and prospect to this development. But at the same time, it offers the practical prospect of a new community of learning with schools at the centre. This prospect is now reflected in the Green Paper on Education *Building on Success*, which is committed to expanding out of school learning opportunities for the benefits they bring, not least to citizenship.[10]

Second, within the past two years new infrastructure has been put in place which can develop provision and plan for the future. There are now OSHL officers in the great majority of local authorities across the UK, charged with developing policy and practice in OSHL and making effective links with the continuum of education, from Sure Start to the University of the Third Age. There will be no new NOF grants from March 2001, funding will roll out over the next 2–3 years, enabling additional resources and partnerships to be developed. This will be complemented by new sources of local funding designed to replicate good ideas and practice. In particular, the Children's Fund and the new Creative Partnerships in England, and the new Community Partnership funding in Wales, could make a significant difference to local developments in out of school learning. In addition, at national level, the New Deal for Communities, and the continuing priority given to tackling underachievement, delinquency, poor housing and crime in acutely deprived neighbourhoods promises a lively future for schemes which offer young people challenging activities, an alternative to acute boredom, and greater opportunities to show what they can do.

Third, there has been, throughout education policy in the past three years, a greater priority given to schools' partnership of all kinds, not least with business, and to schools working together, than for many years. The experience of OSHL in recent years has been to take advantage of – or even to create – a new climate for schools to work together and with local

---

[10] Green Paper on Education, *Building on Success* (February 2001) p 41. The government is also determined that children should have greater access to extra-curricular activities and after-school clubs. Already 97 per cent of schools provide some support of this sort and 7 out of 10 schools increased their provision between 1998 and 2000. We intend to move further, so that in time, every child at primary school who wants to has the opportunity to learn a musical instrument or try one of a range of sports. To make this possible we will expand the availability of out of school learning opportunities and continue to invest in school music at the new higher levels

communities, and for closer connections between school and community as a whole. Providing a glimpse of the future, from two very different geographical perspectives, are Langdon School, LB Newham and Mullion School in Cornwall, both of which have an outstanding belief in the benefits of out of school hours activities.

EXTRA

Langdon School

The school's overall aim is to provide a fully inclusive programme of enrichment, extension, and support activities for students seven days per week, 52 weeks per year, from primary through to secondary school and post-16, designed to equip them with the knowledge, skills and values and attitudes to enjoy lifelong learning. The school has been supported by organisations in the private, public and voluntary sectors.

Students across the whole spectrum of ability and motivation are involved and the school seeks maximum participation from male and female students. Learning opportunities are provided for all students, especially those unable to participate in out of hours activities during the school day due to time and other constraints. The curriculum out of hours consists of a vast array of before-school, lunchtime and after-school clubs, literacy and numeracy intervention programmes, Easter Revision School, Saturday School and Summer University.

Both the Saturday School and the borough's Summer University are open to Langdon students and those of the five partner primary schools. The teachers work collaboratively with their primary colleagues and there are plenty of opportunities to share good practice, eg work shadowing, team teaching, planning and evaluating learning outcomes. Many visitors have reported on the rapport between Langdon staff and their primary school colleagues and the raised achievements of the young people attending. This year, the school is running KS3 SATS revision classes and master classes for gifted and talented students from Langdon and other secondary schools.

The schools use the Excellence Model to help evaluate the effectiveness of the out of hours provision. They monitor student attendance to ensure equality of opportunity and have targeted groups of students who need additional support.

All staff are committed to enhancing and supporting the individual needs of each student. Social inclusion is central to the ethos at Langdon.

Over 90 per cent of students attend at least two out of hours activities per term. In 2000, over 24,000 student attendances were recorded at the Study Centre before school, lunchtime and after school to develop their learning skills. Over 400 students regularly attended the Summer University and 300 students continue to attend Saturday School.

The Lizard Outreach Trust/Mullion School

In Cornwall, Lizard Outreach Trust (LOT) set up a project with Mullion School, which in 1997–98, with additional funding from the DfEE, undertook a major project to take study support out into the community.

LOT provided out of school hours sessions for 70–80 Year 6 children from nine feeder primary schools and 140–180 young people from the secondary school. The scheme, which lasted a year, was not only intended to support transitional, but also to help develop key skills, and to enable 'the pupils of the Lizard peninsular to gain more skills, leading to better prospects of employability'.

The key school – Mullion School – was the location for LOT in an area where many traditional industries have disappeared, and there is extremely high unemployment and virtually no public transport. The scattered nature of the population makes for great difficulty in organising activities outside school hours. The scheme built extensively on an existing base of study support activities in the school (ICT, homework, music, sport and curricular support) and built new links and new provision for and with the primary schools. An ICT course, for example, for Year 6 children (with groups from paired primary schools attending an ICT centre once a week for half a term) was regarded as highly successful. And many examples of increasing confidence and self-esteem were quoted by teachers. One marked success was a 20-week boat building course, supported by local experts and volunteers in a local workshop. Other activities ranged from regular art, drama and music clubs, to short courses in Latin, sailing and soccer refereeing – which provided, on demand, what the young people thought they would need for future employability and access to HE.

LOOKING FOR THE FUTURE IN THE PRESENT

A fourth reason to be cheerful is the prospect of a new, modern model of community education, revitalised after decades of frustration. As a recent report has explained it:

> Stretching from the pre-war Cambridgeshire Village College movement, through the compensatory education and community school movements of the 1960s and 1970s, through to the 'new' community schools of the 1990s there is a view that schools can serve, not merely to remove 'able' children from their communities, but make a positive contribution to those communities. Moreover, communities in general and families in particular are seen, not as a source of disadvantage, but as capable of making a positive contribution to the school and the children within them. In this way, the

school acts as a resource for the community and the community, in turn, acts as a resource for the school.[11]

There are, at the moment, many within the education community who are questioning the place and role of the school in the future – that 'schools are designed for a time and a purpose that no longer exist. . .' Consider the fact that it is as easy (perhaps easier) to communicate with a country on the other side of the world as with your neighbour, and all forms of information are now accessible to everyone in the world with a computer. How will this affect schools? Where will learning take place? Who will be the teachers and mentors of the future?[12]

One role for OSHL in the development of this new thinking has been that of educational test bed, and this will continue. Many new ideas such as family learning and peer mentoring have entered or enhanced educational thinking through the OSHL route and will in time become part of mainstream provision. Increasingly, accepted concepts such as the role of the school, the shape of the school day, and the relationship between the school and other members of its community are being challenged and OSHL will have an important role to play, for example in bringing together learners of different ages and in providing mechanisms by which the accepted framework of the school day and school curriculum can be expanded and changed.

It may well be that the first step towards answering these questions – and to building the learning centres of the future – whatever they may look like or what they may be called – will be to ensure that all schools and communities can draw upon an OSHL programme offered by the school in partnership. As many of the case studies throughout the book have shown, OSHL is making a unique contribution towards bringing the community into the school – and taking the school out to the community. Putting that contribution together with ICT is a powerful combination. Peters Hill School, in the West Midlands, provides one example.

EXTRA

Peters Hill Primary School

This school received an Education Extra award in 1999 towards the cost of its after-school Internet storytelling project. Portable laptops enabled children to work at home with their parents gathering stories of local history for inclusion on a Web site (Homelink2000). The Web site will contain children's stories, and tales and anecdotes collected from parents, grandparents and

[11] Dyson, A and Robson, R (1999) *School, Family, Community: Mapping School Inclusion in the UK*, Joseph Rowntree Foundation, p 1
[12] See, for example, The School of the Future: A view from the Secondary Heads Association, pp 102–06 and other essays in *Schools in the Learning Age* (October 2000) Campaign for Learning

members of the community. Everyone who visits the school is recorded. Budding journalists work with an artist in residence to prepare the resulting poems, stories and animations for the Web site.

The community school of the future can, however, certainly do more – and the way forward for the immediate future is clearly set out in the concept of the extended learning day, and the entitlement of every child to a minimum amount of OSHL activity time. These are neither simple nor inexpensive propositions. But they are an ambitious and credible statement of what the learning of the future might look like, particularly as set out in the *Schools Plus* agenda. This report reaffirms that the relationship schools have with their communities – and in particular with parents and carers – can contribute to improving pupil attainment. *Schools Plus*, with its emphasis on OSHL, on the school as a community resource, and links with local business and industry, 'dares schools [as one key agency has put it] to think beyond simple structures and organisational arrangements'. It urges schools to examine the impact that their work with the community can have on the school's ethos, its curriculum and the use of its facilities. It poses a fundamental question: 'Can schools continue to raise standards by constantly improving the quality of classroom teaching or does continual improvement depend upon engagement with the wider community?'[13]

Making a reality of Schools Plus and its equivalents across the UK could empower both individual and community learning, offers OSHL the best hope of overcoming the most stubborn contradiction uncovered in the past few years: that (as Chapters 1–3 explored) those for whom OSHL activities have most to offer – pupils for whom the family and community are unlikely to compensate – are those who are least likely to participate. While sterling efforts have been made through development programmes, NOF money and community action, to direct resources to these pupils and these areas, there is still a long way to go to overcome the cultural, structural and personal barriers which prevent participation. This is where evidence and persuasion will have to be backed up by provision and leadership at local and national level on a guaranteed basis.

Reaching the hard to reach will depend not only on an extension of partnership, but on sustained partnership , so that the excellent start which has been made will continue to expand and flourish. This, in turn, will depend on several things, principally:

- The core values of OSHL – of voluntarism, of enjoyment, and of the rights of all pupils to an education which is not merely rich but responsive to individual learning needs and strengths – must be maintained. To make

---

[13] Phil Street, Director of CEDC, in *Network*, (May 2000) **20** (2)

OSHL compulsory, or to transpose it into the concept of an extended teaching day rather than a learning day, will destroy the very reason for its success.

- OSHL must be seen as effective for all schools and children and not merely a particular boon and benefit for the most disadvantaged; so that it remains a positive ideal rather than a default model.
- Resources and support provided must be sufficient for local and national partnerships, to build capacity for and with schools, make seamless policy at all levels, and create a stakeholding in education across the community.
- Sufficient support must be provided for the research, development and policy initiatives which will underpin OSHL's value and drive it into all related areas of policy.
- All teachers in training must learn the value of OSHL, its relationship to the core school functions, and its links with wider community and society interests. They should be encouraged to develop individual experience and to see this commitment as a fundamental and enjoyable part of the teaching experience. All teachers in post must be enabled to pursue professional development, as appropriate in this area. All adults and volunteers drawn from partnerships and the community must have the support and training to ensure that their contribution is as effective and rewarding as possible. As we have shown, some university departments of education are already leading the way in this.

In March 2001 the new grants for OSHL will cease, £180 million will be in circulation in the four countries of the UK, and new activities and programmes will be in development and active over the next five years. NOF has already indicated that it is looking to build continuity into its new programme areas and we are optimistic that the next round of initiatives, as discussed above, will see OSHL as one vehicle for their delivery. Once the present OSHL programmes are established, we believe that there will be an irresistible momentum to ensure that they will grow and develop and that new funding streams will be identified to enable them to do so.

Schools, local authorities and voluntary organisations working together have a fundamental role in making sure that this happens. First, in England they can use Standards Funding 'to maintain and improve arrangements for study support' over the next few years to secure the base of activity, and extend it to other schools. In Scotland, the Excellence Fund will provide additional resources.[14] In England, however, continued funding will depend on local authorities giving study support within its host programme of

[14] Wales and Northern Ireland are committing funds through other community and partnership routes

social inclusion – which also includes reducing exclusion, raising attendance and providing full-time education for children out of school. Second, local authorities can develop the role of the OSHL officers so that they become a permanent and creative element of local government policy, linking OSHL activities to all other parts of local government policy from literacy to arts development programmes. The OSHL officers will play the critical role in exploring and supporting partnerships, helping schools and other partners to access new forms of support, for example, from the new Children's Fund, Creative Partnerships for the Arts, new lottery opportunities or local and national enterprises.

Most important, OSHL officers also have a key role in opening up new incentives and professional development opportunities for teachers. As Chapters 1–4 of this book made clear, running activities for children in out of school hours is quite different from teaching during school time. All schools find it difficult to make the time available for additional training, yet, with the right support from headteachers and LEAs, teachers and other adults who offer their time on a voluntary basis can now access an increasing range of incentives, including accreditation for the work done. The Teacher Education in Study Support materials, referred to in Chapter 4, will bring these possibilities nearer schools, and are being helped in many instances by proactive OSHL officers in local authorities. This must, however, become a priority in practice if the benefits of the knowledge, evidence and good practice are to make the widest impact – and draw in schools which are still reluctant to invest more in OSHL. In doing so, they will enrich and energise the in-school curriculum as well.

The prescription is clear enough. There is no need for a crystal ball or for expensive consultancy; all that is required is to make a reality of the entitlement of all pupils to guaranteed extra learning; making the extra learning day a reality in all communities. This way all young people and adults who want to do so, can get the extra help, the enthusiastic mentor and the expertise that will take them on to the next step. That is a major challenge, but if it is met, to paraphrase William Morris, our education service will be genuinely building on the desire to know – an aspiration to which everyone has an equal right. And if that could happen, more teachers might say: 'The response of the students was a revelation to me. . .'[15] and more students would say: 'It was the best idea in the world'.

[15] Teacher quoted in Education Extra (1999) *Museums and Galleries Report* p 35

Index